Lecture Notes in Business Information Processing   **369**

More information about this series at http://www.springer.com/series/7911

Jaap Gordijn · Wided Guédria ·
Henderik A. Proper (Eds.)

The Practice of
Enterprise Modeling

12th IFIP Working Conference, PoEM 2019
Luxembourg, Luxembourg, November 27–29, 2019
Proceedings

 Springer

Editors
Jaap Gordijn ⓘ
Vrije Universiteit Amsterdam
Amsterdam, Noord-Holland
The Netherlands

Wided Guédria
Luxembourg Institute of Science
and Technology
Esch-sur-Alzette, Luxembourg

Henderik A. Proper ⓘ
Luxembourg Institute of Science
and Technology
Esch-sur-Alzette, Luxembourg

ISSN 1865-1348   ISSN 1865-1356 (electronic)
Lecture Notes in Business Information Processing
ISBN 978-3-030-35150-2   ISBN 978-3-030-35151-9 (eBook)
https://doi.org/10.1007/978-3-030-35151-9

This Springer imprint is published by the registered company Springer Nature Switzerland AG
The registered company address is: Gewerbestrasse 11, 6330 Cham, Switzerland

Preface

The 12th IFIP Working Conference on the Practice of Enterprise Modeling (PoEM 2019), was held during November 27–29, 2019, in Luxembourg, hosted by the Luxembourg Institute of Science and Technology (LIST).

PoEM is supported by the IFIP WG 8.1 and is a conference to stimulate the interaction between practitioners in the field of enterprise modeling, and researchers in this interesting discipline, with the goal to inform and learn from each other. After all, enterprise modeling methods and approaches should be usable in practice.

Concretely, the conference presented a wide variety of topics in the realm of enterprise modeling (EM) including requirements engineering, modeling and ontologies, reference architectures and patterns, methods for developing models and architectures, and security and privacy. Additionally, two interesting EM related workshops preceded the conference: the Third International Workshop on Practicing Open Enterprise Modeling within OMiLAB (PrOse 2019) and the Second Workshop on Teaching and Learning Conceptual Modelling (TLCM 2019). Finally, interesting new topics were presented using the format of PoEM Forum papers with their own online proceedings. These Forum papers were integrated in the main program of the conference using a slightly different format.

This year, PoEM received 35 paper submissions covering a wide variety of EM topics. Each paper was evaluated by at least three members of our expert Program Committee, providing constructive feedback. In total 15 high-quality papers were accepted, which can all be found in this volume. The acceptance rate for full papers was thus below 43%.

This conference would not have been possible without the hard work of the Program Committee members and additional reviewers. Additionally, we are thankful to the authors of the papers who submitted and presented their high-quality papers at the conference. We thank the session chairs for ensuring a smooth organization of the sessions and stimulating interesting discussions. We also acknowledge the PoEM Steering Committee chairs for their continuous assistance and the chairs of the Forum for creating an exciting event. Finally, we thank LIST/Luxembourg for the organization of the PoEM conference this year.

September 2019

Jaap Gordijn
Wided Guédria
Erik Proper

Organization

Steering Committee

Anne Persson	University of Skövde, Sweden
Janis Stirna	Stockholm University, Sweden
Kurt Sandkuhl	University of Rostock, Germany

General Chair

Erik Proper	LIST, Luxembourg

Program Chairs

Jaap Gordijn	VUA Amsterdam, The Netherlands
Wided Guédria	LIST, Luxembourg

Forum Chairs

Paul Johannesson	University of Stockholm, Sweden
Christophe Feltus	LIST, Luxembourg

Industry Chairs

Frank Harmsen	PNA Group, The Netherlands
Hans Mulder	Antwerp University, Belgium
Yannick Naudet	LIST, Luxembourg

Organization Chair

Noémie Courtois	LIST, Luxembourg

Program Committee

Wided Guedria	LIST, Luxembourg
Sybren De Kinderen	University of Luxembourg, Luxembourg
Moonkun Lee	Chonbuk National University, South Korea
Keng Siau	Missouri University of Science and Technology, USA
Jelena Zdravkovic	Stockholm University, Sweden
Janis Stirna	Stockholms Universitet, Sweden
Andrea Polini	University of Camerino, Italy
Ana-Maria Ghiran	Babes-Bolyai University of Cluj-Napoca, Romania
Robert Andrei Buchmann	Babeş-Bolyai University of Cluj Napoca, Romania

Anne Persson	University of Skövde, Sweden
Pnina Soffer	University of Haifa, Israel
Darijus Strasunskas	HEMIT, Norway
Colette Rolland	University of PARIS-1, France
Robert Lagerström	KTH Royal Institute of Technology, Sweden

Contents

Methods for Architectures and Models

Enterprise Architecture for Security, Privacy and Compliance

Requirements

Evaluating the Impact of User Stories Quality on the Ability to Understand and Structure Requirements

Yves Wautelet[1]([✉])[iD], Dries Gielis[1], Stephan Poelmans[1], and Samedi Heng[2][iD]

[1] KU Leuven, Leuven, Belgium
{yves.wautelet,stephan.poelmans}@kuleuven.be
[2] HEC Liège, Université de Liège, Liège, Belgium
samedi.heng@uliege.be

Abstract. Scrum is driven by user stories (US). The development team indeed uses, to fill the project's and the sprints' backlog, sentences describing the user expectations with respect to the software. US are often written "on the fly" in structured natural language so their quality and the set's consistency are not ensured. The Quality User Story (QUS) framework intends to evaluate and improve the quality of a given US set. Other independent research has built a unified model for tagging the elements of the WHO, WHAT and WHY dimensions of a US; each tag representing a concept with an inherent nature and granularity. Once tagged, the US elements can be graphically represented through an icon and the modeler can link them when inter-dependencies are identified to build one or more Rationale Trees (RT). This paper presents the result of an experiment conducted with novice modelers aimed to evaluate how well they are able to build a RT out of (i) a raw real-life US set (group 1) and (ii) a new version of the US set improved in quality using QUS (group 2).The experiment requires test subjects to identify the nature of US elements and to graphically represent and link them. The QUS-compliant US set improved the ability of the test subjects to make this identification and linking. We cannot conclude that the use of the QUS framework improved the understanding of the problem/solution domain but when a QUS-compliant US set is used to build a RT, it increases the ability of modelers to identify Epic US. Building a RT thus has a positive impact on identifying the structure of a US set's functional elements.

Keywords: User Stories · Rationale Tree · Quality User Story · Modeling experiment

1 Introduction

Agile methods often describe software requirements with *User Stories (US)*. *User stories are short, simple descriptions of a feature told from the perspective*

© IFIP International Federation for Information Processing 2019
Published by Springer Nature Switzerland AG 2019
J. Gordijn et al. (Eds.): PoEM 2019, LNBIP 369, pp. 3–19, 2019.
https://doi.org/10.1007/978-3-030-35151-9_1

of the person who desires the new capability, usually a user or customer of the system. US are generally presented in a flat list which makes the nature and structure of the elements constituting them difficult to evaluate [3]. Commonly, US templates relates a WHO, a WHAT and possibly a WHY dimension and in practice different keywords are used to describe these dimensions (e.g. Mike Cohn's *As a <type of user>, I want <some goal> so that <some reason>* [2]). In the literature no semantics have been associated to these keywords. Thus, Wautelet et al. [9] collected the majority of templates used in practice, sorted them and associated semantics to each keyword. The key idea is that, using a unified and consistent set of US templates, the tags associated to each element of the US set provide information about its nature and granularity. Such information could be used for software analysis, e.g., structuring the problem and solution, identifying missing requirements, etc. Most of the concepts of [9] are related to the i* framework [12] so that a visual *Goal-Oriented Requirements Engineering (GORE)* model, the *Rationale Tree (RT)*, has been formalized for graphical representation of US sets in [8,10].

In parallel, Lucassen et al. [4] have proposed the Quality User Story (QUS) framework, a linguistic approach to evaluate and improve the quality of individual US and US sets. US are often written with poor attention and their quality can be improved by applying a set of 13 criteria. QUS is supported by the *Automatic Quality User Story Artisan (AQUSA)* software tool. Based on natural language processing techniques, AQUSA detects quality defects and suggests remedies. Domain experts also need to be involved in the US quality improvement process to fine tune the US set. Overall, a QUS-compliant US set is aimed to enhance readability and better support the human understanding of the software problem and solution than its non-compliant counterpart; this further helps stakeholders during all of the software development activities.

Even if they are basically independent researches, an experiment has been conducted to test whether the usage of the QUS framework leads to a US set allowing a modeler to build a RT of higher quality than one that would have been built with the original US set. For this purpose, a real-life US set has been selected and enhanced in quality using the QUS approach with the help of the AQUSA tool and domain experts (we have then a "raw" and a QUS-compliant US set). Students from the master in Business Administration (with a major in IT and familiar with various modeling techniques) at KU Leuven campus Brussels have served as test subjects. A first group was required to perform small exercises and build a RT out of the raw US set, the second one out of the QUS-compliant US set. The difference in quality of the RTs built and their constituting elements' relevance are studied in this paper.

2   Related Work

The need to test different decomposition techniques of US with different agile methods and kinds of stakeholders has been identified in [6]. In this paper we only consider US as structured in the Cohn's form, independently of a specific agile method and evaluate the perspective of the modeler only. Trkman et al. [7] propose an approach for mapping US to process models in order to understand US dependencies. Their approach is oriented to building an operational sequence of activities which is a dynamic approach not targeted to multiple granularity levels representation. We, however, aim to build a rationale analysis of US elements which allows to represent and identify at once multiple granularity levels but does not show explicitly the sequence of activities. As identified by Caire et al. [1], the representation symbols in a visual notation have an impact on the modelers' understanding. We by default used the symbols of i* but this parameter could be further studied.

Wautelet et al. [11] made an experiment using the unified model of [9] for tagging the elements of the WHO, WHAT and WHY dimensions of a US; each tag representing a concept with an inherent nature and defined granularity. Once tagged, the US elements were graphically represented by building one or more RTs. The research consisted of a double exercise aimed to evaluate how well novice and experienced modelers were able to build a RT out of an existing US set. The experiment explicitly forced the test subjects to attribute a concept to US elements and to link these together. On the basis of the conducted experiment, difficulties that the modeler faces when building a RT with basic support were identified but overall the test subjects produced models of satisfying quality. The experiment of Wautelet et al. [11] can be seen as preliminary to the one conducted in this paper. We indeed here also guide subjects into the tagging of US elements and build a RT out of US sets. The main innovation here is that there is a variation of quality among the US sets submitted to the subjects.

3   Research Approach and Background

3.1   Research Hypothesis and Goals

Research Hypotheses. According to Lucassen et al. [5] the use of the QUS framework effectively decreases the quality defects within US. One of the main expectations towards the use of the QUS framework in the experiment is thus that the quality (evaluated by scores) of the represented RTs will be higher with the QUS-compliant US set. This specifically means that we expect an improvement in identifying relevant **software functions** and elements like **Epics, Themes, Non Functional Requirements (NFRs)** and possibly **missing requirements**. The interference of the RT to identify the concepts is expected to be positive, especially for Themes and Epics because their identification is specifically supported by the RT. The **goals** of the experiment are then:

- To analyze the ability of the subjects to understand and identify different concepts (NFRs, missing requirements, Epics & Themes) related to US sets;
- To analyze and verify the ability of the subjects to build a RT from a set of US taken from a real-life case;
- To analyze the impact of the RT on the subjects' ability to identify and distinguish the previously mentioned concepts related to US sets;

– To analyze and measure the impact of the QUS-compliant US set on (i) the
ability of the subjects to identify and distinguish the nature and granularity
of elements present in US (before and after the use of the RT) and (ii) to
build a RT.

3.2   Building the Experiment

A BPMN workflow of the followed research steps can be found in Appendix
C[1]. We have created two versions of the experiment and randomly divided the
subjects in two groups. One group that receives the experiment with the "raw"
US set (available in Appendix A & B), and the other group that receives the
experiment with the "QUS-compliant" set (also available in Appendix A & B).

The real-life US set has been furnished by an organization that wants to
remain anonymous; it is called "Company X" here. The latter furnished a document with US sets concerning the development of a web-application. From the
original document, 2 (raw at this stage) US sets were selected (1 set for each part
of the experiment). Then, several exercises were built together with theoretical
explanations and instructions.

Fabiano Dalpiaz, involved as a promoter in the development of the QUS
framework, ran the raw US sets through the AQUSA tool and delivered the
generated reports. The tool does not include all the criteria so that a manual
tagging was done by Fabiano to evaluate the US sets based on all the criteria (see
Appendix D). Fabiano also added some comments to some of his tags to clarify
his answer (Appendix D). Note that tagging a US means here to answer "yes"
or "no" to the 13 criteria. The research team then met with an IT manager and
a developer of company X to re-discuss and improve the US set. Both employees
were involved in writing the US; they clarified some aspects allowing to build
the final version of the two QUS-compliant US sets. With the raw and QUS-
compliant US sets at disposal, the final version of the experiment was discussed
by the research team. Based on this, some layout was changed and more context
and explanations were added to the experiment document.

The last step was to create a well-founded solution. Each of the research team
members created individually a possible solution for the RT. These solutions
were compared among each other and discussed. After that, a joint solution that
became the "moving golden standard" was set-up, meaning the solution of the
RT could evolve during the corrections of the experiment. Indeed, when a subject
modeled an element or link that was valid but not considered previously, it could
be added to the solution after discussion among the research team members. The
solutions of the exercises of both groups, with the moving golden standard of the
RT included, are shown in appendix G & I. Appendix E contains a timetable that
gives an overview of the iterations that were made to conduct the experiment.
Each time information about when and how the meeting took place, who was
involved and what the outcome was, is given. The conducted experiments of

---

[1] All appendices are available at: http://dx.doi.org/10.17632/st8byw8hkz.1.

both groups are depicted in Appendix F (group 1) & H (group 2), followed by the solutions of the experiments in Appendix G (group 1) & I (group 2).

3.3   Assignment and Measured Variables

In an introductory part, questions have been asked to gather additional information that could be used as variables for the analysis. The following list of questions were asked: (i) educational background; (ii) primary occupation (student, researcher, teacher, ...); (iii) experience with software modeling (Likert-scale from 1 to 5): if they had experience, we further asked what languages they worked with; (iv) amount of years of experience with software development; and (v) 8 Likert-scale questions, from 1–5, about their knowledge of US, User Story Mapping (USM), NFR, US as requirements in agile methods, Epics, Themes, missing requirements and Entity Relationship Diagram (ERD).

Exercises Part 1: The exercises for the first part consist in the identification of the following concepts: (i) non-functional requirements (exercise 1); (ii) Epics (exercise 2); (iii) Themes (exercise 2 (as well)); and (iv) Missing requirements (exercise 3). The subjects received some context information about the application to develop together with a reference in the document's appendix where a list of US-related concepts were explained. The exercises of part 1 were based on the first US set of Company X. The first US set consists in 13 US in its "raw" form (thus for group 1, see Appendix A) and in 11 US in its QUS-compliant form (thus for group 2, see Appendix A). The entire sets were nevertheless split into small samples for the needs of each exercise containing 3 to 4 US. After having made the exercises, the subjects were asked to quantify, by using a Likert-scale from 1 to 5, the clarity of the explanations of the concepts and the difficulty they perceived in identifying these concepts.

Exercises Part 2: The exercise for the second part consists in one global modeling exercise to build a RT. Theoretical background about the different types of elements (i.e., *role, task, capability, hard-goal* and *soft-goal*) and links (i.e., *means-end, decomposition* and *contribution*) used in the RT was given together with a running example of 4 US. The exercise of part 2 is based on the second US set of Company X. The latter US set consists in 7 US in its "raw" form (thus for group 1, see Appendix B) and in 7 US in its QUS-compliant form (thus for group 2, see Appendix B).

The subjects received information about the context of the application development in company X together with a second set of US. Based on a study by Wautelet et al. [11], the test subjects had to execute the following steps to model a RT (see the experiment document in the Appendix F for group 1 and Appendix H for group 2):

- **Step 1**: Identify the WHO element from each US;
- **Step 2**: Identify the elements from the WHAT- and WHY-dimension in every US;

- **Step 3**: Identify, for each element of the WHAT- and WHY-dimension, the construct that will be used for their graphical representation, according to the theory;
- **Step 4**: Graphically represent all elements identified in steps 2 & 3 and create a RT by linking them;
- **Step 5**: Identify the possible missing links to complete the graphical representation.

For steps 2 and 3, the first US was given as an example. The subjects were asked to identify the same concepts as in part 1 but this time using the RT to support them in the process. Note that the ability of identifying a NFR was not explicitly asked again because it was implicitly included in the modeling exercise. The last part consisted in 4 Likert-scale questions about the understandability and easiness of using the RT.

3.4   Data Collection

To collect the data, the experiment has been executed by 34 Business Administration students with a specialization in Business Information Management at the KU Leuven campus Brussels. Before the start of the experiment, Yves Wautelet gave a 30 min introduction about US to both groups at the same time. The subjects were then divided in two groups of 17, one that used the raw set as input and the other that used the QUS-compliant one. The subjects were randomly divided by "blindly" giving them a piece of paper on which "1" or "2" was written. Subjects that received "1" stayed in the same room and were given the experiment with the raw set. Subjects that received "2" had to go to a second room where they were given the experiment with the QUS-compliant set.

3.5   Evaluating the Experiment's Results

The solutions used to evaluate the subject's representations are depicted in Appendix G for group 1 and Appendix I for group 2. Due to their small size, the solutions for the exercises in part 1 did not lead to much discussions and were rapidly adopted. For the large exercise of part 2, the solution is based on a "moving golden standard". Although all of the solutions are highlighted within the appendices, some more explanation about the RT of part 2 should be given. The research team chose to distinguish three hard-goals within the solution that were all separately connected with a task by a means-end link. The following three hard-goals were chosen because they all express a coarse-grained functionality: *Correct errors in personal information*, *Sign in with user account*, and *Register myself*. Besides identifying those elements, the test subjects also had to identify Epics, Themes and missing requirements using of their RT. *As an End User I want to register myself So that I can sign in with a user account* is considered an Epic US. The US indeed contains clear high-level elements while US 2, US 4 and US 5 are related to US 3.

4   Analyzing the Results of the Experiment

4.1   Preparing the Data for Analysis

Data was analyzed with SPSS. Variables have been defined and it has been ensured that their results could be compared by rescaling their total score. The latter was done because there was a difference in the value of the total score within some exercises between the experiment in group 1 and 2. Also, the relevant variables have been put in percentages so scores from different exercises within and between groups could be compared in a consistent way. The next step has been to evaluate and define useful factors. A short description of the used variables is given hereafter.

Description of the Variables. As previously mentioned, an introductory part of the experiment document given to the subjects collected some additional information about them. The variables that were collected are the following:

- EduBackground: highest education level obtained (high school, bachelor, master);
- Experience: the experience in software modeling (Likert-scale[2]);
- KnownModelingLanguage: what modeling languages they have experience with;
- MonthsOfExperience: how many months of experience with software development, regarding any method or technique;
- KnowledgeUserStories: their knowledge about US (Likert-scale);
- KnowledgeUserStoryMapping: their knowledge about USM (Likert-scale);
- KnowledgeNFR: their knowledge about NFRs (Likert-scale);
- KnowledgeUSInAgile: knowledge about US as requirement artifacts in agile software development methodologies (Likert-scale);
- KnowledgeEpicUS: their knowledge about Epic US (Likert-scale);
- KnowledgeUSThemes: their knowledge about Themes in US (Likert-scale);
- KnowledgeMissingRequirements: their knowledge about MR (Likert-scale);
- KnowledgeERD: their knowledge about Entity-Relationship (Likert-scale).

The variables that measure the score of the subjects on the different exercises were named *ScoreNFR*, *ScoreTheme*, *ScoreEpic* and *ScoreMR*. A distinction was made between the exercises of parts 1 and 2.

The ability of the subject to identify a NFR in part 2 was a part of the exercise on the RT and was named *ScoreSoft_Goal*. After the exercises, the subjects' perception on their ability to solve the exercises was asked and transformed into variables *DifficultyNFR*, *-Themes*, *-Epics* and *-MR* for part 1 as well as *FindMR*, *-Epic* and *-Theme* for part 2. The perception of the subjects' ability to identify soft-goals[3] in part 2 was not asked explicitly because it was captured in the

---

[2] A Likert-scale from 1-5 that goes from "never heard of it" to "expert in topic", is used in every variable with a "Likert-scale".

[3] Typically in the RT, a NFR is represented as a softgoal so that, in the rest of this paper, every time we refer to softgoal we implicitly mean a NFR.

Table 1. Factor analysis.

Factors	Factor loadings of items	KMO	Total variance	Cronbach's alpha
F1: KnowledgeUS	**KU1:** 0,845; **KU2:** 0,785; **KU3:** 0,676; **KU4:** 0,672	0,722	55,987	0,731
F2: KnowledgeMacro-ConceptsUS	**KMC1:** 0,900; **KMC2:** 0,935; **KMC3:** 0,742	0,619	74,470	0,806
F3: Understandabili-tyMacroConcepts	**UMC1:** 0,718; **UMC2:** 0,731; **UMC3:** 0,920; **UMC4:** 0,920; **UMC5:** 0,607	0,796	62,246	0,797
F4: EasinessMacro-Concepts_Part2	**EMC1:** 0,709; **EMC2:** 0,910; **EMC3:** 0,895	0,627	71,051	0,792
F5: HelpOfTreeMacro-Concepts_Part2	**HTMC1:** 0,890; **HTMC2:** 0,870; **HTMC3:** 0,891	0,733	78,085	0,857
F6: ClearnessEasines-sOfUseTree	**CET1:** 0,826; **CET2:** 0,768; **CET3:** 0,885; **CET4:** 0,844	0,751	69,211	0,848

perception of modeling the overall diagram. After the first part, the subjects were also asked to give their perception on the understandability of the concepts explained, respectively named *UnderstandUS, -NFR, -Epic* and *-Theme*. While Epics and Themes are related concepts, *ClearDifferenceEpic_Theme* asked whether the difference between both concepts was clear.

The modeling exercise in part 2, regarding the RT, measured the ability of the subjects to model each construct separately. *ScoreCoarseGrainedFunctionality, -Hard_Goal, -Soft_Goal, -Task, -Capability, -Links, -ConsistentTree* and *-MissingLink* were used as variables to measure their performance. Subjects received points on their ability to identify the coarse-grained functionalities from the US. They also received points when they indicated these functionalities as hard-goals, could identify the soft-goals, tasks and capabilities and connect the relevant elements by using the correct links. The RT was also analyzed on its consistency and could be divided into 3 levels. A consistently modeled RT was considered *a clear hierarchical structure were most of the relevant elements were linked*, subjects received the full points in this case. A partially modeled RT combines *at least 2 different US with no clear hierarchical structure*; this was given half of the points. A graphical model were *no US were linked*, was given 0.

Table 2. Comparing the means of the overall scores.

Variables	Mean group 1	Mean group 2	Mean difference (% points)
Percentage of score of the exercises in part 1	64,71	51,70	13,01*
Percentage of the score of the exercises in part 2	49,91	57,62	7,71
Percentage of the score of modelling the Rationale Tree	55,54	64,67	9,13

*: $p<0,05$; **: $p<0,01$

After the exercise, a few questions about the use of the RT were asked. *HelpTree_MR*, *-_Epic*, *-_Themes* are the variables that captured the perception of the subject on how the RT helped in identifying the concepts. To end the experiment, 4 variables about the subjects' perception on the RT: (i) *IntroTree_Clear_Understandable* and *TheoryElementsLinks_Clear_Understandable*, measured how clear and understandable the introduction and the theory about the different elements and links was; (ii) *SkilfulAtUsingTree* measured whether the subjects would find it easy to become skilful at using the RT; and (iii) *ApplyTreeDailyWorkLife* measured whether the subjects would find it easy to apply the RT in their daily work life to evaluate US sets. The perceptions, mentioned above, were measured by a Likert-Scale from 1 to 5 where 1 means "Not at all" and 5 means "Extremely".

Factor Analysis. A Principal Component Analysis was executed to reduce the amount of unstructured information from variables that are associated with a common latent (i.e., not directly measured) variable. Table 1 shows the relevant factors that were found and used during the analysis of the results. A total of six factors was found, Appendix J shows which items are related to which factors within the component matrix. The table shows all factors were usable because they all had an acceptable Kaiser-Meyer-Olkin (KMO) test (above 0, 5). Besides that, the Bartlett's Test of Sphericity was significant in every factor. Every factor had a sufficient percentage of total variance explained and a reliability analysis showed the Cronbach's alpha was high enough (above 0, 6).

4.2 A Between-Group Comparison: Analyzing the Impact of the QUS Framework

The first comparison that is made is the between-group one. The different scores on the exercises are compared by testing whether there is a significant difference between the means of group 1 and 2. In that way, there will be checked whether the use of a QUS-compliant US set improves the ability of the subjects to identify the different concepts before and after using the RT and improves the ability to build a graphical representation.

The **experience in software modeling** of respondents has also been analyzed. Due to a lack of space and because it is not fundamental for the overall understanding of the paper, it has been placed in Appendix K.

Analyzing the Scores. In this section some analysis regarding the scores of the exercises will be compared between both groups to check whether the QUS framework had a possible effect on the scores. Table 2 shows the overall scores of the exercises in part 1, part 2 and the modeling exercise of the RT.

The variables that are included in the overall scores are the following: *ScoreNFR* (*ScoreSoft_Goal* for part 2), *-Theme*, *-Epic* and *-MR*. The exercises concerning the latter concepts can be found in Appendix F and H. The overall score of the modeling exercise is the sum of the scores of all separate elements that had to be modeled. As mentioned previously, the scores are expressed as percentages for consistency reasons.

As seen in Table 2, there is only one significant mean difference. The mean score, expressed as a percentage, of the subjects in group 1 and thus with the raw US set, score a mean of 13,01% points significantly higher than the subjects in group 2. In other words, there is a significant decrease in the mean of the score of 20,11% in group 2, compared to group 1. Part 2 and the exercise on the RT show no significant difference in means. The expectation that the QUS-compliant US set would improve the overall scores of the exercises that are executed by the subjects is not confirmed. On the contrary, subjects from group 1 score higher on the exercises in part 1. Although, the means of the scores from the exercises for part 2 and the RT are higher in group 2, they are not significant. A plausible explanation for the mean difference in the exercises of part 1 is rather hard to find while similar, but improved, US sets are used in group 2. It might be possible that the effect of the QUS framework, that changed some of the US, and the selection of a few different US influenced the ability of the novice modelers to identify the concepts in part 1. To test whether the mean differences are significant, an independent t-test was conducted for part 1 and 2 (Appendix N). The means for the modeling exercises are tested according to the Kruskall-Wallis test, because in group 1 the variable is not normally distributed (Appendix L).

Besides the overall score, the scores of the separate exercises in part 1 and 2 have also been analyzed. Table 3 shows the differences of the separate exercises between group 1 and group 2 and indicates whether they are significant. Again, percentages are used to ensure consistent comparisons. The mean differences are tested by a Kruskall-Wallis test (Appendix M & L). The mean difference

Table 3. Separate scores of the exercises in part1 and part2.

Variables	Mean group 1	Mean group 2	Mean difference (% points)
Percentage of score NFR part 1	74,26	70,00	4,26
Percentage of score Themes part 1	82,35	55,88	26,47*
Percentage of score Epic part 1	73,53	20,59	52,94**
Percentage of score MR part 1	23,53	26,47	2,94
Percentage of score NFR part 2	73,53	73,53	0,00
Percentage of score Themes part 2	47,84	62,75	14,91
Percentage of score Epic part 2	41,18	64,71	23,53
Percentage of score MR part 2	35,29	29,41	5,88

*: $p < 0,05$; **: $p < 0,01$

of the scores in identifying Themes and Epics in part 1 between both groups is significant. There is a decrease of 32,14% in the mean score from group 1 to group 2 in identifying Themes. The mean score of the identification of Epics in group 1, is significantly higher than in group 2. These differences explain the mean difference of the overall score in part 1. Another explanation could be that the QUS-compliant set had a negative impact on the subjects' abilities to identify Epics and Themes from a short set of US. Although the mean scores' differences are not significant, Table 3 shows that the mean scores of identifying Themes and Epics are higher in group 2 from a between-group point of view, but especially from a within-group point of view. From these results, a new hypothesis can be raised: *the subjects' ability to identify Themes and Epics within a high-quality set of US improves while using a RT to identify them.* The hypothesis that a QUS-compliant set will improve the identification of Epics, Themes, NFRs and missing requirements is rejected in both the cases before and after the use of the RT.

Table 4 shows the means of the scores (in points, not as percentages) for the separate modeled elements of the RT. To clarify the figures, the maximum amount of points that could be given to a subject for each variable is indicated. According to the table, the subjects could best identify the coarse-grained functionalities in both group 1 and 2. The average score of the subjects was also high for modeling a consistent RT. That finding can be linked to the research of

Wautelet et al. [11] which concluded that most of the subjects could create an acceptable graphical US model. The subjects scored the least points in identifying the missing links, an error that also frequently occurred in the mentioned study. When looking at the mean differences, there are three values that show a significant difference. The mean score for modeling the tasks, the capabilities and the links is significantly higher in group 2. This implies that some of the expectations are partially confirmed. In both exercises the same US set was used, the only difference was the interference of the QUS framework to improve the quality of the US set. A plausible explanation for the significant difference might be that a US set of better quality (i.e., improved by the QUS framework) helps the modeler to identify some elements of the RT better, specifically tasks, capabilities and links. This could be an interesting finding, while Wautelet et al. [11] mentioned a lot of modeling errors concerning the capability element. The interference of the QUS framework could be a possible solution to easily identify atomicity in functional elements.

A non-parametric Kruskall-Wallis test (Appendix M) was used to compare the means of all the variables in Table 4, except for the score attributed to identifying the links. For the latter, an independent t-test (Appendix N) was executed because the normality condition was met (Appendix L).

The **perceptions** of respondents have also been analyzed. Due to a lack of space and because it is not fundamental for the overall understanding of the paper, it has been placed in Appendix M.

Table 4. Comparing scores on the elements of the Rationale Tree.

Variables	Mean group 1	Mean group 2	Mean difference
Score modelled 3 coarse-grained functionalities in Tree (3p)	2,4118	2,5294	0,1176
Score modelled 3 hard-goals in Tree (3p)	1,2353	1,5882	0,3529
Score modelled 2 soft-goals in Tree (2p)	1,4706	1,4706	0,00
Score modelled 4 tasks in Tree (2p)	0,8824	1,2353	0,3529*
Score modelled 2 capabilities in Tree (1p)	0,6176	0,8824	0,2648*
Score modelled 8 links in Tree (4p)	1,6471	2,3765	0,7294*
Score modelled a consistent Tree (1p)	0,8824	0,7941	0,0883
Score identifying missing links (1p)	0,2941	0,1176	0,1765

*: $p<0,05$; **: $p<0,01$

4.3   A Within-Group Comparison: Analyzing the Impact of the Rationale Tree

In this section, a within-group analysis is made. Like in the previous section, the different scores will be compared by testing whether there is a significant difference, but the means of the exercises from the different parts are here compared in both groups separately. The main goal is to evaluate whether the use of the RT improves the ability of the subject to identify different concepts and to test whether the impact of the RT improves while using a US set of higher quality. Within this section, the new conducted hypothesis from Sect. 4.2 will be tested.

Analyzing the Scores. First, the overall scores of the exercises in both parts are compared. Figure 1 depicts the overall mean scores, as percentages, of the exercises from part 1 and 2 for both groups. The figure depicts the previously identified significant difference in the exercises of part 1 between both groups. Within group 1 (0 in the chart) and group 2 (1 in the chart), the paired t-test is used to test whether there was a significant difference between both parts. The t-test shows there is a significant ($p<0,01$) difference in group 1 between the exercises of part 1 and 2. The tests show there is no significant difference in group 2. With respect to the previous tests, analyzed in Sect. 4.2; it is clear that differences exist in the overall score of the exercises in part 1, both within and between the groups. An explanation for the within-group difference might be that the RT does not help the test subjects to identify the concepts when using a US set of lower quality. Besides that, part 2 introduces something totally new to the test subjects, the RT, that could also have an influence on the ability of the modelers to make the exercises. Another possible explanation of the difference could be the usage of different US sets in both parts. Additionally, the US set in part 1 of group 1 was slightly different from the US set in part 1 of group 2.

A second within-group comparison is done by analyzing the mean differences in the scores of the separate exercises. Table 5 explains the significant difference between the overall scores of the exercises in part 1 and 2. According to a non-parametric Wilcoxon Signed Ranks test, the mean differences of the scores on the exercises regarding Themes and Epics are significantly different. The data shows that group 1 better identified Themes and Epics in part 1. That finding also aligns with the significant difference in the means of the scores on iden-

Table 5. Comparing separate exercises group 1.

Variable	Mean part 1	Mean part 2	Mean difference
Percentage of score on exercise Theme	82,35	47,84	34,51**
Percentage of score on exercise Epic	73,53	41,18	32,35*

*: $p<0,05$; **: $p<0,01$

tifying Themes and Epics between both groups. With respect to the possible other explanations for the significant difference, the explanation in the previous paragraph could be refined into the following: *the RT does not help the test subjects to identify Themes and Epics when using a US set of lower quality.*

In the Table 6, the same comparison is made but now from the point of view of group 2. As in Table 5, only the relevant variables are depicted. The data shows that test subjects can better identify Epics after using the RT. The difference is significant. A plausible explanation might be that the RT helps identifying Epics when using a high-quality set of US. The new hypothesis can thus be partially accepted (only concerning Epics).

Table 6. Comparing separate exercises group 2.

Variable	Mean part 1	Mean part 2	Mean difference
Percentage of score on exercise Epics	20,59	64,71	44,12**

*: $p<0,05$; **: $p<0,01$

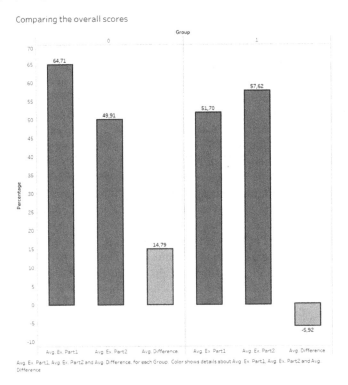

Fig. 1. Comparing the overall scores of the two parts.

5 Threats to Validity, Future Work and Limitations

The first and main threat to validity comes from the "distance" between the raw and QUS-compliant US sets. We have selected two sets of US that have been improved using the QUS framework without having a quantitative evaluation of the distance between the two sets (it is up to the reader to evaluate this distance by tracing the revision procedure and/or reading the initial and QUS-compliant sets). It could be that (raw) US sets of various initial qualities do exist within real-life US sets and that the QUS application will bring more value to initial US sets with lower quality. This would have a direct impact on the ability of the modeler to understand the software problem, to identify functions, their abstraction and complementarity as well as elements like NFRs, Epics, Themes and missing requirements. We need to establish a way to measure/quantify the distance between the raw and QUS-compliant US sets and reproduce the experience with sets having different distances to better understand this. Another threat comes from the quoting system itself. The latter has been built through an analysis of default solutions and a moving golden standard with the aim to define the criteria making the representations relevant and of high quality. While we have included all of the possibilities we found and justified the importance of the criteria we used, other solutions could perhaps have been included.

We also point out two limitations. First, the experiment was only executed by students that, despite some different educational backgrounds, all studied Business Administration. In future research, it would be interesting to compare the ability of different sample groups like agile/requirements specialists, business analysts or other students with a different background (e.g., computer science students). A second limitation concerns the limited amount of information that was given to the subjects. Despite the previously mentioned introduction about US and the information given about the different concepts related to US sets, the amount of information was still limited for students without any previous knowledge about the concepts. Also, the presentation of the RT and its concepts was kept as limited as possible so subjects could execute the experiment within the time frame (approximately 2 h). An introduction and explanation about the unified model for US modeling, for example, was not given to the subjects, although knowledge about that would have been useful.

6 Conclusion and Future Work

After describing the data and creating factors, two types of comparisons were made. A between-group comparison and a within-group comparison were indeed conducted to measure the impact of both the QUS framework and the RT. Some significant differences were found from which the following main conclusions could be drawn. Applying a high-quality US set compared to a US set of lower quality did not improve the test subjects' ability to identify the US related concepts (themes, epics, NFRs or even missing requirements) that were tested in the exercises, both with and without the use of the RT. A possible explanation for the rejection of the hypothesis was that group 2 received a slightly different US set than group 1 in the first part. The improved US set could have been experienced as more difficult for the novice modelers in group 2. The non-significant differences in part 2 between both groups might be explained by the interference of a new framework that the novice modelers did not know. Neither did the interference of the QUS framework improve the overall scores of the exercises compared to the US set of lower quality. Overall, we thus cannot conclude that the effect of the QUS framework, compared to a US set of lower quality, had any benefits to understand the problem/solution domain of the real-life case. A finding that did confirm an expectation was that the QUS-compliant US set improved the ability of the test subjects to identify and model some parts of the RT better, specifically Tasks, Capabilities, and links. This could be due to the fact that the QUS-compliant US set is more consistent and less overlapping than the raw one so helping the modeler to better separate and structure the elements present in US. While analyzing the data, a new hypothesis could be developed. According to some clear differences in means, there was expected that a QUS-compliant US set could improve the test subjects' ability to identify Themes and Epics with the use of the RT compared to identifying the same concepts without using the RT. That expectation was only partially confirmed because there was only a significant difference regarding the identifications of Epics. Even if building a RT out of a US set of a higher quality level does not impact the ability of test subjects to identify Themes, Epics or missing requirements, we can conclude that building the RT from a QUS-compliant US set improves the ability of the novice modeler to identify Epics. By helping in this identification, a RT built out of a QUS-compliant US set improves the ability to understand the problem/solution domain in a real-life case.

Acknowledgement. The authors would like to thank Fabiano Dalpiaz for having evaluated the raw US set with the AQUSA tool and Duje Delic for his involvement in the experiment.

References

1. Caire, P., Genon, N., Heymans, P., Moody, D.L.: Visual notation design 2.0: towards user comprehensible requirements engineering notations. In: 21st IEEE International RE Conference, Rio de Janeiro-RJ, Brazil, 2013, pp. 115–124. IEEE Computer Society (2013)
2. Cohn, M.: Succeeding with Agile: Software Development Using Scrum. 1st edn. Addison-Wesley Professional (2009)
3. Liskin, O., Pham, R., Kiesling, S., Schneider, K.: Why we need a granularity concept for user stories. In: Cantone, G., Marchesi, M. (eds.) XP 2014. LNBIP, vol. 179, pp. 110–125. Springer, Cham (2014). https://doi.org/10.1007/978-3-319-06862-6_8
4. Lucassen, G., Dalpiaz, F., van der Werf, J.M.E., Brinkkemper, S.: Improving agile requirements: the quality user story framework and tool. Req. Eng. **21**(3), 383–403 (2016)
5. Lucassen, G., Dalpiaz, F., van der Werf, J.M.E.M., Brinkkemper, S.: Improving user story practice with the grimm method: a multiple case study in the software

industry. In: Grünbacher, P., Perini, A. (eds.) REFSQ 2017. LNCS, vol. 10153, pp. 235–252. Springer, Cham (2017). https://doi.org/10.1007/978-3-319-54045-0_18

6. Taibi, D., Lenarduzzi, V., Janes, A., Liukkunen, K., Ahmad, M.O.: Comparing requirements decomposition within the scrum, scrum with Kanban, XP, and banana development processes. In: Baumeister, H., Lichter, H., Riebisch, M. (eds.) XP 2017. LNBIP, vol. 283, pp. 68–83. Springer, Cham (2017). https://doi.org/10.1007/978-3-319-57633-6_5

7. Trkman, M., Mendling, J., Krisper, M.: Using business process models to better understand the dependencies among user stories. Inf. Softw. Technol. **71**, 58–76 (2016)

8. Wautelet, Y., Heng, S., Kiv, S., Kolp, M.: User-story driven development of multi-agent systems: a process fragment for agile methods. Comput. Lang. Syst. Struct. **50**, 159–176 (2017)

9. Wautelet, Y., Heng, S., Kolp, M., Mirbel, I.: Unifying and extending user story models. In: Jarke, M., et al. (eds.) CAiSE 2014. LNCS, vol. 8484, pp. 211–225. Springer, Cham (2014). https://doi.org/10.1007/978-3-319-07881-6_15

10. Wautelet, Y., Heng, S., Kolp, M., Mirbel, I., Poelmans, S.: Building a rationale diagram for evaluating user story sets. In: 10th IEEE International Conference on Research Challenges in Information Science, RCIS 2016, Grenoble, France, 1–3 June 2016, pp. 477–488 (2016)

11. Wautelet, Y., Velghe, M., Heng, S., Poelmans, S., Kolp, M.: On modelers ability to build a visual diagram from a user story set: a goal-oriented approach. In: Kamsties, E., Horkoff, J., Dalpiaz, F. (eds.) REFSQ 2018. LNCS, vol. 10753, pp. 209–226. Springer, Cham (2018). https://doi.org/10.1007/978-3-319-77243-1_13

12. Yu, E., Giorgini, P., Maiden, N., Mylopoulos, J.: Social Modeling for Requirements Engineering. MIT Press, Cambridge (2011)

Requirements for Observing, Deciding, and Delivering Capability Change

Georgios Koutsopoulos[✉], Martin Henkel, and Janis Stirna

Department of Computer and Systems Sciences, Stockholm University,
Stockholm, Sweden
{georgios,martinh,js}@dsv.su.se

Abstract. Dynamic business environments create the need for constant change in modern enterprises. Enterprise transformation is associated to changes in enterprise capabilities since capabilities are an essential element in business designs. Capability modeling methods need to evolve accordingly and the development of such methods needs to be systematic. This study, as part of a Design Science project, aims to elicit requirements for a capability modeling method for addressing change. Literature sources and a case study at a healthcare organization that undergoes several changes are used to elicit requirements. The requirements are presented in the form of a goal model for the method under development.

Keywords: Capability · Enterprise modeling · Adaptation · Transformation

1 Introduction

The degree of dynamism in business environments is on the rise, leading to organizations constantly trying to adapt according to situations existing in their external or internal environment. Organizations struggling to "catch-up" is a common phenomenon and the distance is only going to be amplified as the organizations' rate of change is usually lower than their environment's [1]. Therefore, in the area of Information Systems (IS), a challenging task has emerged in the form of providing support methods and tools for the organizations facing constant change. As a response to this situation, various methods have been developed, for example [2, 3] in order to support the adapting organizations in their constantly changing needs.

Enterprise Modeling (EM) is a discipline that has attempted to tackle the above-mentioned challenge in various ways. It captures organizational knowledge and provides the necessary motivation and input for designing IS [4]. In addition, the notion of capability has emerged in IS engineering as an instrument for context-dependent design and delivery of business services [5]. Capability modeling is one specific area of EM that utilizes the concept of capability. Capabilities are an important aspect of enterprises, since they encompass the majority of the concepts relevant to change, such as, goal, decision, context, process, service, and context [5, 6].

In a way similar to any method supporting enterprise transformation, modeling methods need to evolve as well, in order to improve the organizations' ISs. Capability modeling should therefore evolve accordingly, improving not only the way capabilities

J. Gordijn et al. (Eds.): PoEM 2019, LNBIP 369, pp. 20–35, 2019.
https://doi.org/10.1007/978-3-030-35151-9_2

are implemented during design phase of the system, but also adjustments and changes performed during run-time [5].

This study is part of a research project aiming to provide methodological and tool support for changing organizations by supporting capability modeling within dynamic contexts. It follows the framework of Design Science research [7, 8] and this study concerns the step of the elicitation of requirements for the design artifact, in particular, the envisioned method for capability modeling and analysis. Goals, being a type of requirement [9], are elicited from two different sources, literature and a case study in the public healthcare sector of Sweden, and presented as a goal model for the envisioned method. They can be seen as relevant to any similar approach.

The rest of the paper is structured as follows. Section 2 consists of a brief presentation of the basic concepts and related literature. Section 3 describes the methods used for this study. Section 4 presents the requirements elicited from literature. Section 5 introduces the case, along with two specific change implementations and the requirements elicited from the case. Section 6 summarizes the elicited requirements in a goal model. Section 7 presents a discussion of the elicited requirements and Sect. 8 provides concluding remarks and briefly explains the next steps of this research project.

2   Background

EM is defined as the process of the creation of an enterprise model that captures all the enterprise's aspects that are required for a given modeling purpose. A key aspect in EM is the integrated view on the various aspects of the enterprise. An enterprise model therefore consists of a set of interlinked sub-models, each of them focusing on a specific aspect like processes, goals, concepts, business rules [10]. Concerning applicability, EM is applicable for any organization, public or private, or its part.

The focus for *capability modeling* is enterprises ability and capacity to deliver value, to achieve goals, or to sustain a long term function. The importance of capabilities lies in the fact that it assists a holistic view of the enterprise since it encompasses several aspects due to the association of the concept with several key concepts such as goals, business services, processes, actors, environment. EM has been used to depict enterprise capabilities in several ways including stand-alone modeling approaches like VDML (Value Delivery Modeling Language) [11] and CDD (Capability-Driven Development) [5]. Several Enterprise Architecture (EA) frameworks include the concept of capability and offer capability viewpoints. Popular EA frameworks that include capability modeling are (i) Department of Defense Architecture Framework (DoDAF) [12], (ii) NATO Architecture Framework) (NAF) [13], (iii) Ministry of Defence Architecture Framework (MODAF), and (iv) Archimate [14]. There have also been research contributions that provide suggestions on how to model capabilities based on existing modeling methods like i* [15] or Capability Maps [16] or introducing new notations like CODEK [2] to include the elements required to capture how a capability can change or be changed in dynamic environments.

3   Methods

This study belongs to a project elaborated within the Design Science paradigm, in particular, following the guidelines of [7], according to which a method is considered a design artifact. As with any other artifact, a capability modeling method needs to be scoped and have requirements defined for it. The activity aims to answer the question "What artifact can be a solution for the explicated problem and which requirements on this artefact are important for the stakeholders?" [7]. In this study, the defined requirements concern the method and not the case since the method developer is considered as the stakeholder and not the case study's organization's stakeholders. Thus, the task performed is defining requirements for the method; not for the included use case. The requirements for a method for modeling changing capabilities have been elicited by using a *literature review* and a *case study* and visualized as a *goal model*.

3.1   Literature Review

In an earlier study [17], a literature review concerning capability meta-models was conducted. The papers identified in that study are useful for this study as well, often including requirements for modeling capability changes. A part of that study was to identify papers using a snowballing technique on the initial set of papers that was identified through systematic literature review. Several of the papers that were excluded during snowballing for not including a meta-model have been deemed useful to include in this study as a means to identify capability change requirements. The requirements were either directly extracted from papers related to capabilities or indirectly from papers that addressed issues related to change and enterprise information. In the former case, the requirements for capability change were identified using observation, decision support and delivery as the main change functionalities [17]. In the latter, the requirements concerning change were identified in the related papers and were associated to enterprise capabilities.

3.2   Case Study

The case study was performed at a regional public healthcare organization, which we refer to as RH, responsible for healthcare provision in a Swedish county. The organization desired to remain anonymous, therefore, its real name is not published, along with the names of any collaborating companies. The studied part was the organization's capability to provide its residents with healthcare guidance via phone. To get information about what kind of change request the organization needs to handle, a number of meetings were held. The following activities took place in iterations.

Unstructured group interviews were used to identify change requests that the RH Guidance service had received recently. For this, four meetings were held, initially engaging two experts/strategists at RH, and the last three sessions involving one.

Workshops were held to identify the main actors and their relationships, this resulted in the creation of a value network model; three workshops were held.

Document studies were performed to study the current documentation of the capability under study.

For the analysis of how the identified change request would impact the organization, an *experiential approach* [18] was applied. That is, for each identified change request the interviewers also asked the experts to identify the potential change impact.

3.3 Requirements – Goal Modeling

The activity of defining requirements is associated to Requirements Engineering (RE). The aim of RE is to change the current reality by defining briefly and precisely the essence of the desired change [9]. In other words, it defines a goal but not how the goal should be fulfilled. The core activities of RE are (i) elicitation, which concerns the identification of requirements from relevant sources which are also identified during this activity, (ii) documentation of the identified requirements and (iii) negotiation, which concerns the identification and resolution of any possible conflicts. Two more cross-sectional activities are validation and management. The result of the process is a set of goals, scenarios or solution-oriented requirements which are generally known as requirement artifacts and comprise a requirements specification.

Various research methods can be applied to define requirements for an artifact like survey, action research, observation, case study, interview and document studies. In this study, literature review and case study are the two methods employed. The overall requirements are expressed in the form of a goal model. Goal, as a type of requirement artifact [9], is defined as a desired state of affairs that needs to be attained [10]. Goals are often refined into sub-goals forming a goal hierarchy.

The goal model in this study has been developed using the "For Enterprise Modeling" (4EM) method [10]. The available components in a 4EM Goals Model are goal, problem, cause, constraint and opportunity, however, the model in this study consists only of goals. Regarding the design of the model, the 4EM modeling toolkit used for creating the 4EM Goals Model has been developed in the University of Rostock using the ADOxx meta-modeling platform.

4 Requirements from Literature Review

This study is a continuation of a capability literature review [17], from which the majority of the requirements for capability change have been derived. That study involved the development of a framework that facilitated the classification of change concepts in the current literature. The main classification found was the division of key concepts into three functionality parts: (i) observation, (ii) support change decision and (iii) delivery [17]. These three should be the main concerns for a method.

The *observation* part directly refers to the context of the organization and its capabilities. Observing context has been identified as an essential element of change in several studies concerning capabilities and/or change [19–21]. What has also been emphasized is that the context that is relevant to an organization and its capabilities remains unclear, therefore, effort is needed to identify which contextual factors are relevant to a capability's performance [22]. Indirectly, these factors are also affecting whether a capability change is needed and thus should be taken into consideration for inclusion by a capability change method developer. Another part that concerns the context observation is the functional differentiation between a system monitoring itself and the environment [23, 24], or in other words, the internal and external context. This fact is another requirement for a capability change. Finally, any identified relevant contextual factors need to be measured [5], therefore, these factors need to be associated to Key Performance Indicators (KPIs). KPIs are the way to monitor capability performance and fulfillment of the enterprise. If the goal model does not include ways to measure the goals, KPIs need to be established [10]. Summarizing, the identified goals that are associated to observing are 2, 9 and 12–15 as shown in Table 1.

Regarding *supporting change decisions*, the decision needs to be associated to a set of criteria [17, 24], for example, rules and constraints [21] that need to be identified prior to not only the decision, but also the processing and analysis of the relevant data captured through observation. This analysis of captured context data needs to be addressed by the method as well, for example with algorithms that monitor the need for adjustments [25]. Regarding the decision itself, it may concern selecting among existing variants or alternatives [19–21, 24] or deciding on the development of an existing alternative. A capability change method is required to provide support for the identification of existing or new capability alternatives that can efficiently produce the same valuable outcome employing variable delivery behaviors. Finally, since capabilities aim to fulfil intentions, a decision needs to comply with these intentions. Goals, objectives, needs, business requirements, desires states etc. are different concepts of intentions [17] that the decision needs to comply with. Table 1 includes goals 3 and 5–8 that have been identified through these findings and are associated to decision support.

The last part of capability change that the method is required to address is the *delivery* of the capability. Initially, this concerns both the delivery of the capability and the delivery of any change to the capability, or, in other words, the delivery of the transition from an as-is state of a capability to a desired to-be state. Also referred to as transformation or adjustment [5], it may have several forms. A new capability can be introduced or an existing capability can be modified or retired. This is in line with [26], with replacing the concept of maintenance with modification in order to reflect the change to a capability. A significant finding in capability and change delivery literature is the association between capability and resource. Besides the fact that the concept of resource is the most commonly encountered concept in existing capability modeling approaches [17], it has also been associated to capabilities in several studies like [19, 27–29]. Several ways to associate the two concepts have been suggested, for example, as a constraint, but the most common type is that a capability consists of resources. The combination of these resources along with the information describing the relationships and capacities of the resources comprise the capability configuration. In addition, capabilities are also interrelated [17]. Therefore, the method artifact under development needs to address the capability configuration and the allocation of resources to capabilities along with the architecture of capabilities within an enterprise. Based on these findings, goals 4, 10, 11 and 16–20 are associated to capability delivery.

Table 1 summarizes the goals for the capability change modeling method that were elicited from the literature review.

Table 1. Goals elicited from the literature review.

No	Name	Description
1	To manage capability change	Changing an enterprise capability is the primary goal of the method as a response to the ever-changing environment of the enterprise
2	To observe business context	Considering the organization as a system, the environment of the system needs to be monitored to increase awareness of the factors that significantly affect changes
3	To support decision on capability change	Deciding whether a change is needed and how it should be performed is an essential part of any change process. The method should support decision making about change of enterprise capabilities
4	To manage capability delivery	The method should support capability delivery. A capability may be delivered by several activities that need to be analyzed
5	To identify decision criteria	Any decision on a capability change needs to be based on a structured set of relevant criteria. The method should support its identification
6	To identify capability alternatives	The method should support identification of alternative capability configurations during design time, or new alternatives identified through monitoring the capability delivery at run-time
7	To analyze observed context data	The data captured from the environment need to be analyzed and processed according to the factors relevant to the change. The method should support these activities
8	To ensure that decision complies with intentions	Intentional elements reflect the goals that a capability fulfills. The method should facilitate the inclusion of relevant intentional elements in the decision towards a capability change
9	To elicit internal and external business context	It is important to identify which contextual factors are affecting the capability so that they can be monitored properly
10	To manage transition delivery	The method should support addressing the change to an existing capability and to introduce an entirely new way to deliver
11	To manage capability architecture	The capabilities associated to a capability, along with their relationships of various types need to be modeled in order to facilitate positioning the capability and identify the change's impact
12	To observe external business context	Decomposing goal no2, it is important to support the enterprise's awareness of its external dynamic environment and the factors that affect its capabilities
13	To observe internal business context	There is great value in monitoring the internal environment of the enterprise systematically to identify possible required changes and their possible impact. The method should facilitate this task

(continued)

Table 1. (*continued*)

No	Name	Description
14	To measure relevant properties	Not only measuring but also identifying the external and internal properties that are relevant to an existing or incoming capability's performance is essential to assess whether a change is needed or not, and this needs to be addressed by the method artifact
15	To establish KPIs	KPIs are an established approach to evaluate performance. The method should include associating the capability's relevant properties to KPIs
16	To manage introduction of a new capability	A significant characteristic of a changing enterprise is introducing new capabilities that aim to address emerging needs derived and affected from dynamic factors of the enterprise's environment. This goal refers to the introduction of using a configuration that produces a new capability
17	To manage retirement of existing capability	Outdated or harmful enterprise capabilities need to be removed [30]. The sustained existence of an outdated capability may hinder the delivery of other capabilities, therefore, it should be removed. The method should support the retirement of an organization's capabilities
18	To manage modification of existing capability	Modifying a capability refers to changing the way an existing outcome is delivered. In other words, a new configuration that delivers an already existing outcome. The method aims to facilitate this process
19	To manage capability configuration	Capabilities consist of various resources of different types like material resources, human resources, time etc. The method should support configuring a capability as a structured set of resources
20	To allocate resources to capability	Based on the configuration of the capability, the allocation of resources may support enabling a potential and turning it into a capability. Thus, it is important for a capability change method to assist in the association of resources to a capability

5   Requirements from the Case Study

5.1   Case Overview

RH is a public organization that is responsible for healthcare in a Swedish county. One of the organization's capabilities is to provide healthcare advice via phone to any resident and visitor of the county. The task is performed by specially trained professional nurses. They are being supported by specialized software that incorporates various information sources. The abovementioned capability is known by the 4-digit phone number used by the persons contacting the nurses, namely 1177. The strategic goal of 1177 is to reduce the workload of other healthcare organizations by filtering the cases that are not in urgent need of physicians' attention and support these cases by providing useful advice.

RH owns 1177, however, several collaborating public and private organizations are involved by providing resources for it. Being inter-organizational, the configuration of the capability is complex. The complex configuration results in any proposed change in the capabilities of RH to require an in depth analysis of which parts will be affected and how. There are changes proposed that not only affect what is being done but also influence the collaborations with partner organizations in the form of needed or existing contractual agreements.

RH and its capabilities associated to 1177 constantly change. The driving forces for change come both via top-down and bottom-up developments. The top-down perspective is associated to politicians pushing for reforms not only to improve overall quality but also to facilitate the residents using the service and reduce costs. The bottom-up perspective concerns changes proposed by the employees and partners involved in the delivery of the capabilities. In addition, the capability needs to be updated because of new technological developments, for example, the desire to use video calls.

Any incoming change request involves an analysis to determine its effects. The method artifact developed needs to address all the relevant aspects. In order to assist the elicitation of requirements for the method, two recent change requests have been selected, (i) an improvement in the guidance support that enables the responding nurses to guide the callers directly to a healthcare provider by assessing their symptoms and (ii) enabling the nurses performing health guidance to book times directly at local emergency clinics. These two change requests have been selected because they include both internal improvements that the callers may be unaware of, as in case 1, and external improvements that affect external partners that the callers are in contact with, as in case 2. Both cases, which are explained in detail below, concern changes affecting external parties and IT systems.

5.2   Change Case 1: Guidance Support Improvement

The nurses are using a Guidance support system while handling a caller's case. The system has been developed and is being used nationwide. The caller states existing symptoms and the system presents possible sub-symptoms to the nurse. Different levels of emergencies are handled in different manners, from advising on self-treatment, which is also included in the system, to calling an ambulance or suggesting a healthcare provider. A part of the system provides the nurses with a catalogue of healthcare providers. The provider catalogue is developed and maintained by a private provider, in comparison to the guidance system, which is developed by a national public provider.

An improvement that has been proposed is to associate each provider in the catalogue to a specific set of symptoms that the provider is likely to handle. In this way, the callers can be directed to a provider without the need to reach a diagnosis of their situation in advance. On the contrary, the diagnosis part is skipped and a relevant provider is identified directly through stated symptoms. There are multiple benefits from this improvement. Initially, the delivered service is improved since the patient is guided to providers with the best expertise. In addition, the capability becomes more efficient in terms of cost and effort, along with the fact that there is better use of human resources, especially physicians, who can spend time on handling only the cases that are really relevant to their expertise. While this research project was running, a group of expert physicians had already been formed and started mapping providers to symptoms. The idea was to create a web system that can be used directly, and an XML file containing symptoms and providers that could be used in other systems.

5.3   Change Case 2: Time Booking at Emergency Clinics

Another proposed change for RH concerns the 1177 capabilities' direct association to the actual healthcare providers, and in particular, to the local emergency clinics which are also governed by RH. These clinics are meant to treat acute, yet, not life-threatening health problems. For example, they can treat severe allergic reactions, bone fractures or concussions. A resource that is worth noting is the journal system used in the local clinics, developed by a private journal system provider, since it is the one that needs to be accessed by the nurses. More specifically, it has been proposed that 1177's nurses should be enabled to book time slots in emergency clinics while handling acute cases. To date, the nurses can only suggest a clinic to the caller if they estimate that the clinic can handle the case. This change will benefit not only the callers, providing the convenience of having a booked time which also increases the feeling of safety, but also the main emergency units of major hospitals, whose workload will be reduced by directing less severe cases to the local clinics. In addition, it improves RH's ability to control the flow of the patients, directing them through the booked timeslots to the clinics with the shortest queue at the moment.

5.4   Analysis of Changes

This section discusses how the changes related to the three areas of capability change: observation, decision, and delivery relate requirements in the literature.

Concerning the impetus for changing the capabilities is the RH ability to perform *observation*, which can be seen as related to detecting changes in political, social, technological and economic factors. This is an important fact regarding monitoring of capability context because it provides initial guidelines concerning the selection of contextual factors that should be monitored to identify needed changes or possibilities for improvement. In addition, the contracts needed to perform the changes, as discussed below, also require monitoring the legal context of the organization and the capability. To measure the capability delivery, RH has a number of KPIs established that measures for example the number of residents that ask for guidance. Goal 28 was derived from these findings.

Regarding the *decision* on capability change in the case, it can be concluded that an important aspect in the two changes was the ownership of capabilities and associated resources. An important finding from the first change is that the ownership of the capability and the resources is significant for the configuration of the capability, along with any included tasks that have been outsourced. Developing new resources as part of the changes requires using existing resources owned by different organizations. For example, developing the symptom-provider system relies on data from the provider catalogue, owned by the private provider, and the expert group, owned by RH. The developed system and XML will in return, feed data to the provider catalogue system. A potential source of conflict and problems lies in the fact that an organization that collaborates with external partners to improve the efficiency of its services needs to have clear organizational boundaries set. This was derived from the case concerning the interactions and agreements among RH, the private provider and the national public provider in the first change, and RH, the journal system provider and the local emergency clinics in the second one. Using an external organization's resources or outsourcing tasks requires clearly stated boundaries set in the form of informal agreements or formal contracts. This will provide certain control over the cross-organizational configuration of the capability. The method should provide support for this type of capabilities and should assist the identification of resource ownership and contact points, either manual or automated, for example in APIs. An additional finding is that configuring a capability through a resource allocation supports the identification of alternatives. That is, reallocating resource sets may enable an existing potential and turn it into a new capability or alternative. The important association between goals 6 and 19 was identified based on these findings, along with the complementary goals 21–28.

Regarding the *delivery* of changes in the case it could be observed that the first change is a capability modification. Existing resources will be used in different ways to create new resources, and improve the delivery process, without changing the final outcome that is delivered, since it will be still fulfilling the same goal. The second change is a case of introducing a new capability. Even though the resources allocated to the capability are already existing, a new goal has been set and the delivered value is new. Both cases concern the reuse of resources in different manners. Goals 21–28 are also associated to delivery findings.

Considering the interrelated capabilities, it is important to identify new resources, like the symptom-provider system, created through the capability delivery and to take into consideration the needed resources, not only to develop the new resources, but also to maintain it. That may be a way to identify new capabilities.

5.5 Requirements

A summary of the goals elicited through the RH case are shown in Table 2. They complement the goals elicited from literature, therefore the numbering continues.

6 Goal Model for Capability Changes

The requirements for business capability change are expressed in the form of a goal model using the 4EM approach. Figure 1 depicts the Goals model that integrates goals elicited from both sources used in this study.

The main goal 1 in the model is managing capability change. It is refined in goals 2–4 reflecting the three main functionalities, observation, decision support and delivery. Observation, in return, is refined into goals 12 and 13, distinguishing between the internal and external context that needs to be observed and supported by goal 9, the elicitation of the context to observe. Goal 14, which concerns measurement, supports

Table 2. Additional goals elicited from the case study.

Goal	Name	Description
21	To specify capability ownership	The ownership of the capability facilitates positioning a capability within its ecosystem. The method should support identifying which actor, organization, unit etc., owns the given capability
22	To specify resource ownership	The ownership of resources may be different than the ownership of the capability they are associated with and allocated to. This is common for inter-organizational capabilities. The method should address the possible ownership conflicts and their resolution
23	To manage internal resources	In comparison to the external resources that can only be identified, the internal resources of the organization can also be managed and assigned to one or more capabilities
24	To identify external resources	External resources associated to a capability may not be owned by the same organization as the capability. Identifying them defines resource ownership and the method should support it
25	To identify outsourced tasks	Capabilities are associated to tasks as components of processes that deliver the capabilities. Inter-organizational capabilities include tasks that have been outsourced to external collaborators. The method should support their identification
26	To support defining organizational boundaries	Task and resource ownership identification is associated to the limits of the organizations, also known as organizational boundaries. The method artifact should include their definition
27	To identify collaborating organizations	Organizations providing resources allocated to a capability should be identified as part of the capability's and organization's ecosystem. The method should facilitate capability configuration
28	To monitor political, economic, social, technological and legal context	Political, economic, social, technological and legal contextual factors are important for the elicitation of the context, which is relevant to a capability's performance

goals 12 and 13 and is supported by goal 15, which concerns establishing KPIs to facilitate measurement. Goal 9 is supported by goal 28 depicting specific context fields that can assist the elicitation of contextual factors. Decision support is supported by goals 5–8, which depict the analysis of context data, the identification of decision

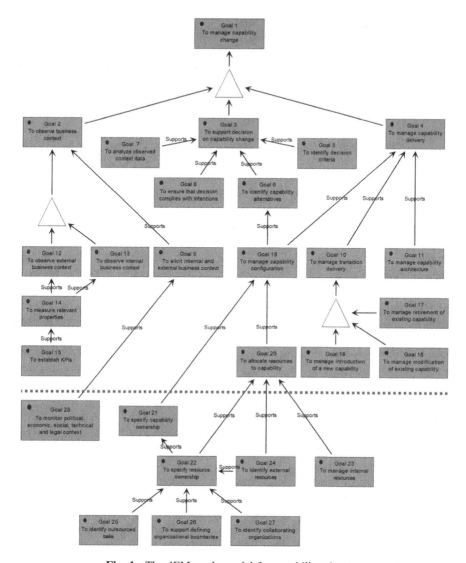

Fig. 1. The 4EM goals model for capability change.

criteria and capability alternatives, and ensuring that the decision complies with intention elements. Finally, delivery is supported by goals 10, 11 and 19, depicting management of transition delivery, capability architecture and capability configuration accordingly. Goal 19 also supports goal 6. Goal 10 is refined into goals 16-18 to depict the different categories of transition, which are the introduction of a new capability and the modification or retirement of an existing capability. Goal 19 is supported by goal 20, allocating resources to a capability. It is, in return, supported by goals 22–24, that depict the specification of resource ownership, the identification of external resources and management of internal resources. Goal 22 is also supporting goal 21 and goal 24 is supporting goal 22. Goal 22 is supported by goals 25–27 which concern the identification of outsourced tasks, supporting the definition of organizational boundaries and the identification of collaborating organizations accordingly.

Visually, the model consists of two parts. The upper part, which includes the goals elicited through the literature review, and the lower part, which includes the goals that were elicited from the case study and complement the initial set. The red dashed line depicts the border between the two sets of goals.

7 Discussion

The two sources of requirements for the method under development have provided requirements that were not only consistent, but also complementary to each other. The fact that the initial set of literature requirements are not all included in the case study requirements does not mean that they do not exist. On the contrary, the majority of requirements are overlapping. This applies to several goals from the literature. For example, in the case study, the need to monitor specific contextual fields, i.e. political, social, economic, technological and legal fields, supports the more generic goal found in the literature; to observe the business context. Therefore, the initial goal of the need to perform observations is present in the case. Even though there has been no explicit mention of the observation part, there were implications of different sources of observed data that motivated change requests. For example, there was political influence and pushing from employees to improve the service and reduce costs using new technologies. Additionally, the attributes of any relevant method supporting observation like PESTLE analysis [31] which seems highly consistent with this study's findings, should be taken into consideration.

The two change requests tackled in the case study have provided the opportunity to elaborate requirements on two types of capability change. Change 1 concerns the modification of an existing capability and change 2 concerns the introduction of a new capability. An interesting observation is that both cases are resolved by the reallocation of existing resources, both internal and external to the organization. This resulted in emphasizing the need for a clear definition of the boundaries of an organization, a task which can be assisted by identifying the resources and tasks that belong to collaborating organizations. Contracts may not be needed in every possible occasion, however, any type of boundary needs to be controlled in order to avoid possible conflicts and problems, even by informal agreements. Any method that aims to support changes and include inter-organizational capabilities should take this into consideration. In addition, as depicted in the goals, there is a significant difference between internal and external resources and tasks. The former can be managed while the latter can only be identified and the method should tackle these specific activities. The goal model has also made possible to emphasize the importance of capability configuration, since it is the only goal that currently supports both decision support and delivery.

A noteworthy fact concerns the increasing frequency of inter-organizational collaborations [32], leading to inter-organizational capabilities, however, the literature sources have not addressed this issue to date. Capability modeling has not elaborated on inter-organizational capabilities and this provides a great opportunity for the method under development to contribute to this part of changing capabilities as well. The inter-organizational capabilities studied in this case can prove as a starting point for researching the behavior of changing inter-organizational capabilities, being private to private, public to public or public to private as in the RH case.

8   Conclusion

In this paper, we have elicited requirements for developing a modeling method that uses the concept of capability to manage enterprise transformation in dynamic environments. Reusing the systematic literature review findings of our previous work has provided a set of goals. A case study from a public healthcare organization in Sweden has confirmed the main goals derived from literature and complemented the final set with goals concerning inter-organizational capability changes. The result has been presented in the form of a goal model that integrates all requirements from both sources.

Concerning future work, the requirements elicited from literature need to be practically validated. In addition, the requirements elicited from the case study belong to a single case and should be validated and possibly refined by enterprise transformation practitioners. The goal model presented in this study is the first step of an iterative process that is planned to proceed in the near future. When defining requirements will have been completed, the development of the method will begin.

Acknowledgment. We would like to express our gratitude to the employees of RH who took their time in letting us interview them to identify and describe the cases presented in the paper.

References

1. Burke, W.W.: Organization Change: Theory and Practice. Sage Publications, Thousand Oaks (2017)
2. Loucopoulos, P., Kavakli, E.: Capability Oriented Enterprise Knowledge Modeling: The CODEK Approach. In: Karagiannis, D., Mayr, H.C., Mylopoulos, J. (eds.) Domain-Specific Conceptual Modeling, pp. 197–215. Springer, Cham (2016). https://doi.org/10.1007/978-3-319-39417-6_9
3. Proper, H.A., Winter, R., Aier, S., de Kinderen, S. (eds.): Architectural Coordination of Enterprise Transformation. Springer, Cham (2017). https://doi.org/10.1007/978-3-319-69584-6
4. Persson, A., Stirna, J.: An explorative study into the influence of business goals on the practical use of enterprise modelling methods and tools. In: Harindranath, G., et al. (eds.) New Perspectives on Information Systems Development, pp. 275–287. Springer, US, Boston, MA (2002). https://doi.org/10.1007/978-1-4615-0595-2_22
5. Sandkuhl, K., Stirna, J. (eds.): Capability Management in Digital Enterprises. Springer, Cham (2018). https://doi.org/10.1007/978-3-319-90424-5
6. Loucopoulos, P., Stratigaki, C., Danesh, M.H., Bravos, G., Anagnostopoulos, D., Dimitrakopoulos, G.: Enterprise Capability Modeling: Concepts, Method, and Application. Presented at the October (2015)

7. Johannesson, P., Perjons, E.: An Introduction to Design Science. Springer, Cham (2014). https://doi.org/10.1007/978-3-319-10632-8

8. Hevner, A.R., March, S.T., Park, J., Ram, S.: Design science in information systems research. MIS Q. **28**, 75–105 (2004)

9. Pohl, K.: Requirements Engineering: Fundamentals, Principles, and Techniques. Springer, Heidelberg (2010)

10. Sandkuhl, K., Stirna, J., Persson, A., Wißotzki, M.: Enterprise Modeling: Tackling Business Challenges with the 4EM Method. Springer, Berlin, Heidelberg (2014). https://doi.org/10.1007/978-3-662-43725-4

11. Object Management Group (OMG): Value Delivery Modeling Laguage (2015). https://www.omg.org/spec/VDML/1.0

12. USA Department of Defense: Department of Defense Architecture Framework 2.02 (2009). https://dodcio.defense.gov/Library/DoD-Architecture-Framework/

13. NATO: NATO Architecture Framework v.4 (2018). https://www.nato.int/nato_static_fl2014/assets/pdf/pdf_2018_08/20180801_180801-ac322-d_2018_0002_naf_final.pdf

14. The Open Group: Archimate 3.0.1. Specification (2017). https://publications.opengroup.org/i162

15. Danesh, M.H., Yu, E.: Modeling enterprise capabilities with i*: reasoning on alternatives. In: Iliadis, L., Papazoglou, M., Pohl, K. (eds.) Advanced Information Systems Engineering Workshops, pp. 112–123. Springer International Publishing, Cham (2014). https://doi.org/10.1007/978-3-319-07869-4_10

16. Beimborn, D., Martin, S.F., Homann, U.: Capability-oriented modeling of the firm. Presented at the IPSI Conference, Amalfi, Italy January (2005)

17. Koutsopoulos, G., Henkel, M., Stirna, J.: Dynamic adaptation of capabilities: exploring meta-model diversity. In: Reinhartz-Berger, I., Zdravkovic, J., Gulden, J., Schmidt, R. (eds.) Enterprise, Business-Process and Information Systems Modeling, pp. 181–195. Springer International Publishing, Cham (2019). https://doi.org/10.1007/978-3-030-20618-5_13

18. Kilpinen, M.S.: The emergence of change at the systems engineering and software design interface (2008)

19. Bērziša, S., et al.: Deliverable 1.4: requirements specification for CDD, CaaS–capability as a service for digital enterprises. Riga Technical University (2013)

20. Fleurey, F., Dehlen, V., Bencomo, N., Morin, B., Jézéquel, J.-M.: Modeling and Validating Dynamic Adaptation. In: Chaudron, M.R.V. (ed.) Models in Software Engineering, pp. 97–108. Springer, Berlin, Heidelberg (2009). https://doi.org/10.1007/978-3-642-01648-6_11

21. Andersson, J., de Lemos, R., Malek, S., Weyns, D.: Modeling dimensions of self-adaptive software systems. In: Cheng, B.H.C., de Lemos, R., Giese, H., Inverardi, P., Magee, J. (eds.) Software Engineering for Self-Adaptive Systems, pp. 27–47. Springer, Berlin, Heidelberg (2009). https://doi.org/10.1007/978-3-642-02161-9_2

22. Zdravkovic, J., Stirna, J., Kuhr, J.-C., Koç, H.: Requirements engineering for capability driven development. In: Frank, U., Loucopoulos, P., Pastor, Ó., Petrounias, I. (eds.) The Practice of Enterprise Modeling, pp. 193–207. Springer, Berlin, Heidelberg (2014). https://doi.org/10.1007/978-3-662-45501-2_14

23. Weyns, D., Malek, S., Andersson, J.: FORMS: unifying reference model for formal specification of distributed self-adaptive systems. ACM Trans. Auton. Adapt. Syst. **7**, 1–61 (2012)

24. Morandini, M., Penserini, L., Perini, A.: Towards goal-oriented development of self-adaptive systems. In: Proceedings of SEAMS 2008, p. 9. ACM Press, Leipzig (2008)

25. Grabis, J., Kampars, J.: Adjustment of Capabilities: How to Add Dynamics. In: Sandkuhl, K., Stirna, J. (eds.) Capability Management in Digital Enterprises, pp. 139–158. Springer International Publishing, Cham (2018). https://doi.org/10.1007/978-3-319-90424-5_8

26. Henkel, M., Bider, I., Perjons, E.: Capability-based business model transformation. In: Iliadis, L., Papazoglou, M., Pohl, K. (eds.) Advanced Information Systems Engineering Workshops, pp. 88–99. Springer International Publishing, Cham (2014). https://doi.org/10.1007/978-3-319-07869-4_8

27. Azevedo, C.L.B., Iacob, M.-E., Almeida, J.P.A., van Sinderen, M., Pires, L.F., Guizzardi, G.: Modeling resources and capabilities in enterprise architecture: a well-founded ontology-based proposal for ArchiMate. Inf. Syst. **54**, 235–262 (2015)

28. Rafati, L., Roelens, B., Poels, G.: A domain-specific modeling technique for value-driven strategic sourcing. Enterp. Model. Inf. Syst. Arch. **13**, 1–29 (2018)

29. Loucopoulos, P., Kavakli, E., Chechina, N.: Requirements engineering for cyber physical production systems. In: Giorgini, P., Weber, B. (eds.) Advanced Information Systems Engineering, pp. 276–291. Springer International Publishing, Cham (2019)

30. Koutsopoulos, G.: Modeling organizational potentials using the dynamic nature of capabilities. In: Joint Proceedings of the BIR 2018 Short Papers, Workshops and Doctoral Consortium co-located with 17th International Conference Perspectives in Business Informatics Research (BIR 2018), Stockholm, Sweden, 24–26 September 2018, pp. 387–398 (2018)

31. Law, J.: A Dictionary of Business and Management. Oxford University Press, Oxford (2009)

32. Ziemann, J., Matheis, T., Freiheit, J.: Modelling of Cross-Organizational Business Processes - Current Methods and Standards. Enterprise Modelling and Information Systems Architectures, vol. 2, 23–31 pp. (2015)

Towards Architecting a Knowledge Management System: Requirements for an ISO Compliant Framework

Dmitry Kudryavtsev[1(✉)] and Dinara Sadykova[2(✉)]

[1] Graduate School of Management, Saint-Petersburg University,
Volkhovsky per., 3, 199004 Saint-Petersburg, Russia
d.v.kudryavtsev@gsom.spbu.ru
[2] Financial University Under the Government of the Russian Federation,
Leningradsky Prospect, 49, 125993 Moscow, Russia
ddsadykova@gmail.com

Abstract. Nowadays, enterprises must be knowledge-driven to be competitive and survive in knowledge economy. It means that knowledge must be a key value-creating resource for such organizations, and knowledge management system shall be embedded into overall enterprise management system. Today, knowledge management is not only a possible best practice of industrial leaders and a topic of academic research, but also a "must have" element of every company. Accordingly, knowledge management has been recently included into ISO 9001:2015 and ISO 30401 standards specifying requirements for knowledge management systems. The main research question of the current paper is how to embed knowledge management requirements of ISO into frameworks for enterprise architecture modeling and management? This paper analyses and summarizes knowledge management-related ISO requirements for enterprise management system and transform them into requirements for domain-specific modeling language. Knowledge management-oriented enterprise modeling frameworks are further studied and compared against ISO requirements. This comparison demonstrates fragmented support of ISO requirements. Thus, the research highlights the need for ISO compliant knowledge-oriented extension for existing, proven EM frameworks and provides requirements for it.

Keywords: Knowledge company · Knowledge management system · Enterprise architecture management · Enterprise modeling · Knowledge mapping

1 Introduction

1.1 Motivation and Problem Statement

Knowledge has become a key resource in modern economy. Companies need to learn how to create value and make money out of knowledge. Key capabilities of a 21st-century company are acquiring new knowledge, applying current knowledge, retaining current knowledge and handling outdated or invalid knowledge. Knowledge management (KM), a rather new discipline, helps companies to establish these capabilities.

© IFIP International Federation for Information Processing 2019
Published by Springer Nature Switzerland AG 2019
J. Gordijn et al. (Eds.): PoEM 2019, LNBIP 369, pp. 36–50, 2019.
https://doi.org/10.1007/978-3-030-35151-9_3

"The inclusion of Knowledge Management within the recently released ISO 9001:2015 marks a huge change within the world of KM. For the first time, one of the global business standards explicitly mentions knowledge as a resource, and specifies expectations for the management of that resource. This provides a long-awaited level of legitimacy for KM which could be a game-changer." [1] Even more, ISO 30401 was published in 2018, and it contained requirements for knowledge management system (KMS). Thus, today many companies begin to implement knowledge-related ISO requirements. These implementations require enterprise trans-formation.

On the other hand, enterprise modeling (EM), enterprise engineering (EE) and architecture management (EAM) are proven approaches for coordinating business transformations [2–4]. Enterprise Modelling, according to [5] "is concerned with representing the structure, organisation and behaviour of a business entity, be it a single or networked organisation, to analyse, (re-)engineer and optimise its operations to make it more efficient". Enterprise models include "concepts that are suited to support the conjoint analysis and design of information system and action system" [6]. Enterprise engineering (EE) and architecture management (EAM) are strongly connected to EM. These disciplines are concerned with designing or redesigning business entities, typically, using enterprise models. EAM and EE "provide methods and techniques for an aligned development of all parts of an enterprise" [7].

It seems reasonable that knowledge-driven companies and KMS (as management systems) complying with ISO requirements should be designed and implemented involving EM and EAM frameworks. So the final goal of our research is to suggest ISO compliant knowledge-oriented extension for existing, proven EM and EAM frameworks. Such an extension will not only help to design, implement and support KMS, but also seamlessly integrate it into overall enterprise architecture of a company. This extension will be used by enterprise architects and their teams; it can be also useful for chief knowledge officers or knowledge managers, if they are familiar with EM and EAM.

It seems reasonable that knowledge-driven companies and KMS (as management systems) complying with ISO requirements should be designed and implemented involving EM and EAM frameworks.

Although there are many papers integrating EM/EA and KM (e.g. [8–11]), they consider this link from very different perspectives, and it is unclear if there are existing KM-oriented enterprise modeling frameworks which satisfy requirements on domain-specific modeling language and EAM method.

1.2 Research Questions and Approach

The current paper addresses the following research question:

How to embed KM-related requirements of ISO into frameworks for enterprise architecture modeling?

In order to answer this question, the following subquestions are suggested:

- What are KM-related ISO requirements for EM language?
- Do existing KM-oriented enterprise modeling frameworks satisfy the requirements for this language?

Answers to these questions will provide the basis for the future design-oriented research [12] aimed at creating and evaluating of ISO compliant knowledge-oriented extension for existing, proven EM frameworks.

Although it is also necessary to have ISO compliant EAM method for architecting, implementing and supporting KMS and knowledge-driven organization, due to the size limitations the analysis of requirements for EAM method is out of the scope of the current paper.

Specification of the KM-related ISO requirements for EM language is based on the [13]. In order to find or design the necessary extension for EM languages/framework, we follow the method proposed by Frank (2010), which has already been successfully applied in other projects. The method suggests a macro process model for developing domain-specific modeling languages. The macro process consists of 7 steps [13]: 1. Clarification of scope and purpose, 2. Analysis of generic requirements, 3. Analysis of specific requirements, 4. Language Specification (abstract syntax), 5. Design of Graphical Notation (concrete syntax) and 6. optional Development of Modelling Tool. The process ends with the evaluation and iterative refinement of developed artefacts (7). Within this paper, we focus on the first 3 steps.

The current paper starts with the analysis of KM-oriented requirements for enterprise management system within ISO 9001:2015 and ISO 30401:2018 standards (Sect. 2). Then it synthesizes KM-oriented ISO requirements for EM language (Sect. 3). Overview and categorization of approaches at the intersection of KM and EM/EAM helped to identify relevant KM-oriented enterprise modeling approaches (Sect. 4.1). The selected modeling approaches were compared with the KM-oriented ISO requirements for EM language (Sect. 4.2).

2 Analysis of KM-Oriented Requirements in ISO Standards

KM-related ISO requirements for enterprise management system are provided in ISO 9001:2015 and in ISO 30401:2018. This section analyzes these two standards and elicit integrated KM-related ISO requirements for EM language from them. The analysis starts from informal description of main KM-related elements within the standards, after that a detailed semantic analysis of the texts of standards is provided. The text analysis identifies required concepts for ISO compliant knowledge-oriented EM extension.

ISO 9001 was revised in 2015. The revised standard, ISO 9001:2015, includes the new clause 7.1.6 Organizational knowledge. The requirements of this clause are:

"Determine the knowledge necessary for the operation of its processes and to achieve conformity of products and services.

This knowledge shall be maintained and made available to the extent necessary.

When addressing changing needs and trends, the organization shall consider its current knowledge and determine how to acquire or access any necessary additional knowledge and required updates.

NOTE 1: Organizational knowledge is knowledge specific to the organization; it is generally gained by experience. It is information that is used and shared to achieve the organization's objectives.

NOTE 2: Organizational knowledge can be based on: (a) Internal Sources (e.g., intellectual property, knowledge gained from experience, lessons learned from failures and successful projects, capturing and sharing undocumented knowledge and experience; the results of improvements in processes, products and services); (b) External Sources (e.g., standards, academia, conferences, gathering knowledge from customers or external providers)."

As Nick Milton of Knoco Limited notes, "this new clause is not a Knowledge Management standard, nor does it require an organization to have Knowledge Management in place as a formal requirement. As a clause in a Quality standard, it simply requires that sufficient attention is paid to knowledge to ensure good and consistent quality of goods and services" [1].

The text analysis of the KM-related fragment is presented in Table 1.

Table 1. Analysis of clause 7.1.6 Organizational knowledge in ISO 9001:2015

Text of the ISO standard	Required objects	Required activities
Determine the knowledge necessary for the operation of its processes and to achieve conformity of products and services	Knowledge Necessary knowledge Knowledge necessary for the operation of its [organization] processes Processes Knowledge necessary to achieve conformity of products and services Products and services	Determine necessary knowledge
This knowledge shall be maintained and made available to the extent necessary		Maintain knowledge Make knowledge available
When addressing changing needs and trends, the organization shall consider its current knowledge and determine how to acquire or access any necessary additional knowledge and required updates	Needs Trends Organization Current knowledge	Consider its [organization] current knowledge Determine how to acquire any necessary additional knowledge Determine how to access any necessary additional knowledge Determine required knowledge updates

ISO 30401:2018 "Knowledge management systems – Requirements" was published in November 2018.

"The purpose of this standard for knowledge management is to support organizations to develop a management system that effectively promotes and enables value-creation through knowledge" [14].

This standard is led by principles – it starts from KM guiding principles: Nature of knowledge; Value; Focus; Adaptive; Shared understanding; Environment; Culture; Iterative. These principles can be transformed into the corresponding principles of EAM framework.

Main KM definitions in ISO 30401:2018 standard:

"Knowledge – human or organizational asset enabling effective decisions and action in context" [14].

"Knowledge management – management with regard to knowledge" [14]. Where management is considered as "management process of planning, organizing, directing and controlling the outcomes of people, groups or organizations" [15].

"Knowledge management system – part of a Management system with regard to knowledge. Note 1 to entry: The system elements include the organization's knowledge management culture, structure, governance and leadership; roles and responsibilities; planning, technology, processes and operation, etc." [14]. Where management system according to [14] is a set of inter-related or interacting elements of an organization to establish policies, and objectives and processes to achieve those objectives.

According to [14] "the organization shall establish, implement, maintain and continually improve a knowledge management system, including the strategy, processes needed and their interactions, in accordance with the requirements of this international standard."

ISO 30401:2018 includes KM-specific part and universal part, which is applicable for any management system. The description of a KM system is a specific part, while management activities, which "establish, implement, maintain and continually improve" KM system, are standardized and follows the template from the proposals for management system standards (see ISO/IEC Directives Part 1 and Consolidated ISO Supplement, Annex SL [16]). These management activities correspond to steps of PDCA-cycle and are the following: Context of the organization; Leadership; Planning; Support; Operation; Performance evaluation & Improvement.

Clause 4.4 of the ISO 30401:2018 includes the description of KMS, which shall be established, implemented, maintained and continually improved by an organization. This clause was used for eliciting the requirements for KM-oriented EM language (see Table 2). In several cases, when the standard referred to other clauses, such clauses were analyzed and necessary concepts were extracted. Some fragments of ISO standards text were considered as explanatory and were not used for extracting required concepts (objects and activities).

3   KM-Oriented ISO Requirements for Enterprise Modeling Language

Based on the analysis of ISO standards, the following requirements for EM language were synthesized:

Table 2. Analysis of clause 4.4 Knowledge management system in ISO 30401:2018

Text of the ISO standard	Required objects and activities
4.4.1 General The organization shall **establish, implement, maintain and continually improve a knowledge management system**, including the processes needed and their interactions, in accordance with the requirements of this document	Establish a KMS Implement a KMS Maintain a KMS (Continually) Improve a KMS
4.4.2 to 4.4.4 include requirements, each representing **a dimension of the knowledge management system**, which are interdependent. Acknowledging and incorporating these dimensions within the knowledge management system and putting them in place through a managed change process is required for the implementation of an effective and holistic knowledge management system within the organization	Dimension of the KMS
4.4.2 Knowledge development The organization shall demonstrate that the knowledge management system covers the following activities, for effectively managing knowledge through **its stages of development** through systematic **activities and behaviours**, supporting the **knowledge management system objectives** and covering the **prioritized knowledge domains** defined in 4.3	Knowledge development Stages of knowledge development Activities and behaviours KMS objectives Prioritized knowledge domains
(a) Acquiring new knowledge: means to provide the organization with knowledge that was previously unknown or unavailable within the organization	New knowledge Acquiring new knowledge Means
(b) Applying current knowledge: means to make knowledge effective, integrating the current relevant knowledge of the organization in order to enable improved actions and decision making	Current knowledge Applying current knowledge Means
(c) Retaining current knowledge: means to safeguard the organization from the risks of knowledge loss	Current knowledge Retaining current knowledge Means
(d) Handling outdated or invalid knowledge: means to protect the organization from making mistakes or working inefficiently, as a result of use of knowledge inappropriate within the current organizational context	Outdated knowledge Invalid knowledge Handling outdated or invalid knowledge Means
4.4.3 Knowledge conveyance and transformation The organizational knowledge management system shall **include activities and behaviours**, supporting all different **types of knowledge flows**, through systematic activities and behaviours, supporting the **knowledge management system objectives** and covering the **prioritized knowledge domains** defined in 4.3	Knowledge conveyance and transformation Activities and behaviours Types of knowledge flows KMS objectives Prioritized knowledge domains

(*continued*)

Table 2. (*continued*)

Text of the ISO standard	Required objects and activities
(a) Human interaction: exchange and co-creation of knowledge through conversations and interactions; between individuals, teams and across the organization	Human interaction
(b) Representation: making knowledge available through demonstrating, recording, documenting and/or codifying	[Knowledge] representation
(c) Combination: synthesis, curating, formalizing, structuring or classifying of codified knowledge, making the knowledge accessible and findable	[Knowledge] combination
(d) Internalization and learning: reviewing, assessing and absorbing knowledge; incorporating it into practice	[Knowledge] internalization and learning
4.4.4 Knowledge management enablers The organizational knowledge management system shall include and integrate elements of all the following enablers to create an effective knowledge management system. This shall support the **knowledge management system objectives** and cover the **prioritized knowledge domains** defined in 4.3	KM enablers KMS objectives Prioritized knowledge domains
(a) Human capital: roles and accountabilities, including all **knowledge management system stakeholders**; making sure that knowledge management is encouraged within the organization (covered in detail in Clause 5)	Human capital Roles and accountabilities KM stakeholders
(b) Processes: defined **knowledge activities** applied and embedded within **organizational processes**, including procedures, instructions, methods and measures (covered in Clause 8)	Processes Knowledge activities Organizational processes
(c) Technology and infrastructure: digital channels, virtual and physical workspace and other tools	Technology and infrastructure Digital channels Virtual workspace Physical workspace
(d) Governance: Strategy, expectations and means of ensuring the knowledge management system is working in alignment (covered in detail in Clauses 5 to 10)	Governance KM strategy KM expectations KM policy (from clause 5.2)
(e) Knowledge management culture: Attitudes and norms regarding sharing, learning from mistakes (covered in detail in 4.5)	KM culture Attitudes [regarding sharing, learning from mistakes ...] Norms [regarding sharing, learning from mistakes ...]
4.5 Knowledge management culture Embedding a knowledge management culture across the organization is critical for sustained application of knowledge management. A culture where connections and knowledge activities are encouraged, and knowledge is valued and actively used, will support the establishment and application of the knowledge management system within the organization	KM culture

R1: An EM language for ISO compliant design of KMS should provide concepts for modeling **organizational context for KM and KMS**. Concepts:

1.1. Organizational Processes, which requires knowledge;
1.2. Products and Services, which requires knowledge;
1.3. KMS objectives.

R2: An EM language for ISO complient design of KMS should provide concepts for modeling **Knowledge and its status**. Concepts: Knowledge; Knowledge domain; Status of knowledge (Necessary knowledge; Current knowledge; New knowledge; Outdated knowledge; Invalid knowledge; Prioritized knowledge domains).

R3: An EM language for ISO complient design of KMS should provide concepts for modeling **Stages of knowledge development**. Concepts: Acquiring new knowlede; Applying current knowledge; Retaining current knowledge; Handling outdated or invalid knowledge.

R4: An EM language for ISO complient design of KMS should provide concepts for modeling **Types of knowledge flows within Knowledge conveyance and transformation**. Concepts: Human interaction; [Knowledge] Representation; [Knowledge] Combination; [Knowledge] Internalisation and learning.

R5: An EM language for ISO complient design of KMS should provide concepts for modeling **Activities, behaviours, means for knowledge development and knowledge conveyance and transformation**.

R6: An EM language for ISO complient design of KMS should provide concepts for modeling **KM enablers**. Concepts:

6.1. Human capital (Roles and accountabilities, KM stakeholders);
6.2. Processes (Knowledge activities, Organizational processes);
6.3. Technology and infrastructure (Digital channels, Virtual workspace, Physical workspace);
6.4. Governance (KM strategy, KM expectations, KM policy);
6.5. KM culture (Attitudes, Norms).

Management activities, which "establish, implement, maintain and continually improve" KM system are not reflected in these requirements since they mostly correspond to activities in EAM method, rather than enterprise modeling language (see conclusion for areas of further research).

4 Study of KM-Oriented Enterprise Modeling Approaches

4.1 Overview of Approaches at the Intersection of KM and EM/EAM

There are many research papers studying a link between KM and EM or EA. In order to select the right approaches for further analysis (see Sect. 4.2), we analyzed and organized existing into the following categories (Fig. 1):

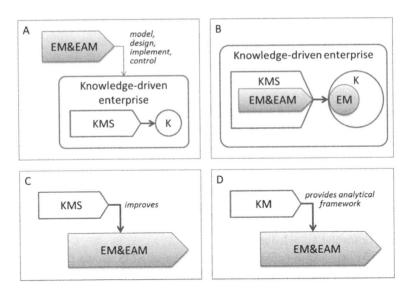

Fig. 1. Categories of approaches at the intersection of KM and EM/EAM

A. Enterprise modeling and/or enterprise architecture management are used for designing and implementing KMS;

B. Enterprise model is a codified organizational knowledge describing the way enterprise operations are organized;

C. Knowledge management helps to improve enterprise architecture management practices;

D. Knowledge management provides analytical framework for EM&EAM.

A. Enterprise modeling and/or enterprise architecture management are used for designing and implementing KMS

Focus: analysis and design of an effective and efficient KMS

"Modeling is one of the key tasks that helps on the one hand to understand, analyze and improve business processes (business process reengineering), organizational structures in general and structures and processes of KM initiatives in particular. On the other hand, modeling supports the design, implementation and management of information systems, in this case of knowledge management systems" [17].

Modeling approaches in this category can be subdivided into the next groups:

A.1. Design of a KMS as a management system (Focus of our analysis)

A.1.1. Business process-oriented approaches

- KM extensions to ARIS (KM ARIS) [18],
- PROMOTE – a framework for process-oriented KM, which includes modeling language and method. The focus of this approach is on "modelling, identification, accessing, storing, distribution, and evaluation of knowledge in a process-oriented manner." [8],
- B-KIDE: A Framework and a Tool for Business Process-Oriented Knowledge Infrastructure Development (B-KIDE) [19].

A.1.2. Knowledge work-oriented approaches
This group partially intersects with the previous one, but has many special features.

- KIPO (the knowledge-intensive process ontology) [20] & corresponding KIPN (Knowledge Intensive Process Notation) [21],
- Knowledge modelling in weakly-structured business processes (KM-WSB) [22],
- Rapid knowledge work visualization for organizations (Know Flow toolset) [23].

A.1.3. Agent-Oriented KM Modeling

- An agent oriented approach to analyzing knowledge transfer [24] (Knowledge Transfer) [24],
- Modelling knowledge transfer: A knowledge dynamics perspective [25] (KDP) [25].

A.1.4. Holistic KM modeling approaches

- Modeling Knowledge Work for the Design of Knowledge Infrastructures [26], where the concept of knowledge stance was discussed to integrate the process oriented and the activity-oriented perspective (Knowledge stance modeling).
- Knowledge-MEMO [27] – is a multi-perspective modeling method for knowledge management.

A.2. Design of a KMS as an information system
Some research papers focus on the specification of IT infrastructure of KMS, e.g. [28].

B. Enterprise model is a codified organizational knowledge, which describes how enterprise operations are organized
Focus: capturing, externalization, formalization, structuring and distribution of knowledge about an enterprise.

Enterprise model development is considered as creating and populating knowledge repository.

Examples of typical publications in this category: [11, 29, 30].

"Process modeling as a tool that allows the capturing, externalization, formalization and structuring of knowledge about enterprise processes" [11].

"Models of an enterprise capture knowledge" [31].

"Enterprise Modeling has been defined as the art of externalizing enterprise knowledge, i.e., representing the core knowledge of the enterprise" [5].

"The Active Knowledge Modeling (AKM) technology is about discovering, externalizing, expressing, representing, sharing, exploring, configuring, activating, growing and managing enterprise knowledge" [30].

"Building knowledge repositories with enterprise modelling and organizational patterns" [29].

Limitations: enterprise models cover only a fragment of enterprise knowledge (tacit knowledge is not covered; knowledge about product, customer, partners external environment etc. is only partially represented in enterprise models), so methodologies from this category are not sufficient for designing and implementing KMS.

C. Knowledge management helps to improve enterprise architecture management practices

Focus: Knowledge management methods and techniques are used to improve EAM practices.

Examples of typical publications in this category: [10, 32].

"EA projects generate a series of artifacts that contain knowledge directly or indirectly which can be reused or transferred from project to project. In this paper, the interest in providing a KM framework for TOGAF-based EA, to capture, store and reuse lessons learned in the first phases of the project" [10].

"KM in general has 3 processes, i.e. create, classify, and retrieve. These three processes can be utilized to support EA Team in formulation of enterprise architecture. This paper suggests the use of knowledge chain, labels (tagging), and taxonomy to develop knowledge base that can helps EA Team in formulation process of enterprise architecture" [32].

In [32] authors present a step-by-step model of knowledge management in an enterprise architecture is proposed with reference to a business strategy. This model suggests the use of knowledge chain, labels (tagging), and taxonomy to develop knowledge base that can helps EA Team in formulation process of enterprise architecture.

Also, in [10] was covered the similar problem, in this paper, the authors propose a KM metamodel for the EA based on TOGAF for the collection, storage and reuse of knowledge. Validation is presented by examining a specific case in a consulting company.

D. Knowledge management provides analytical framework for EM&EAM

Examples of typical publications in this category:

- Business process modeling through the knowledge management perspective [33].
- Future research topics in enterprise architecture management–a knowledge management perspective [9].

4.2   Analysis of the KM-Oriented Enterprise Modeling Approaches

Based on the requirements listed in Sect. 3, an analysis of the approaches in Table 3. The columns describe the main approaches for KM-oriented enterprise modeling (see category A in previous section). The rows list the requirements. The results of the analysis are at the intersection.

Most approaches define links between KM and business process management. KM has links to processes, roles and organizational units (KM ARIS, PROMOTE, KM-WSB, KIPO, B-KIDE, Knowledge-MEMO, Know Flow toolset). Only a little part of approaches models technology and infrastructure, but not to the full extent (e.g. PROMOTE, B-KIDE, Know Flow toolset). Relationships between knowledge and products/services of an enterprise are lacking. Some modeling approaches partially fulfill requirements (see "±" sign), which mostly means that a modeling approach suggests similar concepts and/or uses them in a limited way. KM Culture is not

Table 3. Analysis of approaches based on required elements in way of modeling

Required elements in way of modeling/ approaches	KM ARIS [18]	PROMOTE [8]	B-KIDE [19]	KIPO&KIPN [20, 21]	KM-WSB [22]	Know Flow toolset [23]	Knowledge Transfer [24]	KDP [25]	Knowledge stance modeling [26]	Knowledge-MEMO [27]
R1. Organizational context for knowledge, KM and KMS										
1.1. Organizational processes, which requires knowledge	+	+	+	+	+	+	+	−	+	+
1.2. Products and services, which requires knowledge	−	−	−	−	−	−	−	−	−	−
1.3. KM objectives	−	−	−	±	−	−	+	−	±	+
R2. Knowledge and its status	+	+	+	−	+	−	−	+	+	±
R3. Stages of knowledge development	−	±	+	+	+	+	−	+	−	−
R4. Types of knowledge flows	−	±	−	−	−	−	±	−	±	±
R5. Activities, behaviours, means [for knowledge development and/or for knowledge conveyance and transformation]	−	+	+	+	+	+	+	−	+	−
R6. KM enablers										
6.1. Human capital (Roles and accountabilities, KM stakeholders)	+	+	±	±	±	+	+	+	+	+
6.2. Processes (knowledge activities applied and embedded within organizational processes)	+	+	+	+	+	+	+	−	+	+
6.3. Technology and infrastructure	−	+	±	−	−	±	−	−	+	+
6.4. Governance	−	−	−	−	−	−	−	−	±	±
6.5. KM culture	−	−	−	−	−	−	−	−	−	−

Legend: + fulfilled; ± partly fulfilled; − not fulfilled

modeled, however, it is unclear if it is worth modeling or not. Holistic KM modeling approaches [26, 27] better fulfil the requirements, but not completely. Thus, we can conclude that there is no approach meeting requirements outlined in Sect. 3.

5 Conclusion

ISO has recently included KM-related requirements into its standards, i.e. ISO 9001:2015 Quality Management Systems – Requirements and ISO 30401:2018 Knowledge Management Systems – Requirements. Many organizations started implementing these ISO requirements. EM and EAM may be used to support organizations within this process. The final goal of our research is to suggest ISO compliant KM-oriented extension for existing, proven EM and EAM frameworks. Such extension will not only help to design, implement and support KMS, but also to seamlessly integrate it into overall enterprise architecture of a company.

This paper analyses and summarizes KM-oriented ISO requirements for enterprise management system. This analysis helped to specify KM-oriented ISO requirements for EM language. Existing research papers integrating KM and EM/EA were subsequently studied. Research categorization was suggested. KM-oriented modeling frameworks were studied and compared against KM-related ISO requirements. This comparison demonstrated fragmented support of ISO requirements. Thus, the research highlighted the need for ISO compliant KM-oriented extension for existing, proven EM frameworks.

Further research is needed to achieve the final goal of the research, which is to suggest ISO compliant KM-oriented extension for existing proven EM and EAM frameworks. Thus, the research needs to:

- Analyse management activities required by ISO, which "establish, implement, maintain and continually improve" KM system, and compare them with existing EAM methods (both generic and KM-oriented). Since the description of these activities for KMS mostly follows the ISO template for other management systems (see ISO/IEC Directives Part 1 and Consolidated ISO Supplement, Annex SL [16]), it seems reasonable to compare this generic ISO template with existing EAM methods;
- Compare methods and techniques for knowledge and knowledge assets mapping [34, 35] with determined requirements. These approaches have a long history and provide many ways for describing organizational knowledge, its sources, application areas (strategic themes, business processes) and development plans, but they are less formalized than modeling approaches that we have analyzed in the Sect. 4.2.
- Develop, demonstrate and evaluate ISO compliant knowledge-oriented extension for existing, proven EM and EAM frameworks.

References

1. Fry, I.: Knowledge Management and ISO 9001:2015. Real KM, 4 October 2015. https://realkm.com/2015/10/14/knowledge-management-and-iso-90012015/
2. McGinnis, L.F.: Enterprise modeling and enterprise transformation. Inf. Knowl. Syst. Manag. **6**(1, 2), 123–143 (2007)

3. Harmsen, F., Proper, H.A.E., Kok, N.: Informed governance of enterprise transformations. In: Proper, E., Harmsen, F., Dietz, J.L.G. (eds.) PRET 2009. LNBIP, vol. 28, pp. 155–180. Springer, Heidelberg (2009). https://doi.org/10.1007/978-3-642-01859-6_9
4. Proper, H., Winter, R., Aier, S., de Kinderen, S.: Architectural Coordination of Enterprise Transformation. Springer, Cham (2018). https://doi.org/10.1007/978-3-319-69584-6
5. Vernadat, F.B.: Enterprise Modeling and Integration: Principles and Applications. Chapman & Hall, London (1996)
6. Frank, U.: Multi-perspective enterprise modeling: foundational concepts, prospects and future research challenges. Softw. Syst. Model. **13**(3), 941–962 (2014)
7. Sandkuhl, K., Stirna, J., Persson, A., Wißotzki, M.: Enterprise Modeling: Tackling Business Challenges with the 4EM Method. The Enterprise Engineering Series. Springer, Heidelberg (2014). https://doi.org/10.1007/978-3-662-43725-4
8. Woitsch, R., Karagiannis, D.: Process oriented knowledge management: a service based approach. J. UCS **11**(4), 565–588 (2005)
9. Buckl, S., Matthes, F., Schweda, C.M.: Future research topics in enterprise architecture management – a knowledge management perspective. In: Dan, A., Gittler, F., Toumani, F. (eds.) ICSOC/ServiceWave-2009. LNCS, vol. 6275, pp. 1–11. Springer, Heidelberg (2010). https://doi.org/10.1007/978-3-642-16132-2_1
10. Meneses-Ortegón, J.P., Gonzalez, R.A.: Knowledge management in enterprise architecture projects. In: Fred, A., Dietz, J., Aveiro, D., Liu, K., Bernardino, J., Filipe, J. (eds.) IC3 K 2016. CCIS, vol. 914, pp. 287–305. Springer, Cham (2019). https://doi.org/10.1007/978-3-319-99701-8_14
11. Kalpic, B., Bernus, P.: Business process modelling in industry—the powerful tool in enterprise management. Comput. Ind. **47**(3), 299–318 (2002)
12. Österle, H., et al.: Memorandum on design-oriented information systems research. Eur. J. Inf. Syst. **20**(1), 7–10 (2011)
13. Frank, U.: Outline of a method for designing domain-specific modelling languages (No. 42). ICB-research report (2010)
14. International Organization for Standardization – ISO. ISO 30401:2018 Knowledge management systems – Requirements. Geneva, Switzerland: ISO (2018)
15. International Organization for Standardization – ISO. ISO 30400:2016 Human resource management—Vocabulary. Geneva, Switzerland: ISO (2016)
16. International Organization for Standardization – ISO. Proposals for management system standards. Geneva, Switzerland: ISO. (ISO/IEC Directives Part 1 and Consolidated ISO Supplement, Annex SL) (2018)
17. Maier, R.: Knowledge Management Systems: Information and Communication Technologies for Knowledge Management, 3rd edn. Springer, Heidelberg (2007). https://doi.org/10.1007/978-3-540-71408-8
18. Allweyer, T.: Modellbasiertes Wissensmanagement. Inf. Manag. **1**(1998), 37–45 (1998)
19. Strohmaier, M., Tochtermann, K.: B-KIDE: a framework and a tool for business process-oriented knowledge infrastructure development. Knowl. Process. Manag. **12**(3), 171–189 (2005). https://doi.org/10.1002/kpm.227
20. França, J.B.S.: KIPO: the knowledge-intensive process ontology. Softw. Syst. Model. **143**, 1127–1157 (2015)
21. Netto, J.M., França, J.B., Baião, F.A., Santoro, F.M.: A notation for knowledge-intensive processes. In: Proceedings of the 2013 IEEE 17th International Conference on Computer Supported Cooperative Work in Design (CSCWD), pp. 190–195. IEEE (2013)
22. Papavassiliou, G., Mentzas, G.: Knowledge modelling in weakly-structured business processes. J. Knowl. Manag. **7**(2), 18–33 (2003)

23. Strohmaier, M., Lindstaedt, S.: Rapid knowledge work visualization for organizations. J. Knowl. Manag. **11**(4), 97–111 (2007)

24. Strohmaier, M., Yu, E., Horkoff, J., Aranda, J., Easterbrook, S.: Analyzing knowledge transfer effectiveness–an agent-oriented modeling approach. In: 2007 40th Annual Hawaii International Conference on System Sciences (HICSS'07), p. 188b. IEEE (2007)

25. Mougin, J., Boujut, J.F., Pourroy, F., Poussier, G.: Modelling knowledge transfer: a knowledge dynamics perspective. Concurr. Eng. **23**(4), 308–319 (2015)

26. Maier, R.: Modeling knowledge work for the design of knowledge infrastructures. J. UCS **11**(4), 429–451 (2005)

27. Schauer, H., Schauer, C.: Modeling techniques for knowledge management. In: Knowledge Management Strategies: A Handbook of Applied Technologies, pp. 91–115. IGI Global (2008)

28. Maier, R., Hädrich, T., Peinl, R.: Enterprise Knowledge Infrastructures. Springer, Heidelberg (2009). https://doi.org/10.1007/3-540-27514-2

29. Stirna, J., Persson, A., Aggestam, L.: Building knowledge repositories with enterprise modelling and patterns-from theory to practice. In: ECIS, pp. 937–948 (2006)

30. Lillehagen, F., Krogstie, J.: Active Knowledge Modeling of Enterprises. Springer, Heidelberg (2008). https://doi.org/10.1007/978-3-540-79416-5

31. Frank, U.: Multi-perspective enterprise models as a conceptual foundation for knowledge management. In: Proceedings of the 33rd Annual Hawaii International Conference on System Sciences, pp. 1–10. IEEE (2000)

32. Wibowo, A.: Knowledge management support for enterprise architecture development. Int. J. Knowl. Eng. **3**(1), 25–31 (2017)

33. Kalpič, B., Bernus, P.: Business process modeling through the knowledge management perspective. J. Knowl. Manag. **10**(3), 40–56 (2006)

34. Balaid, A., Rozan, M.Z.A., Hikmi, S.N., Memon, J.: Knowledge maps: a systematic literature review and directions for future research. Int. J. Inf. Manag. **36**(3), 451–475 (2016)

35. Schiuma, G., Carlucci, D.: The next generation of knowledge management: mapping-based assessment models. In: Bolisani, E., Handzic, M. (eds.) Advances in Knowledge Management. KMOL, vol. 1, pp. 197–214. Springer, Cham (2015). https://doi.org/10.1007/978-3-319-09501-1_9

Modeling and Ontologies

The OntoREA© Accounting and Finance Model: Inclusion of Future Uncertainty

Walter S. A. Schwaiger$^{(\boxtimes)}$, Aqif Nasufi, Natalia Kryvinska,
Christian Fischer-Pauzenberger, and Ömer Faruk Dural

Institute of Management Science, Technische Universität Wien,
Theresianumgasse 27, 1040 Vienna, Austria
walter.schwaiger@tuwien.ac.at

Abstract. The OntoREA© accounting and finance model [1] indicates already in its name a fundamental distinction, i.e. the distinction between the accounting related backward looking perspective into the past and the finance related forward looking perspective into the future. Accordingly, in accounting current economic events are recorded and persisted and in finance future related commitments are addressed. Concerning the completeness of accounting and finance concepts there is an asymmetry in the OntoREA© model. The accounting concepts are completely covered, whereas in the coverage of the forward looking finance perspective one main deficiency exists: The uncertainty surrounding the forward looking perspective is not specified.

In this article the problem of the missing uncertainty representation in the OntoREA© accounting and finance model is explicitly addressed. The novel approach consists in directly linking uncertainty to commitments. By conceptualizing uncertainty according to the stochastic concepts that underlie the option pricing [2–4] and the intertemporal equilibrium pricing theory [5], the missing representation is solved. Furthermore, the stochastic concepts have a precise ontological meaning [6, 7]. Hence, the extension of the current model with the proposed uncertainty representation gives a well-founded stochastic model of the accounting and finance domain.

Keywords: REA business ontology · OntoREA© accounting and finance model · Uncertainty representation · Stochastic process concept · UFO-B

1 Introduction

Conceptual modeling provides concise knowledge representations for the domain under investigation. In the OntoREA© accounting and finance model [1] the domains of accounting and finance are conceptually modelled with the Unified Foundational Ontology (UFO)-based modeling language OntoUML [8]. OntoUML is an UML extension that incorporates the metaphysical nature of the modelled "things" – like the principle of essence and rigidity, identity, unity and dependency – and makes them accessible in ULM class diagrams via UFO metaphysical stereotypes.

The origins of the OntoREA© accounting and finance model trace back to the *REA business ontology* [9, 10]. In the accounting and policy infrastructure of this ontology

© IFIP International Federation for Information Processing 2019
Published by Springer Nature Switzerland AG 2019
J. Gordijn et al. (Eds.): PoEM 2019, LNBIP 369, pp. 53–67, 2019.
https://doi.org/10.1007/978-3-030-35151-9_4

the informational and procedural elements, which are needed for accounting and finance purposes, are specified. Due to the focus on economic transactions with real (physical) assets the accounting infrastructure of the REA business ontology had a deficiency with respect to representation of financial assets and liabilities. This deficiency was solved by integrating the requirements from Asset-Liability-Equity (ALE) accounting [11] and the forward looking perspective from finance [12]. By using the OntoUML language [8] the integration of the forward looking perspective also was accompanied by an *ontological turn*. Instead of using the "specification of a conceptualization" definition of ontology [13], a metaphysical definition of ontology from philosophy was applied, i.e. the Unified Foundational Ontology (UFO) with respect to *endurant* (static, structural) entity types (UFO-A) [14]. The ontological turn by switching from UML modeling language to the OntoUML language enhances the expressiveness of the conceptual model by adding to each concept applied in the model its UFO-metaphysical (ontological) nature.

The ontological expressiveness provided by the OntoUML language underlying the OntoREA© accounting and finance model showed especially useful for the modeling of the *temporal modal* behavior of derivative financial instruments [15, 16]. Depending on the market value, derivative instruments can be assets, if the value is positive, or liabilities, if the value is negative. If the value is zero, then derivative instruments are off balance positions. In the case of forward contracts, which are unconditional derivatives compared to conditional derivatives in form of options, the value can change randomly in either direction, so that they can randomly switch between asset, liability and off balance positions.

The expressiveness of the OntoUML modeling language with respect to the characterization of a temporal modal behavior is fine, but it can only trace the behavior as time goes by, i.e. online. This is sufficient for accounting purposes as it allows the recognition of the (random) value changes in the ALE accounting systems. With respect to the forward looking perspective of finance, this restriction is quite severe. It prohibits the modeling of a temporal model behavior on an ex-ante basis. In order to overcome this shortcoming the future related uncertainty has to be specified explicitly. In the *probabilistic extension* of the REA business ontology, the concept of a *filtered probability space* [17, p. 350] was applied to model future events as *probabilistic events*. As probabilistic events are elements of probability spaces, they are obviously of a different type compared to economic events which represent transactions in the REA business ontology. Recognizing this difference, the probabilistic events are not connected neither to economic events nor to commitments in the extended REA business ontology. Consequently, the probabilistic events are (only) proposed for carrying objectives in form of target values for planning and control purposes that are attached to different future occurrences.

The usage of filtered probability spaces for characterizing future uncertainty is a solid conceptualization. It stems from the "golden", i.e. Nobel-laureates age of finance from the 1970's. At that time both, the option pricing theory [2–4] as well as the intertemporal equilibrium pricing theory [5] used filtered probability spaces for modeling the uncertainty that surrounds the corresponding forward looking perspectives. The main question now is, how the integration of such a stochastic conceptualization of the future uncertainty into the OntoREA© accounting and finance model can be achieved?

This question leads to the primary research objective of this article, i.e. the adequate extension of the OntoREA© model that allows the modeling of a temporal modal behavior also on an ex-ante basis like in the option pricing theory and the intertemporal equilibrium pricing theory. Furthermore, the extension should be that generic so that it can also be applied to other valuation systems as well as planning and control systems like real option pricing and decision analysis [18, 19], stochastic control problems [20, 21], approximate control problems [22] and control problems with augmented states in form of exogenous and endogenous state variables [23].

In order to achieve this objective the "event" mismatch has to be disentangled first. For this purpose *perdurant* (dynamic, non-structural) entity types – called *Event* type in UFO-B [6] – are used to define the economic events in the OntoREA© model. For precisely expressing the different concepts in the OntoREA© model the types in the model will be written with capital letters and the corresponding *perdurant* UFO-B type will be specified in *Italics*, e.g. *Event* type Economic Event, and the same notation applies to *endurant* UFO-A types, e.g. *Kind* type Economic Resource.

In the next step the future uncertainty related to filtered probability spaces will be defined in terms of the *stochastic process* concept. The advantage of using this concept is the distinction between the *sample space* that specifies the uncertainty structure and the *state space* that specifies the mapped values from the stochastic process. This distinction allows the coupling of the *Kind* type Economic Commitment to its corresponding *uncertainty information structure* without having to specify probabilities for the commitments' possible states over time. Finally, this structure, i.e. the *Kind* type Uncertainty Sample Space provides the uncertainty representing information structure upon which in the planning process future economic events (plan events) – that are specified in the *Event* type Plan Event Tree – are committed.

The structure of this article is as follows: The next section *OntoREA© accounting and finance model: Stochastic extension* gives a compact overview of the OntoREA© model expressed with the OntoUML modeling language. In the following section the meaning of the *Kind* type Uncertainty Sample Space and *Event* type Plan Event Tree – that are the central elements in the model's stochastic extension – is elaborated. The next chapter deals with the *ERP-Control Application* in order to show for demonstration purposes the stochastic foundation of the production planning module and its IT implementation. In the final section the main contribution of the paper is concluded and future research directions are given.

2   OntoREA© Accounting and Finance Model: Stochastic Extension

The OntoREA© accounting and finance model [1] formalized in the OntoUML language can be seen in Fig. 1. The metaphysical, i.e. UFO-ontological meaning of the entity types and relationship types is specified in the stereotypes, e.g. the perdurant UFO-A type «Kind». For the exploration of the model it's advisable to start with the *identity providing backbone* in form of the *Kind* types Economic Resource and

Economic Agent from the *endurant* universal types («Kind») of UFA-A as well as the Economic Event from the *perdurant* universal types («Event») of UFA-B. The Balanced Duality type expresses the *Formal* reification relationship between the *Subkind* type Debit Event and the *Subkind* type Credit Event and their monetary balancing within each economic transaction in the spot market. The *Relator* stereotype indicates that in double-entry bookkeeping accounting systems the Debit Event and the Credit Event of a *spot market contract* have the property to balance in monetary terms. Consequently, there is a legal truthmaker that mediates between individual debit and credit events.

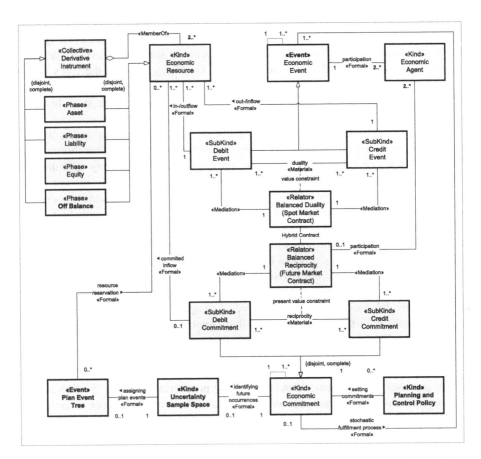

Fig. 1. OntoREA© accounting and finance model with stochastic extension (Color figure online)

A similar reasoning holds true for the *Formal* type Balanced Reciprocity that relates to the *Kind* type Economic Commitment. "Commitments are different from Economic Events since they represent obligations (of various degrees of enforceability) to trading or production partners instead of actual consumption or acquisition transactions. An example of a Commitment is a reservation for an airline flight or a reservation for a hotel stay." [9, p. 10]. Like Economic Event types the *Kind* type Economic Commitment is distinguished between *atomic* commitments and *complex* commitments that consist of more than one atomic commitment. The Balanced Reciprocity relationship related to Economic Commitment types comes from the fundamental pricing principle of finance that requires from *future market contracts* the balancing in monetary terms of a Debit and a Credit Commitment type. Consequently, the properties enforced by the truthmaker comes from finance theory. The *Relator* stereotype indicates this truthmaker which reifies the *Material* relationship between the *Subkind* type Debit Commitment and the *Subkind* type Credit Commitment and their monetary reciprocity (i.e. monetary balancing) within each economic future market transaction. The balanced reciprocity requires that the present value of the debit commitments is equal to the present value of credit commitments. Furthermore, there are hybrid contracts that are a mixture between a spot and a future contract, e.g. loan contracts settled with a bank.

The *Kind* type Economic Commitment and the *Event* type Economic Event are in a *Formal* fulfillment relationship type. Its cardinalities indicate that a commitment relates to at least one economic event, whereas an economic event can have a commitment. Finally, for completeness it is mentioned that the *Collective* type Derivative Instrument connects derivatives via a *MemberOf* relationship type to the asset and liability resources of their underlying replication portfolio. As derivative instruments are recorded by accounting law on a net basis, their constituting asset and liabilities are off balance sheet positions that are not individually reported in the balance sheet. Consequently, the *Phase* type Off Balance represents these constituting assets and liabilities.

There are five changes (marked in **blue** color in Fig. 1) in comparison to the original OntoREA© accounting and finance model [1] for enhancing understandability. The most importance change relates to the resolution of the "mismatch" problem and it consists of the switch in the Economic Event's type from the *Kind* type (UFO-A) to the *Event* type (UFO-B). According to this switch it is clear that the Economic Event is not of a static but of a dynamic nature. "Events (also called *perdurants*) are individuals composed of temporal parts. They *happen in time* in the sense that they extend in time accumulating temporal parts. Examples of events are a conversation, a football game, a symphony execution, a birthday party, or a particular business process. Whenever an event is present, it is not the case that all its temporal parts are present." [6, pp. 328–329]. Furthermore, the inclusion of an additional reflective relationship indicates that not only *atomic* events, which have no proper parts, but also *complex* events in form of aggregations of at least two disjoint (atomic) events. In complex events the temporal relationship between its constituting events is incorporated via a temporal property in each event. A reflective relationship type is also added – and this is the 2nd change – to the Kind type Economic Commitment to allow the building of *complex* from *atomic* commitments.

The remaining three changes are of minor importance compared to the *Event* type change. They eliminate narrow cardinality restrictions due to specific examples in the original OntoREA© accounting and finance model [1] with respect to Economic Agent's participation relationships and the Derivative Instruments MemberOf relationship. Next, the term *Off Balance* is chosen instead of the term *Claim* to explicitly indicate the off balance nature of claims that are defined as pending businesses. Finally, the ALE phases are specified only once and this specification is connected via generalization relationships to the Derivative Instrument type as well as to the Economic Resource type.

The stochastic extension of the OntoREA© accounting and finance model can be seen by the additional constructs (marked in **red** color) at the bottom of Fig. 1: the three entity types, i.e. the *Kind* type Uncertainty Sample Space, the *Event* type Plan Event Tree and the *Kind* type Planning and Control Policy, as well as the four related relationship types, i.e. the *Formal* relation 'identifying future occurrences', the *Formal* relation 'assigning plan events', the *Formal* relation 'resource reservation' and the *Formal* relation 'setting commitments'. The precise meaning of the additional concepts used in the stochastic extension of the OntoREA© model are given next.

3 Stochastic OntoREA© Model: Meaning of 'Uncertainty Sample Space' and 'Plan Event Tree'

The *Kind* type Uncertainty Sample Space is the information structure of the uncertainty that accompanies the future related Economic Commitment types. This uncertainty information structure is a mathematical construct. Specifically, it is the *sample space* of a stochastic process. "A *stochastic process* is a mathematical model for the occurrence at each moment after the initial time, of a random phenomenon. The randomness is captured by the introduction of a measureable space $(\Omega, \mathcal{F})$, called the *sample space*, on which probability measures can be placed. Thus, a stochastic process is a collection of random variables $X = \{X_t, 0 \leq t < \infty\}$ on $(\Omega, \mathcal{F})$, which take values in a second measurable space $(S, \mathcal{S})$, called the *state space*. ... For a fixed sample point $\omega \in \Omega$, the function $t \to X_t(\omega)$; $t \geq 0$ is a sample path (realization, trajectory) of the process X associated with ω." [24, p. 1].

The sample space of a stochastic process consists of two parts: Firstly, the sample point space Ω containing all possible sample points, i.e. all worlds that possibly occur in the future and secondly, the information structure $\mathcal{F}$ containing all *sample states* in which the possible worlds can occur over the time horizon defined by the stochastic process. The information structure is mathematically defined as a sequence of sample point space partitions. If these partitions are successively finer grained, the partition sequence is a *filtration*. Such a filtration is the core concept for specifying the concept of *revealing information*. "Uncertainties are resolved ... at times $t = 0, 1, ..., T$. Let $\vartheta = \{\gamma_1, \gamma_1, ..., \gamma_S\}$ denote the (finite) set of possible states of the world. The true state of the world is revealed to the firm at time T. At intermediate times t, the firm possesses some information about this final state that we represent as the *time-t state of information* ω_t. Formally, these time-t states of information ω_t, are defined as subsets of ϑ that form a partition of ϑ (the possible ω_t's are mutually exclusive and their union is ϑ) and become successively finer with increasing t (each ω_{t-1}, is the union of states ω_t in the next time period)." [18, p. 797].

The revealing information concept is not only relevant for the domains of finance and decision analysis, but also for the domain of (e.g. inventory) control problems. "In open-loop minimization we select all orders $u_0, \ldots, u_{N-1}$ at once at time 0, without waiting to see the subsequent demand levels. In *closed-loop minimization* we postpone placing the order u_k until the last possible moment (time k) when the current stock x_k will be known. The idea is that since there is no penalty for delaying the order u_k up to time k, we can take advantage of information that becomes available between times 0 and k (the demand and stock level in past periods)." [20, p. 4]

In this article the concept of revealing information is directly connected to the stochastic process concept by defining *possible states of the world* (sample points) that live in the sample point space $\Omega = \{\omega_1, \omega_2, \ldots, \omega_S\}$ and defining *time-t sample states* $s_{t,i}$ in which the possible worlds can appear at time t. An example of a binary uncertainty sample space [3] is given in the left panel of Fig. 2. Furthermore, due to the filtration concept the binary sample space's time-t sample states also contain the corresponding sample points. By specifying the i-th sample point at time-t with $\omega_{i,t}$ the time-t sample state occurrence of the sample point can be traced over the different time points (see right panel of Fig. 2): E.g., the 1st sample point ω_1 is equal to the first time-3 sample state $s_{3,1}$ (that is equal to $\omega_{1,3}$) and it is contained in the subsets constituting the sample states s_0 (that includes $\omega_{1,0}$), $s_{1,1}$ (that includes $\omega_{1,1}$) and $s_{2,1}$ (that includes $\omega_{1,2}$). The set $\{\omega_{1,2}, \omega_{2,2}\}$ is an example of a subset that defines a sample state, i.e. the state $s_{2,1}$ in the time-2 partition.

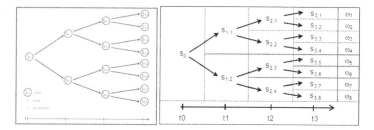

Fig. 2. Binary uncertainty sample space – possible occurrences of the worlds over time

By using the stochastic process concept for modeling the information structure related to the uncertainty of stochastically revealing complex Economic Commitment types, the uncertainty of these types becomes stochastically conceptualized with the *Kind* type Uncertainty Sample Space. This stochastic conceptualization is attached via the *Formal* relationship 'identifying future occurrences' to the *Kind* type Economic Commitment, so that it reifies the type's associated uncertainty information structure in form of a *Kind* type. The assignment of a stochastic information structure to a complex commitment is exemplified by a loan provided by a bank, which is a hybrid contract in the OntoREA© model. In the loan contract the loan taker originally gets a cash amount from the bank and she has the obligation to pay back that amount and the corresponding interest payments in the future. In this contract the balancing requirement means that the cash amount received initially is equal to the present value of the committed payments that have to be paid back in the future. The bank's uncertainty with respect to the loan taker's repayments can be represented by a sample space in form of a truncated binary tree where in each period there is the possibility that the loan taker defaults.

In the planning process future actions are anticipated and committed. In this article the committed future actions are related to the Economic Commitment type that is fulfilled later on with one or more future Economic Event types. In a stochastic planning process the committed future actions are assigned to the time-t sample states defined in the uncertainty information structure that surrounds the Economic Commitment type. E.g., in the *stochastic annual production planning context*, the quarterly production volumes are committed and attached to an Economic Commitment type. If the uncertainty information structure of the quarterly production volumes is defined e.g. according to the quarterly possible sales volumes resulting from a binary sales process then a binary uncertainty sample space arises like in Fig. 2.

The committed production volumes only specify the output that is achieved by performing the anticipated and committed production activities. Consequently, in the planning process not only volume values but beyond this also future Economic Event types in form of physical production processes are anticipated and committed. These anticipated and committed processes are plan events in form of an UFO-B *Event* type. In the case of a complex production Economic Commitment type a structured bundle of plan events is committed, i.e. the *Event* type Plan Event Tree.

In order to assure compatibility in the planning process, the Plan Event Tree type has to be established in conformity with the uncertainty structure surrounding the Economic Commitment type. This conformity is achieved via establishing the *Formal* relation 'assigning plan events' that aligns the *Kind* type Uncertainty Sample Space with the *Event* type Plan Event Tree.

For interpreting the *Event* type used in the stochastic extension of the OntoREA© accounting and finance model an *anti-eternalist* view [7, p. 479] is taken by considering the stochastic, tensed events as *ongoing events* that change over time in line with the successively revealing information. "According to Galton's view, the dynamic behavior of an ongoing event concerns ... the *process* that constitutes it, considered as an object (depending on the event's participants) that is fully present in the thin temporal window where we experience things happening at the present time and moves forward as time passes by, assuming different properties at different times... In this paper I will argue in favor of rejecting ... the view that events are 'frozen in time', by proposing a *tensed* ontological account (contrasted with the dominant *tenseless* tradition) according to which only past events are frozen in time, while ongoing and future events may have modal properties concerning their actual occurrence. At the core of this proposal there is a radical thesis: from the experiential point of view (that is, if we take tense seriously), ongoing events do change. They change by *embodying* temporal parts as time passes by, which *accumulate* with the previous parts. As a new temporal part is embodied, the event's properties and its elapsed duration may change accordingly. ... future events are conceived as *empty embodiments* at the time we refer to them..." [7, p. 480].

For completing the stochastic extension of the OntoREA© accounting and finance model in Fig. 2 three more things have to be explained. Firstly, the specification where the Economic Commitment type from the planning process comes from. For this purpose the *Kind* type Planning and Control Policy is introduced that provides the *Kind* type Economic Commitment via the *Formal* relationship 'setting commitments'. Secondly, the Plan Event Tree type has a *Formal* relationship 'resource reservation' to Economic Resource type. With this relationships materials and capacity resources are reserved that are needed for the future execution of the committed plan events specified in the Plan Event Tree type. Thirdly, the way, the commitments are fulfilled over time. According to the stochastic nature of the Economic Commitment type the fulfilment over time is itself a stochastic process which is represented by the *Formal* relationship 'stochastic fulfilment process'.

4   ERP-CONTROL Application: Stochastic Production Planning and Control

After having specified the uncertainty representation in the stochastic extension of the OntoREA© accounting and finance model the demonstration of its applicability is addressed. For this purpose the ERP-CONTROL application [17] is used. Of special importance it the application's stochastic planning infrastructure for the production domain [25] as it directly incorporates the Plan Event Tree type for capturing the future's uncertainty and it allows the assignment of thereupon contingent future plan events that are planned, committed, reserved and then fulfilled later on.

Figure 3 shows the stochastic production planning infrastructure from the ERP-CONTROL application which is related to the stochastic Annual Planning Process in the module Analytical Planning. The planning task is started by activating the Production Planning entry in the right hand side menu. This initializes a new instance of an annual planning process that requires from the production planner [26] the specification of input information required in: Product Selection, Planned Production Volume, Plan Event Tree and Confirmation.

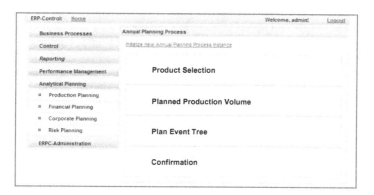

Fig. 3. ERP-CONTROL: annual production planning process

After selecting the product (e.g. bathed candles) to be planned and after inserting the planned production volume for the next year, the binary plan event tree – shown in Fig. 4 – appears and gives the planner the possibility to overwrite the planned production volumes in all quarterly sample states. In the specific examples the binary tree relates to the uncertainty due to the stochastic demand for the selected product that can increase or decrease in each quarter according to a binary stochastic process. In the best case, the demand increases in each subsequent sample state. In this case 10000 kg are planned to be produced over the year (Yearly Quantity). According to the bill of material (BOM) and the routing with respect to the capacity resources, i.e. the personnel and the equipment resources, the resulting production costs (Personnel Costs, Material Costs, Equipment Cost, Total Costs) are calculated and shown as well. The production volume dependent production costs are also shown for the other sample paths that can possibly be realized in the uncertainty sample space.

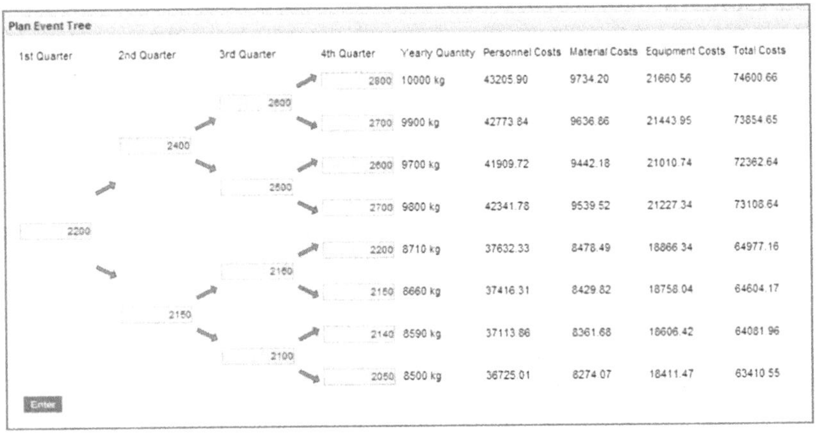

Plan Event Tree

1st Quarter	2nd Quarter	3rd Quarter	4th Quarter	Yearly Quantity	Personnel Costs	Material Costs	Equipment Costs	Total Costs
			2800	10000 kg	43205.90	9734.20	21660.56	74600.66
		2600	2700	9900 kg	42773.84	9636.86	21443.95	73854.65
	2400		2600	9700 kg	41909.72	9442.18	21010.74	72362.64
		2500	2700	9800 kg	42341.78	9539.52	21227.34	73108.64
2200			2200	8710 kg	37632.33	8478.49	18866.34	64977.16
	2160		2160	8660 kg	37416.31	8429.82	18758.04	64604.17
	2150		2140	8590 kg	37113.86	8361.68	18606.42	64081.96
		2100	2050	8500 kg	36725.01	8274.07	18411.47	63410.55

Enter

Fig. 4. Plan event tree – quarterly contingent production volumes and related costs

The last step in the Annual Planning Process is the Confirmation. By confirming the Plan Event Tree, the therein specified sample state contingent production volumes are committed and the corresponding material, personnel and equipment resource requirements are reserved.

The stochastic Annual Planning Process is accompanied by the Quarterly Planning Process. This process gets activated at the beginning of each quarter by inserting the production volumes for the three months of the quarter. In the left panel of Fig. 5 the monthly volumes are inserted for the three months of the first quarter. The right panel of Fig. 5 shows the insertion of the actual realized production volumes that is collected each month. After the third month of the quarter the overall actual production volume of the first quarter is collected. This value can be seen in the left upper part of Fig. 6. The figure also shows that the upper sample state ($s_{1,1}$) has realized which was specified by the controller who selected that state. According to the revealing information concept it can be seen that the lower sample state ($s_{1,2}$) and its following paths are grayed out indicating that they cannot be realized any more in the future. After the realization of the $s_{1,1}$-sample state only the first four sample paths can possibly be realized over the remaining three quarters of the year.

Bathed Candle Product Segment 2013 S0: 2200 kg		**Output Production**	
		Bathed Candle Product Segment 2013 S0	
January*	700 kg	**Planned Output**	700.00 kg
February*	733 kg	**Produced Output**	
March*	767 kg		650.00 kg
Enter		Enter	

Fig. 5. Quarterly production planning and monthly production execution process

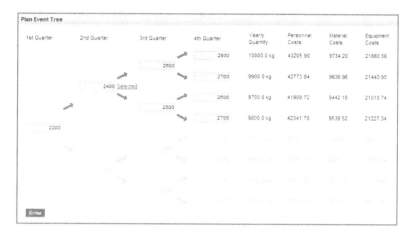

Fig. 6. Plan event tree – resolving uncertainty over time

As already indicated by its name, the ERP-CONTROL application does not provide the stochastic planning infrastructure only for planning but also for controlling purposes by providing monitoring facilities. In the monitoring feature of ERP-CONTROL the planned and committed production volumes are compared to the realized volumes and variances between the two are calculated. In a double loop management system the variance information can be used either to trigger corrective adjustments at the production process level e.g. by correcting the production policy or adaptive adjustments at the production planning level e.g. by adapting the sample state contingent production volumes for the forthcoming periods.

After having demonstrated the functioning of the stochastic production planning infrastructure in ERP-CONTROL, it will be shown now which concepts from the OntoREA© accounting and finance model's stochastic extension are implemented in the application in which way.

Figure 7 shows the excerpt from ERP-CONTROL's data model. It contains the data structure that is placed below the Economic Resource class for delivering the informational basis for the stochastic production planning infrastructure. In order to implement the bill of material (BOM) and the routing through the capacity resources the Economic Resource class is specialized into the three resource classes, i.e. Personnel, Equipment and Material. The Personnel Specification class and the Equipment

Specification class are the compositional parts of the Process Segment class that defines the routing of the production process. The Material Specification class provides the compositional parts of the Product Segment that defines the BOM. For the stochastic production planning infrastructure the Plan Events class is added.

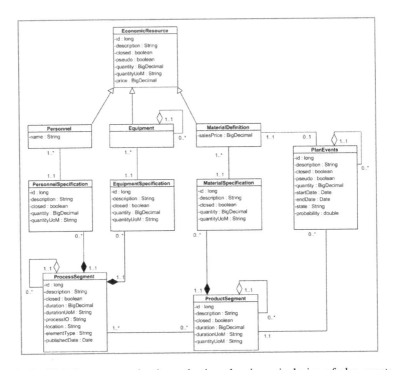

Fig. 7. ERP-CONTROL: stochastic production planning – inclusion of plan events

The attributes of the Plan Events class contain the information with respect to the time dimension (tensed nature of future events) in the startDate and endDate attributes and to the uncertainty dimension (stochastic nature of future events) in the state attribute and the probability attribute. The Boolean pseudo attribute indicates if the instance of the Plan Event class is committed (TRUE) or not (FALSE).

The recursive relationship of the Plan Events class allows the building of tree structures. In the ERP-CONTROL application they are used to build the binary Plan Event Tree structure (Fig. 4). This tree is constructed according to the (binary) Uncertainty Sample Space type and it contains the planned and committed production (plan) events. The committed events reserve the corresponding resources and they are executed according to the realizing sample states over time in a stochastic, i.e. a temporal modal way.

The Plan Events class is implemented – like the other classes in Fig. 7 as well – in the Java Enterprise Edition as a database persisted entity bean.

The state attribute of the Plan Events class contains the reference to the sample states defined in the (binary) Uncertainty Sample Space type. This reference is given by the binary coding of the time-t sample states that can be seen in Fig. 8. The annual production plan is called the "root" in the Plan Event Tree and it includes the planned production volumes for the selected product. To an annual production plan belong 15 possible quarterly production plans which are coded by the sample path "0nnn" where n can be 0, 1 or { }. For example: in the third quarter the four sample states are possible, i.e. 000, 001, 010 and 011. Furthermore, each quarterly production plan has three monthly plans with state 0nnn.m where m stands for the months 0, 1 and 2. For example: 0.0 for January, 0.1 for February and 0.2 for March.

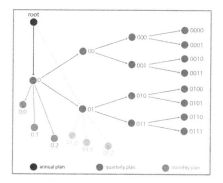

Plan category	Time-t sample state	Binary coding
Annual plan	Root	
Quarterly plan	0nnn	$n : (\{\} \mid 0 \mid 1)$
Monthly plan	0nnn.m	$n : (\{\} \mid 0 \mid 1)$, $m : (0 \mid 1 \mid 2)$

Fig. 8. Binary sample space representation – binary coding of time-t sample state

5 Conclusion

The primary research objective of this article was the extension of the OntoREA© accounting and finance model with an adequate representation of the uncertainty that surrounds the forward looking perspective of finance. This objective was achieved by an UFO-ontological conceptualization of the stochastic concepts, i.e. the stochastic process and the revealing information concepts from the "golden" age of finance and their integrations into the OntoREA© model. Key for the consistent integration is the connection of the Economic Commitment type with the Uncertainty Sample Space and the Plan Event Tree types. Due to the generic nature of the stochastic extension it can be applied not only for financial planning and control but also for decision analysis and different kinds of optimal control problems. The applicability of the OntoREA© model's stochastic extension was demonstrated via the ERP-CONTROL application where elements of this extension were used to provide the application's stochastic production planning and control infrastructure.

By including perdurant Event types from UFO-B for the ontological specification of the Economic Event and the Plan Event Tree types a completely new possibility arises for the conceptual modeling of different processes. Mixing UFO-B with UFO-A constructs in the stochastic OntoREA© accounting and finance model allows a convenient mixture of structural and dynamic concepts. Equipped with this new possibility the UFO-B event-based dynamic modeling can cover different types of processes at the operational level and the different management levels, i.e. operational (business) processes (business domain), managerial processes (management control domain) and policy setting (governmental) processes (governance domain). For future research it seems especially interesting to grab this new opportunity for solving the problem of integrating managerial and governmental processes in form of Balanced Scorecard management systems [27] or in form of more general strategic and management control systems [28] into different versions of the REA model and the stochastic OntoREA© accounting and finance model, respectively.

References

1. Fischer-Pauzenberger, C., Schwaiger, W.S.A.: The OntoREA© accounting and finance model: ontological conceptualization of the accounting and finance domain. In: Mayr, H.C., Guizzardi, G., Ma, H., Pastor, O. (eds.) ER 2017. LNCS, vol. 10650, pp. 506–519. Springer, Cham (2017). https://doi.org/10.1007/978-3-319-69904-2_38

2. Black, F., Scholes, M.: The pricing of options and corporate liabilities. J. Polit. Econ. **81**, 637 (1973)

3. Cox, J.C., Ross, S.A., Rubinstein, M.: Option pricing: a simplified approach. J. Financ. Econ. **7**, 229–263 (1979)

4. Merton, R.C.: Theory of rational theory option pricing. Bell J. Econ. **4**, 141–183 (1973)

5. Merton, R.C.: An intertemporal capital asset pricing model. Econometrica **41**, 867 (1973)

6. Guizzardi, G., Wagner, G., de Almeida Falbo, R., Guizzardi, R.S.S., Almeida, J.P.A.: Towards ontological foundations for the conceptual modeling of events. In: Ng, W., Storey, V.C., Trujillo, J.C. (eds.) ER 2013. LNCS, vol. 8217, pp. 327–341. Springer, Heidelberg (2013). https://doi.org/10.1007/978-3-642-41924-9_27

7. Guarino, N.: On the semantics of ongoing and future occurrence identifiers. In: Mayr, H.C., Guizzardi, G., Ma, H., Pastor, O. (eds.) ER 2017. LNCS, vol. 10650, pp. 477–490. Springer, Cham (2017). https://doi.org/10.1007/978-3-319-69904-2_36

8. Guizzardi, G.: Ontological Foundations for Structural Conceptual Model (2005). http://doc.utwente.nl/50826

9. Geerts, G.L., McCarthy, W.E.: An ontological analysis of the economic primitives of the extended-REA enterprise information architecture. Int. J. Account. Inf. Syst. **3**, 1–16 (2002)

10. Geerts, G.L., McCarthy, W.E.: Policy level specifications in REA enterprise information systems. J. Inf. Syst. **20**, 37–63 (2006)

11. Schwaiger, W.S.A.: The REA accounting model: enhancing understandability and applicability. In: Proceedings of the 34th International Conference on Conceptual Modeling ER 2015, vol. 9381, pp. 566–573 (2015)

12. Fischer-Pauzenberger, C., Schwaiger, W.S.A.: The OntoREA accounting model: ontology-based modeling of the accounting domain. Complex Syst. Inform. Model. Q. **11**, 20–37 (2017)

13. Gruber, T.R.: A translation approach to portable ontology specifications. Knowl. Acquis. **5**, 199–220 (1993)

14. Ontology Project: UFO-A Specification

15. Fischer-Pauzenberger, C., Schwaiger, W.S.A.: The OntoREA© accounting and finance model: a retroactive DSRM demonstration evaluation. In: Poels, G., Gailly, F., Serral Asensio, E., Snoeck, M. (eds.) PoEM 2017. LNBIP, vol. 305, pp. 81–95. Springer, Cham (2017). https://doi.org/10.1007/978-3-319-70241-4_6

16. Fischer-Pauzenberger, C., Schwaiger, W.S.A.: OntoREA© accounting and finance model: hedge portfolio representation of derivatives. In: Buchmann, R.A., Karagiannis, D., Kirikova, M. (eds.) PoEM 2018. LNBIP, vol. 335, pp. 372–382. Springer, Cham (2018). https://doi.org/10.1007/978-3-030-02302-7_24
17. Schwaiger, W.S.A., Abmayer, M.: Accounting and management information systems - a semantic integration. In: 15th International Conference on Information Integration and Web-based Application & Services, pp. 346–352 (2013)
18. Smith, J.E., Nau, R.F.: Valuing risky projects: option pricing theory and decision analysis. Manag. Sci. **41**, 795–816 (1995)
19. Brandão, L.E., Dyer, J.S., Hahn, W.J.: Using binomial decision trees to solve real-option valuation problems. Decis. Anal. **2**, 69–88 (2005)
20. Bertsekas, D.: Dynamic Programming and Optimal Control, vol. I. Athena Scientific, Belmont (2005)
21. Bertsekas, D.: Dynamic Programming and Optimal Control -, vol. II. Athena Scientific, Belmont (2011)
22. Keane, M.P., Wolpin, K.I.: The solution and estimation of discrete choice dynamic programming models by simulation and interpolation: monte carlo evidence. Rev. Econ. Stat. **76**, 648–672 (1994)
23. Denault, M., Simonato, J.G., Stentoft, L.: A simulation-and-regression approach for stochastic dynamic programs with endogenous state variables. Comput. Oper. Res. **40**, 2760–2769 (2013)
24. Karatzas, I., Shreve, S.: Brownian Motion and Stochastic Calculus. Springer, Heidelberg (1991). https://doi.org/10.1007/978-1-4612-0949-2
25. Dural, Ö.F., Nasufi, A.: Produktionsplanung und-steuerung unter Unsicherheit: design und implementierung in integrierten ERP-Systemen. Master thesis, TU Wien (2013)
26. Fellner, D.: Modellbasierte Planung und Steuerung unter Unsicherheit. Master thesis, TU Wien (2010)
27. Church, K.S., Smith, R.E.: An extension of the REA framework to support balanced scorecard information requirements. J. Inf. Syst. **21**, 1 (2007)
28. Schwaiger, W.S.A.: REA business management ontology: conceptual modeling of accounting, finance and management control. In: CAiSE Forum, pp. 41–48 (2016)

A Role-Based Capability Modeling Approach for Adaptive Information Systems

Hendrik Schön[1](✉), Jelena Zdravkovic[2], Janis Stirna[2], and Susanne Strahringer[1]

[1] Business Informatics, esp. IS in Trade and Industry, TU Dresden, Dresden, Germany
{hendrik.schoen, susanne.strahringer}@tu-dresden.de
[2] Department of Computer and System Sciences, Stockholm University, Stockholm, Sweden
{jelenaz, js}@dsv.su.se

Abstract. Most modeling approaches lack in their ability to cover a full-fledged view of a software system's business requirements, goals, and capabilities and to specify aspects of flexibility and variability. The modeling language Capability Driven Development (CDD) allows modeling capabilities and their relation to the execution context. However, its context-dependency lacks the possibility to define dynamic structural information that may be part of the context: persons, their roles, and the impact of objects that are involved in a particular execution occurrence. To solve this issue, we extended the CDD method with the BROS modeling approach, a role-based structural modeling language that allows the definition of context-dependent and dynamic structure of an information system. In this paper, we propose the integrated combination of the two modeling approaches by extending the CDD meta-model with necessary concepts from BROS. This combination allows for technical development of the information system (BROS) by starting with capability modeling using CDD. We demonstrate the combined meta-model in an example based on a real-world use case. With it, we show the benefits of modeling detailed business requirements regarding context comprising environment- and object-related information.

Keywords: Capability modeling · Roles · Context · Business requirements

1 Introduction

Organizations need a rapid response to changes in the business environment in terms of new legislation, changes in customer and supplier behavior, new and often adverse events. Such change cannot always be foreseen at the time of information system (IS) development and hence the current approach that is based on implementing change by redesigning and redeploying applications is no longer sufficient. A strand of approaches aims at continuous development and tightening the gap between development and operations [1]. This is, however, not suitable for developing and customizing enterprise applications that need to respond to change both on the business and IS level. That is, a congruent approach that supports responsiveness to changes in the application context and facilitates the responses to transcend from the business to

Published by Springer Nature Switzerland AG 2019
J. Gordijn et al. (Eds.): PoEM 2019, LNBIP 369, pp. 68–82, 2019.
https://doi.org/10.1007/978-3-030-35151-9_5

the information system is needed. Sandkuhl and Stirna [2] contributed to making IS more flexible with respect to the adaptation to context. The concept of capability was used for this purpose because it unifies the business aspects traditionally used in areas such as enterprise modeling like goals and processes with execution context [3]. Furthermore, it connects context with the specification of algorithms for adjusting the IS once the context changes. The stance of CDD is that any information that influences the IS is to be modeled as context.

BROS (Business Role-Object Specification) [4] is a structural modeling language for design time specification of business objects concerning a domain model as well as specific business logic. Role-fulfilling objects cover the static specification part regarding the separation of concerns, whereas the dynamic specification part of the business logic is expressed via events. The final BROS model serves as a blueprint for development and can be implemented in role-based modeling languages. BROS supports the specification of system-internal variability that is induced by, e.g., the change of role fulfillment. In case of human or organizational roles, changes of this kind often require adaptations in terms of business process variants because the same roles can be fulfilled by several actors each of which having a different skill profile. This aspect has not been elaborated in the CDD approach. *Therefore, the objective of this paper is to explore the integration of the CDD and BROS for the purpose of supporting role-based capability modeling and IS design.* Among the motivators for the CDD [5] are the following goals, to which the proposed integration of the two approaches is set to contribute:

- *To allocate resources to process execution tasks and to provision human resources to process execution.* The integrated proposal addresses this goal by explicitly modeling skill profiles of actors and skill requirements of roles, which allows specifying the actor-role fulfillment by using the concept of *scene* in BROS.
- *To customize services according to context.* The integrated proposal allows designing and monitoring changes in the context caused by actor-role fulfillment.
- *To monitor process execution.* The CDD approach supports model-driven generation of a monitoring application, Capability Navigation Application (CNA) for overseeing context elements, KPIs, and triggering capability adjustments. The proposal allows integration of actor-role fulfillment and skill monitoring in the CNA.

The remainder of the paper is structured as follows. Section 2 covers the related background of our research. Section 3 provides a conceptual overview of the suggested role-based capability approach. Further, in Sect. 4, the abstract and theoretical part of our research is demonstrated via the introduction of the extended meta-model, a core part of the paper. Section 5 demonstrates our new approach by applying it to a real-world use case, a lecture management scenario in higher education, followed by the conclusion in Sect. 6 with summary and outlook.

2   Background

The enterprise modeling discipline endeavors to support businesses by means of IS, which imposes supporting some low-volatile business processes and concepts, but lately even more is required – coping with dynamically changing business environments requiring adaptations of IS at execution time. In this regard, adaptability is seen as an architectural property, enabling a system to efficiently adjust to different or evolving operational or usage circumstances [6, 7].

To achieve adaptability, organizations should be able to, by the support of modeling, master different variations of their businesses, such as user preferences, environmental variations, changes on partners' sides, legislations, and other [8]. This study also investigates the area of dynamic adaptions of IS and finds that there is a plethora of capability modeling approaches that depict adaptability elements in different ways. Many of the existing approaches address capability delivery by means of, for example, services, business processes, or actions. Nevertheless, the current state in capability design does not offer a transition to tasks associated with IS development. The CDD approach (Sect. 2.1) relies on enterprise models for designing IS based business capabilities with inbuilt support for adaptation to changing contexts at the execution time [2]. Amongst Enterprise Architecture frameworks and languages, including TOGAF, Archimate, DODAF, NAF and MODAF, the NAF framework [9] is the closest to CDD in its ability to define local conditions in design, but it does not have a method for capability adjustments at runtime. Also, the work of Rodriguez et al. [10] is related to CDD and includes context-dependency as well. However, this approach focuses more on reliability modeling and transformation with replicas at design time. The specifications of the other frameworks provide methods neither for the use of capability at runtime nor for adjustments [3]. However, its methodology and the underlying architecture for designing variability for the purpose of adaptation lack the support for dynamic roles of the entities being involved in the implementation of the capabilities, such as subjects (persons, organizations) and objects. The BROS language (Sect. 2.2) uses business scenarios as a fitting complement to support the specification of system variability induced by the change of role fulfillment.

2.1 Capability-Driven Development (CDD)

The foundation for CDD is provided by the conceptual Capability Meta-Model (CMM). CMM was developed on the basis of industrial requirements and related research on capabilities. In brief, it consists of the three main parts of the meta-model:

- Enterprise model for representing organizational designs with Goals, KPIs, Processes (with concretizations as Process Variants) and Resources;
- Context model for representing for which context a Capability is designed (represented by Context Set) and Context Situation at runtime that is monitored and according to which the deployed solutions are adjusted; and
- Patterns and variability model for delivering Capability by reusable solutions for reaching Goals under different Context Situations. Each pattern describes how a certain Capability is to be delivered within a certain Context Situation and what Process Variants and Resources are needed to support a Context Set.

The meta-model in Fig. 1 is a simplified version of CMM showing the key components of CDD, also described in Table 1. The full version with complete element definitions is available in [11].

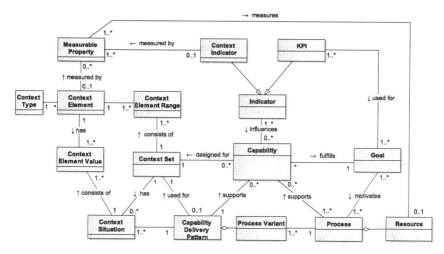

Fig. 1. A conceptual meta-model supporting capability driven development

Table 1. Concepts of the core CDD meta-model

Concept	Description
Capability	Capability is the ability and capacity that enable an enterprise to achieve a business Goal in a certain context (represented by Context Set)
KPI	Key Performance Indicators (KPIs) are measurable properties that can be seen as targets for achievement of Goals
Context Set	Context Set describes the set of Context Elements that are relevant for design and delivery of a specific Capability
Context Element Range	Context Element Range sets boundaries of permitted values for a specific Context Element and for a specific Context Set
Context Element	A Context Element is representing any information that can be used to characterize the situation of an entity
Measurable Property	Measurable Property is any information about the organization's environment that can be measured
Context Element Value	Context Element Value is a value of a specific Context Element at a given the runtime situation. It can be calculated from several Measurable Properties
Goal	Goal is a desired state of affairs that needs to be attained. Goals can be refined into sub-goals. Goals should typically be expressed in measurable terms such as KPIs
Process	Process is a series of actions that are performed in order to achieve particular results. A Process supports Goals and has input and produces output in terms of information and/or material. A process is perceived to consume resources
Pattern	Patterns are reusable solutions for reaching business Goals under specific situational contexts. The context defined for the Capability (Context Set) should match the context in which the Pattern is applicable
Process Variant	Process variant is a part of the Process using the same input and delivers the same outcome as the Process in a different way

The CDD methodology combines three interconnected cycles of working – design, delivery, and feedback. Design starts with configuring existing or creating new enterprise goals and processes combined with captured business contexts and eliciting required capabilities. This is followed by delivery of the capability requiring composition and integration of existing technologies and applications, such as ERP systems. During the execution of the application, the changes of context are monitored, and runtime adjustment algorithms are used to calculate if the context's changes require another capability pattern. Feedback is achieved by monitoring defined KPIs, which enable capability refinement and pattern updating.

2.2 Business Role-Object Specification (BROS)

Roles and the related concepts were investigated in various research areas during the last decades (e.g., theories [12], modeling languages [13], programming languages [14, 15], runtime environments [16], or enterprise modeling [17, 18]). Roles extend the established object-oriented paradigm by the ability to represent an object in different contexts and by changing its behavior and characteristics accordingly. Roles are described in terms of (a) behavioral, (b) relational, and (c) context-dependent properties [12, 13]. This serves a more accurate description of the domain's entities with their context-dependent structure and behavior. BROS uses this advantage of roles to model software based on required business needs.

The BROS modeling language [4] was originally developed for an easy adaptation of (structural) reference models [19], it can also be used for creating role-based software in general. It utilizes the role-paradigm to specify mainly structural models. Via roles, however, BROS (in contrast to traditional modeling languages such as UML) is able to include the behavior-aware specifications in structural models non-invasively.

BROS does not focus on process modeling itself; it explicitly includes events induced in the respective background processes, nevertheless. Via events, temporality, and role-based context-dependent behavior, BROS allows for behavioral modeling constructs within a mainly structural modeling language. Thus, BROS benefits from CDD due to its ability to define the complex business constraints (i.e., when to choose a scene) as a background source of these events.

The main concepts of BROS are objects, roles, scenes, and events (Fig. 2). Objects are selected from an underlying structural domain model and are the target of any use case or enterprise-specific adaptation done by using the remaining concepts. BROS utilizes roles as specific representations of objects in certain scenes (the role's context). The enterprise-specific processes are the main drivers of the adaptation and serve two kinds of information: (a) the scene as an encapsulation context of a use case or task, and (b) the events as certain points in time affecting the roles. The details of the language, as well as an example, are described in [4], based on the research of CROM [13]. For the purpose of this research, the BROS concepts were introduced in the CDD meta-model with the knowledge implied by the BROS meta-model.

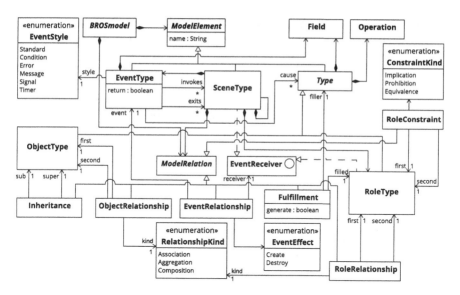

Fig. 2. The basic BROS meta-model [4]

3 Conceptual Approach

According to the motivation for this research, we strive for a framework that extends the CDD approach with the role-based paradigm provided by the BROS approach. Although both approaches are settled on different levels and phases of the software development stack (see Fig. 3), the role concepts introduced by BROS are suitable to be used for fine-grained capability design. CDD and BROS have been developed independently of each other. Nevertheless, they share a common concept of "dedicated context": the process variant in CDD and the scene in BROS. Both are representatives of a special, single task or execution, dependent on the chosen environment.

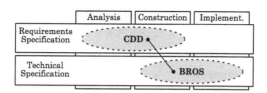

Fig. 3. The connection between both areas

This task may change during runtime since one or more requirements from the given environment is dropped. In CDD, a process variant is derived from a general process description (e.g., giving a lecture). The concrete process variant is then chosen by variation points based on the environment's requirements. Thus, CDD focuses on the conceptual view of the requirements, capabilities, and goals of the respective IS. In contrast, BROS utilizes scenes to describe the behavior of roles for certain tasks or executable procedures. The scene defines the context-dependent boundary of a role's validity (e.g., the role "Teacher" is only valid in the context of the scene "Giving Lecture") in combination with a start and an end as specific points in time.

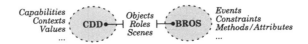

Fig. 4. The set of common concepts

BROS is intended to be an extension to CDD, hence, we integrated its concepts (see Fig. 4) into the already existing CDD methodology. We state that, with the BROS concepts, it is possible, to describe the capabilities of an enterprise with regard to performers that are able to play certain roles (or not). CDD, as presented in [2], is able to model the capability dependence on static environment information (e.g., resource utilization, calendar time or the weather condition), while including BROS enables the modeling of capabilities that depend on the participating performers (that is, actors and objects with abilities), illustrated in Fig. 5.

Technically, our proposal is realized as a meta-model extension to the CDD meta-model. Extending the meta-model also allows maintaining the adaptation and decision mechanisms of CDD. Thus, we strived for a non-invasive adaptation to implement the BROS features for two reasons: (a) to use CDD as a new source of business knowledge usable in BROS, and (b) to include the structural modeling concepts (scenes, roles, and objects) into CDD to provide a more powerful modeling approach.

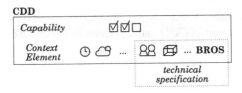

Fig. 5. Adding BROS to CDD

4   Meta-Model Extension

This section introduces the full (extended) meta-model, describes the respective model elements as well as their relationships and purposes.

To achieve the envisioned integration of CDD and BROS and keep the existing CDD method components and method extensions intact, the meta-model has been extended "non-invasively" (c.f. [2] for more information about CDD methods components). The CDD-BROS integration is intended as a method extension. For this purpose, we extended the complete CDD meta-model with a set of new meta-model elements that override or extend already defined elements. As a result, the CDD meta-model ensures that the new extension is compatible with the CDD environment and other CDD extensions. The meta-model depicting CDD with the BROS extension is shown in Fig. 6. The set of BROS elements contains the newly developed elements. While *ProcessVariant* and *ProcessVariantVariationPoint* are overridden (i.e., marked as abstract) and not usable together with the BROS extension, the *ContextElement* and *MeasurableProperty* are extended and can be used simultaneously with the related BROS elements. Apart from the inherited elements, several new elements are used to model the BROS part of the combined approach.

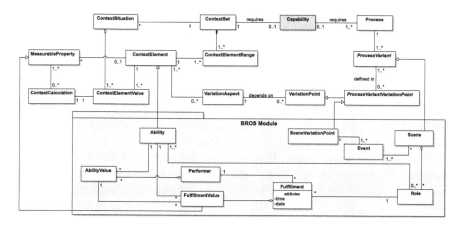

Fig. 6. The small CDD meta-model with the BROS extension

The newly introduced BROS elements are responsible for dedicated context decisions based on provided skills by entities. For that reason, we use the semantics of roles, objects, and scenes established in BROS.

A *Performer* is an entity (type) of the real world that is allowed to take over a *Role* in a *Scene* via *Fulfillment* to provide certain *Abilities*. For example, the performer "professor" is able to fulfill the role "teacher" in the scene "giving lecture" to achieve the ability (and responsibility) of "teaching". This is also possible for non-human objects like, e.g., the entity "room" that may fulfill the role "lecture hall." However, the performer and its roles depend on the use case that has to be modeled. With the meta-model extension, it is stated that the scene (a BROS concept) replaces the *ProcessVariant*. Thus, the process defined by CDD now uses scenes to describe different flows dependent on the chosen context. Scenes contain roles that are determined for a specific temporal execution (e.g., the "giving lecture" scene requires the role "teacher"). The variation mechanisms in CDD then do not point to process variants but specific scenes with roles. The roles are fulfilled by performers (real-world entities). The fulfillment between a performer and a role is annotated with the fulfillment value that quantifies the ability of the performer to fulfill a specific role. E.g., various instances of a performer "professor" fulfill the "lecturer" role in the scene "giving lecture" with their own specific *FulfillmentValue* in term of a skill profile. This value is inherited from *MeasurableProperty*, i.e., the fulfillment value is given by, e.g., a database in the ERP system that lists the employees with their skill profiles and may be time-dependent. There must be at least one role (provided by a scene) that is responsible for providing the necessary abilities. However, at runtime, the concrete *AbilityValue* for the abilities is derived via *ContextCalculation* from the fulfillment value, i.e., dependent on the entity that takes over the specific role. Since the ability is inherited from *ContextElement*, the *ContextElementRange* (from CDD) is assigned to the abilities to limit the possible value range for the context. At runtime, those are concrete value boundaries. If the range is violated (due to not fitting ability values) the adaptation part of CDD uses the *SceneVariationPoint* to define another scene that is able to be used for the new context. However, this paper does not focus on the adaptation part, which is defined in the full CDD meta-model. In the proposed meta-model, we use *Events* since the BROS scene definition includes, inter alia, a start and end via an event. Thus, we use an event as an interface from the scene variation point towards the scene. This allows the start of multiple scenes with triggering a single start event.

The new meta-model elements are listed in Table 2. The M1 level is used for capability design, e.g., specifying that a lecturing capability is based on performers such as professors and roles such as teachers, students, and course assistants. The M0 level of a capability model materializes once the lecturing capability is executed and runtime-specific professors, e.g., "John" and "Alice", perform specific roles for specific scenes. An M1 instantiation example for the new elements in this meta-model is given in the next section. Due to the non-invasive changes to the original meta-model, all mechanisms of CDD, like the capability adjustment algorithms and calculations of KPIs and context, are still operational.

Table 2. New meta-model elements within the BROS method component

Concept	Description	M1 example	M0 example
Performer	A real-world entity on type-level that is able to do something	Person, Room, Computer	Alice, INF003
Role	A context-specific behavior that may be adopted by a performer	Attendant, Teacher, Lecture Hall	Alice's Teacher role, INF003's Lecture Hall role
Scene	A contextual boundary that denotes a temporal execution	Giving Lecture, Checking Exams	Lecture ID 5
Fulfillment	The process of a performer playing a role	Employee-Teacher-Fulfillment	Alice playing the Teacher
Fulfillment value	A runtime value that is related to the profile of a role	–	Profile of room INF003 when fulfilling Lecture Hall
Event	A type of point in time when something may happen	Start, End, Interruption	9am at 24. Dec 2019, Incoming Call ID 42
Scene variation point	A mechanism that decides the triggering of events to start a certain scene	–	–
Ability	An action related to the possibilities of a performer	Heating up, Having capacity, Teaching	Teaching ability of Alice
Ability value	A runtime value that denotes the quantity of a certain ability	–	42, 1337, yes

5 Use Case – Provisioning of Subjects in Higher Education

This section demonstrates the proposed CDD and BROS integration with an example case of the teaching environment at a large university in Sweden.

5.1 Use Case Description

The provisioning of the subjects in Higher Education requires substantial planning and effort. That includes organizing the lecturers' team, scheduling, admission of students, and publishing course materials. Once a course starts, the major activities are teaching sessions, exercises, supervision, and examinations.

Requirements Engineering is a standard subject offered at both the undergraduate and graduate levels to about 250 students in total. The course is given in Swedish at the undergraduate level, and in English at the graduate level. The team of teachers includes several roles: lectures and Q&A seminars are given by professors; exercises are supervised by teaching assistants, PhD students, and professors; tool tutoring and supervision is done in the computer labs and led by teaching assistants, PhD students, and research assistants. The course material includes lectures, tutorials, reading material, and media. It is published on the Moodle online education portal. The platform is managed by the whole teaching team according to the assigned roles and responsibilities. During the course execution, the portal is also used for managing communication among the students and the teachers, management of quizzes, grading of exercises, as well as other activities. Since we investigate a Swedish university, there is the possibility of a sudden and severe snowfall in colder seasons. Hence, the local traffic information system and the weather forecast are analyzed for possible general delays. If severe delays throughout the city are to be expected or are occurring, the course events might be cancelled, rescheduled, repeated, and/or switched to online delivery.

Concerning course scheduling, each classroom has a limit for the maximum number of persons. Because the classrooms are a resource constraint, they need to be booked well in advance. If the number of students exceeds the size of the classroom, it is possible to stream a lecture to another classroom in real-time. This, however, poses additional tasks related to the management of the teaching process. It is not easy to reschedule the rooms in cases when more students than estimated register for the course (the deadline is the day when the course starts), as well as when additional tutoring (and thereby rooms) becomes needed. The final exam is classroom-based and as such requires a sufficient number of places and invigilators for each of the examination rooms, which requires engaging both the teachers as well as additional staff.

5.2 Meta-Model Instance Design

According to the defined schema of model layers by Object Management Group [20, 21], the meta-model is on the M2 layer. An instance of this layer is the M1 layer, which is a model that uses the M2 defined concepts to specify the targeted "real model." An instance of M1 is on the layer M0, which represents "real items" like "Alice" as a person or "INF003" as a room. However, since the CDD and BROS extensions are on

M2, we need to define the capability design on the M1 layer before considering runtime items. However, not all M2 concepts need to be instantiated on the M1 level because concepts that denote runtime concepts, like values of context elements or ability values, belong to M0 (i.e., fulfillment, fulfillment value, ability value, and event). For these values, we model the M1 pendants as a type that needs to be expressed at runtime. Thus, as elaborating the M0 is not our primary goal, we do not go into detail of their runtime assignments.

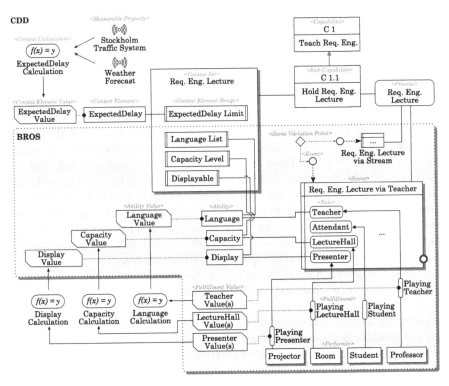

Fig. 7. An example instance of the meta-model for the use case

Figure 7 shows the M1 instance of the M2 meta-model, including the CDD part (white background) and the new BROS concepts (gray background). We derived this instance example from the use case as only one of many different possibilities. The respective M0 types from the meta-model are annotated to the M1 model elements.

The use case requirements are encoded in the context set named "Req. Eng. Lecture", which serves the overall CDD capability of "Teach Req. Eng." The ranges (specified on M0 with concrete range boundaries later on) set the parameters of deciding between different scenes. For this use case, there are several such ranges as parameters: a specific schedule delay, a required teaching language, a device that is able to display the slides, and so forth. If something happens, e.g., there is too little capacity available in the room for the lecture, the adaptation part of CDD (not shown in the meta-model) adapts towards this new situation with triggering changes. By using BROS, the capacity of a lecture room is modeled in Fig. 7 as an ability of a role that is fulfilled by a performer, i.e., any room (e.g., "INF003") that plays the role of the lecture hall at runtime so that its capacity is used for the lecture's capacity.

If at runtime this capacity is outside the range set in the capability design, the adaptation part has two options:

1. It uses a different performer (that is, a new room with higher capacity) that fulfills the role in the same scene so that the scene does not change; or
2. If there is no other performer available, the scene is switched to another scene (e.g., a scene that streams the lecture to various locations) that meets the range requirements with possibly other roles (e.g., a stream receiving device).

If neither of the two possibilities can be applied, then an error occurs since there is no available solution to the new context. The real-world entities, the performers, have to fulfill the roles in a scene, i.e., the CDD environment is able to perform calculations deriving the ability value out of their profile since the real room "INF003" at runtime does not know which abilities one wants to derive (e.g., its capacity or its ability to be ready for exams). The CDD environment delivers the actual runtime value for the ability (e.g., "15" for capacity) that gets checked against the range boundaries, which can be Boolean, lists, formal expressions or simple number ranges (e.g., "1 to 20"). The context set may also contain ranges that are not dependent on entities but on environmental states. In Fig. 7, we modeled the traffic situation and the weather forecast as measurable properties, so that the calculation results in the value of expected delay. This is checked against the range in the context set to decide whether it is possible to hold a lecture or whether one should start streaming (or skip the lecture). This expected delay is an environment-based state and independent from any concrete performers and roles (for demonstration purposes on how to model BROS-independent context elements). Thus, when designing capabilities, one has to decide between environment- or entity-based context elements and their ranges. Regarding the modeling complexity, we only designed a simple CDD-BROS model for one capability with limited scene-based variability. There are plenty of options to extend this design, e.g., multiple abilities or performers per role, performers that fulfill a set of roles in certain scenes, involving different IT supporting tools for teaching and other variants.

5.3 Use Case Discussion

With the modeled use case stated in Fig. 7, we argue that the modeling of entity-based context elements receives more attention in the capability design. Previously, every context element was handled as external. Thus, the modeling of capabilities is enhanced due to additional modeling constructs:

- The construct of scene allows the definition of concrete variations of an executable, providing a set of necessary roles;
- Roles (encapsulated in scenes) enable modeling the necessary entity-based context elements (i.e., abilities of performers);

- Performers are the main constructs to define the concrete entities that are responsible for fulfilling a context element range (indirectly via roles).

This trinity of the role-based BROS paradigm (scene, roles, and performers) is the tool for switching between contexts and related situations at runtime. When encountering an unmet range condition, the new possibility, to switch between fulfillments instead of switching to a whole new scene, is an important improvement. As such, the same context scene may be continued with only changing the performers, who are fulfilling the needed roles and their abilities for the scene.

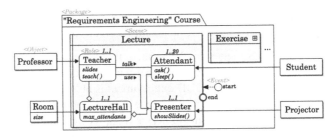

Fig. 8. An example BROS model with objects, roles, events, and a scene

The combination of CDD and BROS allows modeling on multiple levels, i.e., subsequent stages along the model-driven development lifecycle (as shown in Fig. 5). With the usage of the BROS concepts in CDD, the transition towards implementation is simplified. BROS, as intended to be on the technical level, is tightly connected to the underlying software development. Assuming the fact that the CDD modeling would define several scenes, roles, and performers for its contexts, these can also be used for a related BROS model. Figure 8 shows a possible BROS model for software construction that is derived from the CDD model in Fig. 7 with the same scene, its roles, and the related performers. This interrelation of the different abstraction levels while developing IS via CDD and BROS benefits model-driven development.

6 Conclusion

We have shown that two existing approaches, CDD and BROS, which were developed independently and for different purposes, can be combined to complement each other. This was done by integrating the needed BROS elements into the CDD meta-model as an extension. The combined approach was demonstrated with a use case and allowed for a more realistic and fine-grained modeling of an enterprise's capabilities.

The introduction of entity-based abilities, related to roles, grasp the nature of capability responsibility and liability. Thus the CDD-BROS integration contributes to an enterprise modeling approach that can be used for early business-focused modeling as well as for later specification of technical details in a seamless manner. The different facets of adaptation and variation are covered through the combined approach encompassing adaptations at runtime due to resource allocation via performers. This, in general, supports role-based capability modeling and IS design as stated in Sect. 1.

Comparing this overall contribution to Enterprise Architecture approaches, we conclude that the suggested combination supports modeling on the level of detail that is needed for seamless IS development even encompassing runtime aspects like accounting for performers. However, in comparison to MDA-like approaches, which are (by nature) aligned to seamless integration along the development lifecycle, our suggestion is stronger when it comes to early capability driven modeling and context-dependent adaptations. One limitation of our current work is that we cannot ensure that other methodological enhancements in the enterprise architecture, enterprise modeling, or MDA domain may have achieved comparable goals. Also, the CDD-BROS-integration still needs to be fully implemented and supported with tools. This will require that the BROS extension to the CDD meta-model is implemented as a CDD method component. In the realm of a full-fledged integration, examples at the level of complexity of our use case could then be used to demonstrate the full potential of using CDD with BROS – not only at the modeling level but also within the accordingly developed IS.

Acknowledgements. This work is partially funded by the German Research Foundation (DFG) within the Research Training Group "Role-based Software Infrastructures for continuous-context-sensitive Systems" (GRK 1907).

References

1. Hüttermann, M.: DevOps for Developers. Apress, New York (2012). https://doi.org/10.1007/978-1-4302-4570-4
2. Sandkuhl, K., Stirna, J.: Capability Management in Digital Enterprises. Springer, Cham (2018). https://doi.org/10.1007/978-3-319-90424-5
3. Zdravkovic, J., Stirna, J., Grabis, J.: A comparative analysis of using the capability notion for congruent business and information systems engineering. Complex Syst. Inform. Model. Quart. **10**, 1–20 (2017)
4. Schön, H., Strahringer, S., Furrer, F.J., Kühn, T.: Business role-object specification: a language for behavior-aware structural modeling of business objects. In: Proceedings of the 14th International Conference on Wirtschaftsinformatik, Siegen, Germany (2019)
5. Bērziša, S., et al.: Deliverable 1.4: requirements specification for CDD, CaaS–capability as a service for digital enterprises. Riga Technical University (2013)
6. Morin, B., Barais, O., Jezequel, J.-M., Fleurey, F., Solberg, A.: Models@Run.time to support dynamic adaptation. Computer **42**, 44–51 (2009)
7. Engel, A., Browning, T.R., Reich, Y.: Designing products for adaptability: insights from four industrial cases. Decis. Sci. **48**(5), 875–917 (2017)
8. Koutsopoulos, G., Henkel, M., Stirna, J.: Dynamic adaptation of capabilities: exploring meta-model diversity. In: Reinhartz-Berger, I., Zdravkovic, J., Gulden, J., Schmidt, R. (eds.) BPMDS/EMMSAD -2019. LNBIP, vol. 352, pp. 181–195. Springer, Cham (2019). https://doi.org/10.1007/978-3-030-20618-5_13
9. North Atlantic Treaty Organization: NATO Architecture Framework v4. North Atlantic Treaty Organization (NATO) (2019)

10. Rodrigues, G.N., Roberts, G., Emmerich, W.: Reliability support for the model driven architecture. In: de Lemos, R., Gacek, C., Romanovsky, A. (eds.) WADS 2003. LNCS, vol. 3069, pp. 79–98. Springer, Heidelberg (2004). https://doi.org/10.1007/978-3-540-25939-8_4
11. Grabis, J., et al.: Deliverable 5.3: the final version of capability driven development methodology (2016)
12. Steimann, F.: On the representation of roles in object-oriented and conceptual modelling. Data Knowl. Eng. **35**, 83–106 (2000)
13. Kühn, T., Leuthäuser, M., Götz, S., Seidl, C., Aßmann, U.: A metamodel family for role-based modeling and programming languages. In: Combemale, B., Pearce, D.J., Barais, O., Vinju, J.J. (eds.) SLE 2014. LNCS, vol. 8706, pp. 141–160. Springer, Cham (2014). https://doi.org/10.1007/978-3-319-11245-9_8
14. Herrmann, S.: Programming with roles in ObjectTeams/Java. In: Proceedings of the 2005 AAAI Fall Symposium (2005)
15. Leuthäuser, M.: A pure embedding of roles (2017). http://nbn-resolving.de/urn:nbn:de:bsz:14-qucosa-227624
16. Taing, N., Springer, T., Cardozo, N., Schill, A.: A dynamic instance binding mechanism supporting run-time variability of role-based software systems. In: Companion Proceedings of the 15th International Conference on Modularity, pp. 137–142. ACM (2016)
17. Almeida, J.P.A., Guizzardi, G., Santos Jr, P.S.: Applying and extending a semantic foundation for role-related concepts in enterprise modelling. In: Proceedings of the 12th IEEE Intern. Enterprise Distributed Object Computing Conference, EDOC, pp. 31–40. IEEE (2009)
18. Frank, U.: Delegation: an important concept for the appropriate design of object models. J. Object Oriented Program. **13**, 13–17 (2000)
19. Schön, H.: Role-based adaptation of domain reference models: suggestion of a novel approach. In: Drews, P., Funk, B., Niemeyer, P., Xie, L. (eds.) Tagungsband Multikonferenz Wirtschaftsinformatik 2018, pp. 1447–1453. Leuphana (2018)
20. Object Management Group: Meta object facility (MOF) core specification v2.5.1. Object Management Group (2016)
21. Atkinson, C., Kuhne, T.: Model-driven development: a metamodeling foundation. IEEE Softw. **20**, 36–41 (2003)

A Financial Reporting Ontology for Market, Exchange, and Enterprise Shared Information Systems

Ivars Blums[1] and Hans Weigand[2]

[1] SIA ODO, Riga, Latvia
Ivars.Blums@odo.lv
[2] University of Tilburg, Tilburg, The Netherlands
H.Weigand@uvt.nl

Abstract. Enterprises operate in markets by building and fulfilling exchange relationships. However, up to date accounting information systems are organized in an enterprise-specific way. We introduce the Market Information perspective on top of the Exchange (Shared Ledger) and Enterprise-Specific perspectives. The latter, developed earlier, are enhanced and the interplay with the Market perspective elaborated. First, we analyze how are Market related concepts of Offering, Contract, Resource, and Social Interaction represented in UFO ontologies and other ontologies. Second, we propose a Market perspective, and included Exchange, and Enterprise perspective conceptual model of a Shared Information System for Financial Reporting in OntoUML language, and third, we analyze the International Accounting Standards Board (IASB) Conceptual Framework and Standards for Financial Reporting to uncover construct deficit and overload in these Standards and Framework for usage in Shared Information Systems.

Keywords: IFRS · Conceptual model · UFO · COFRIS

1 Introduction

Enterprises operate in markets by building and fulfilling exchange relationships. Traditionally, information systems support the enterprise by collecting and storing data that is available within the enterprise. This holds in particular for Accounting Information Systems (AIS) supporting internal management and, importantly, Financial Reporting (FR). The financial reports give an overview of the financial position and performance of the firm based on the postings in the ledgers of the enterprise. Whereas nowadays, information systems include more and more external relevant data sources, for instance, market information, the Accounting and Financial Reporting Standards [1] hold to an enterprise-specific point of view.

The objective of general-purpose Financial Reporting is to provide financial information about the Reporting Enterprise, which comprises of:

- Economic Resources controlled by the Enterprise – Assets,
- Economic Obligations – Claims against the Enterprise – Liabilities and Equity Claims,

© IFIP International Federation for Information Processing 2019
Published by Springer Nature Switzerland AG 2019
J. Gordijn et al. (Eds.): PoEM 2019, LNBIP 369, pp. 83–99, 2019.
https://doi.org/10.1007/978-3-030-35151-9_6

- Changes within a period in those Assets and Claims – Income, Expenses, and other Equity Changes,
- Enterprise management's stewardship of the Enterprise's Economic Resources.

This information should be faithful and relevant for existing and potential investors, lenders and other creditors in making decisions relating to providing resources to the Enterprise [2, 3]. Assets and liabilities aggregate information about effects of exchanges in the market and other economic events that create and change exchange offerings, contract obligations, economic resources, and underlying objects. The interpreted and aggregated information is audited [9] and disclosed to the authorities and the market.

From this short description it is immediately clear that the *subject* of FR exceeds the borders of the enterprise. Claims are claims to or from other parties; they exist in a relationship. So, there is all the reason for *shared ledger accounting* that takes its starting point not in one or the other party but in the (exchange) relationship. In [7] we have analyzed the advantages of such an approach and have shown how blockchain (DLT) and smart contract technology can support it technically. In this paper, we go one step further and argue that not only the exchanges, but also the market should be included. Markets are not abstract economic entities anymore, but increasingly materialize in platforms and business networks, such as Airbnb and SAP Ariba. With the advent of shared ledger systems and the steady growth of a global information infrastructure, a pure enterprise-specific perspective is becoming obsolete, in our view.

In this paper, we continue building a Financial Reporting Ontology grounded on Unified Foundational Ontology (UFO) and its sub-ontologies. Today, the conceptualization of accounting and Financial Reporting requires precise meaning, enlargement of the scope of concepts and application of new methods for ontological representations to increase interoperability and reuse. What is new in this paper is that we suggest FR to be a subsystem of *Market*, *Exchange*, and *Enterprise* Information Systems, having the FR ontology grounded on upper ontologies and harmonized with Legal, Economic, Business, and IT ontologies, frameworks and standards.

The need for interoperability increases in network-based Market models, such as DLT enabled systems and traditional and new exchange platforms, governmental systems, banks, communities, and corporations of related enterprises, joint ventures, and principal-agent based relationships, all of which require substantial information sharing.

While there are several new papers regarding the development of AIS in blockchain systems e.g., [23, 24], a foundational ontology grounded and fully FR compliant ontology for IS that share Market, Exchange, Business, and FR compliant information does not exist.

Thus, the key research questions for this paper are: (1) how can we benefit from sharing information of Market, Exchange, Business, and Financial Reporting IS; (2) which foundational ontologies, core ontologies, ontological patterns, enterprise related frameworks, and standards can help building a shared IS; (3) what are the deficiencies of current Financial Reporting frameworks and standards when taking the perspective of a shared environment?

In this paper, we continue building a Financial Reporting Ontology grounded on Unified Foundational Ontology (UFO) and its sub-ontologies [12–21]. We introduce the Market Information perspective on top of the Exchange (Shared Ledger) [6, 7] and Enterprise-Specific [5] perspectives and extend the COFRIS ontology accordingly.

To demonstrate some of the value of the ontological analysis, we analyze the IASB Conceptual Framework and show where improvements are possible.

Our research methodology is analytical. We analyzed UFO concepts and models, the existing accounting theories, standards, information systems and integrated them into a conceptual model represented in verified OntoUML [13] diagrams and constraints.

2 Ontological Foundations Background

Enterprise ontologies depict the main objects and relationships of an organization and the functions and activities of a business. Enterprise ontologies and standards tend to take an Enterprise-centric perspective. In contrast, UFO social sub-ontologies are based on UFO Social relator, its disposition and manifestations, which support consensual and correlative relationships and interactions among social agents. As such, it is a good basis for market and exchange perspectives that are the objectives of this paper.

In this section, we briefly recapture UFO and discuss some alternative ontologies in order to answer our second research question.

2.1 UFO Social, Service, Legal Sub-ontologies and Other Relevant Concepts

OntoUML is a language whose meta-model has been designed to comply with the ontological distinctions and axiomatization put forth by UFO [12]. The combination of built-in stereotypes and constraints of the language enforces conformance, making every valid OntoUML model compliant with UFO.

The UFO-A layer of UFO is the Ontology of Endurants. Endurants are entities that exist in time and can change in a qualitative way while maintaining their identity. Objects or Substantials (e.g., Satya Nadella, his car, the Microsoft Corporation), Relators (e.g., Nadella's employment contract with Microsoft, his car ownership) and Qualities (e.g., Nadella's age, Nadella's car market price) are examples of Endurants.

Kinds are types that classify their entities necessarily and provide a uniform principle of identity for their instances. Instances of a kind can (contingently) instantiate different Roles in different relational contexts. This distinction between necessary and contingent types applies to all Endurants and to Relators in particular. For example, while an Employment Contract (e.g., the one connecting Nadella and Microsoft) is necessarily so, it can contingently be classified as an Offered Contract and as an Agreed Contract. Relators (as well as Qualities/Modes) are existentially dependent entities. The Relator of Nadella and Microsoft can only exist if both Nadella and Microsoft exist.

According to UFO-C, the Sub-ontology of Intentional and Social Entities [14], the exchange of Communicative acts creates Social moments such as Commitments and

Claims that inhere in the Social agents involved in these communicative acts. Social agents are Parties' Roles played by Human agents and Institutional agents.

Two or more pairs of mutually dependent Commitments and Claims form a kind of social relationship between the social individuals involved and is termed a Social relator [14]. Social relators are important for our consideration because they are grounding Legal relators that in turn are grounding Economic relators. The latter underlie relationships required for our ontology.

A Commitment (internal or social) is *fulfilled* by an agent A if this agent performs an action x such that the post-state of that action is a situation that satisfies that Commitment's goal. Appointments, are Commitments whose propositional content explicitly refers to a Time interval, and Complex Closed Appointments are composed of a number of Commitments that should be achieved by executing a number of actions of a particular type, under certain types of situations (on the occurrence of a certain triggering event).

Beyond the Ontology of Endurants, UFO also comprises an Ontology of Events as past occurrences (UFO-B) [17]. UFO-B, especially in its new OntoUML 2.0 realization [13, 17], facilitates the building of behavioral models of exchange scenarios.

As noted earlier, conventional accounting is based on a functional classification of transaction effects (recognition) and valuation (measurement) in accounts. In contrast, besides its more faithful and objective character, event information allows the enterprise to benefit from *local, cumulative, contextual*, and *modal* properties of events [18] that happen in a market *scene* [19] and cannot be reduced to properties of their participants' qualities. In particular, to satisfy the growing needs of FR to determine whether an event is unique, infrequent, unusual, routine and whether it could have a continuing effect on routine and frequent business activities of the enterprise [3], grounding must be established in the history and disposition of events.

UFO-S is the Core Ontology for Services [14], which characterizes service phenomena by considering service commitments and claims established between a service parties - provider and a customer along with the service lifecycle phases: Offer, Negotiation/Agreement and Delivery that provides an outline for our Economic Exchange lifecycle model [5]. The detailed exchange scenarios, resources and obligations, their recognition and measurement are outside the scope of UFO-S.

Some Legal aspects of Service Contracts were further elaborated in [16] within the UFO-L Legal Ontology, which is based on Hohfeld/Alexy's theory of fundamental legal concepts. A central element of UFO-L is the notion of legal relator, which is a social relator that is composed of externally dependent legal moments, each of which represents a legal position. The legal positions of UFO-L subsume Claims and Commitments (Rights and Obligations in COFRIS), i.e., Claim-Right and Duty, Permission and No-Right, Power and Subjection, Immunity and Disability, respectively. The above-mentioned Right and Obligation pairs form Correlative associations [16], which are *legal* foundations and benefits of the shared perspective.

UFO [20] describes Resource as a role that an Object plays [or could play] in an action needed to make progress towards the goal. More specifically, Resource is defined as a type-level entity, capturing the role of an (agentive or non-agentive) Object in the scope of a material relation or in the scope of an event [6]. The Object type is restricted to an "allowed type". In FR Resources are represented as Rights over the Objects [2].

UFO [20] regards Product as a subtype of a Resource restricted by creation or change participation. As stated in e.g., ArchiMate [25] a Product represents a coherent collection of (resources) - services and/or passive structure elements, accompanied by a contract/set of agreements which is offered as a whole to (internal or external) customers. From an Enterprise FR perspective, a Performance Obligation of a Contract specifies Product Type. A Contract Asset and Revenue can be recognized, when a Performance Obligation is fulfilled, i.e., Product (collection of services and goods) transferred.

2.2   Other Relevant Ontologies (Not Grounded in UFO)

REA – ISO/IEC 15944-4:2015 [26] Business transaction scenarios—Accounting and economic ontology, introduces economic resources, events, and agents, for business transaction scenarios. Obligations and Claims are described in REA [26] as entities optional to "ontological completeness". Transaction scenarios of exchange lifecycle phases are elaborated in ISO in more detail than in UFO-S.

However, the concepts of assets and liabilities and their economic disposition, perhaps the core of accounting and FR, are not regarded. Thus, REA is sometimes viewed as an "operational ontology" [22] and suggested to be augmented by concepts relevant for accounting and FR by OntoREA [28].

FIBO Standard for Financial Industry [27] covers Assets and Enterprise-Specific modeling, but neither Economic Resources, nor Contract Fulfillment scenarios.

The PROV Ontology [8] introduces a set of concepts to represent provenance information in a variety of application domains. The main concepts and their relation to our ontology is shown in Fig. 1.

The e3value approach supports the modeling of value networks based on the e3-value ontology [10, 11]. It takes an independent view of the enterprise, interestingly assumes an aggregation level of "network" on top of individual enterprises and stresses the importance of reciprocity in value transactions. Although e3value is useful for exploring business models, it is not sufficiently detailed for accounting and FR purposes.

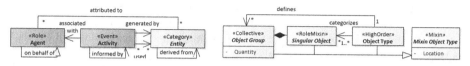

Fig. 1. The Main concepts of PROV ontology.

Fig. 2. Mixin object type pattern.

3   COFRIS V. 0.3. Economic Phenomena

This section describes the COFRIS v. 0.3 redefinition and extension of our Exchange ontology [5] in a shared environment, using OntoUML. We first introduce a view on Market, Exchange, and Enterprise IS. After having clarified some ontological choices, we present an integrated conceptual model of (business) economic phenomena (Fig. 4) and describe it in separate subsections for each of the three IS distinguished.

3.1   Market, Exchange, and Enterprise Shared Information Systems

Traditionally, the AIS takes an internal enterprise-specific perspective to produce financial statements and uses audit to reconcile with exchange and market perspective. Nowadays exchange and market information becomes more and more available and reliable for independent gathering of enterprise related information. Economic activities and relationships should be captured in Market, Exchange and Enterprise Information Systems. This vision is schematized in Fig. 3, explained below.

The **Market IS** includes *facilitation* and recording of exchanges carried out with Market IS involvement. Market IS aggregates them and other disclosed Economic Exchange and Enterprise Experience, including Financial Reporting, Offering, and Market Participant, Contract Obligation, Resource, and Underlying Object Register information. The aggregation results in *typification* and Market Experience that is communicated back to Market Participants for *instantiation* as Market Regulations, Exchange, Contract Obligation, Resource and Underlying Object Types. Typification occurs because the market information is not about an individual transaction and involved prices but is on a generic level – such as "the" market price of some resource type.

Information in the **Exchange IS** is correlative and consensual – symmetrical and agreed among the exchange parties and covers the whole lifecycle of Economic Exchange dispositions, activities, and participants – Offerings, Contract Obligations, and Resources. The exchange and market information undergo [de] *recognition*, [re] *classification*, and [re] *valuation* in Enterprise IS, according to FR Standards.

The information in **Enterprise Financial Reporting IS** is Enterprise-Specific and interpreted per Financial Reporting Standards, Enterprise's Restrictions, Business Model, Policies, Capabilities, Intentions, and generally is neither correlative nor consensual with other Market Participant information. Current FR Standards neither require the capture of a full lifecycle of an economic exchange, nor object provenance, in a systematic way. Instead of capturing information about transactions and events, conventional accounting recognizes, classifies, and valuates prescribed transaction and other event *effects* in assets, liabilities and equity [4].

The *fair* valuation of assets and liabilities is presently required in FR and is inevitably tied to a *customized* market valuation of similar resources and obligations. Until recently market valuation was readily available only in commodity and stock markets, but networks of Market IS open up a new possibility of provenance and *typifying* of economic exchanges, obligations, resources and obtaining valuation.

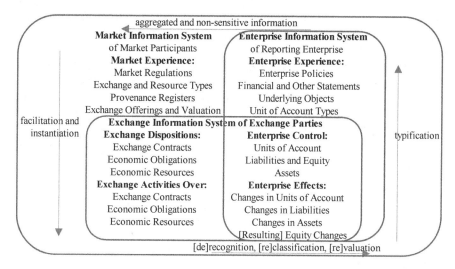

Fig. 3. Market, exchange, and enterprise shared information systems.

The non-sensitive information produced by FR IS can be communicated for mutual benefit to the Exchange and Market IS on a deeper scale and semantics than existing FR.

The importance of observing transactions in the Exchange IS and Market IS context is increasing because their information is becoming more faithful, immutable and more easily captured in Market, Exchange, and Business IS by other than accounting departments. Note that the information of such transactions is grounding, but not substituting, the accounting recognition and measurement.

3.2   Some Ontological Choices of Our Core Ontology

In COFRIS the social relator is assumed to be: CORRELATIVE – meaning that one PARTY's Commitment and its FULFILLMENT is a COUNTERPARTY's Claim and its FUL-FILLMENT and vice versa, CONSENSUAL – meaning that the Commitment and the Claim and their FULFILLMENT are AGREED among PARTIES. Social relator can be OFFERED – meaning that the Commitment is committed (OFFERED) by one PARTY but not yet agreed by the COUNTERPARTY.

The Social Relator Life can proceed through several instantiation phases. Thus, the SOCIAL RELATOR TYPE instantiated and communicated to the community by an agent qua offeror will become an OFFERED Social Relator, accepted by the claimer – AGREED Social Relator, and further possibly LAPSED, SUSPENDED, ENFORCED, BREACHED or FUL-FILLED. For a Complex Closed Appointment, we will distinguish the COMPLEX or CONTRACT FULFILLMENT of all Products committed, PERFORMANCE FULFILLMENT of a sub-goal of a particular Product committed and TRANSFER FULFILLMENT of particular Resource for Performance Fulfillment committed.

Commitment captures the social meaning of FULFILLMENT and assumes providing benefits (products including services) for a COUNTERPARTY. ECONOMIC COMMITMENT [5] assumes a return for providing a benefit (or sacrifice) – a VALUE RIGHT (OBLIGATION) of a PARTY. Thus, Economic Commitment is a Conditional Commitment to EXCHANGE a FULFILLMENT for a VALUE ACCRUAL.

A reciprocal social relator [14], called an ECONOMIC RELATOR [7] is implied to model economic relationships between Market Participants relating Transfer Dispositions over an Object, and Value Accrual. Economic Relator captures Offering, Contract Obligation and Property grounded dispositions to exchange Rights (resp, Obligations) over an Object for Value Rights (resp, Obligations).

To simplify presentation in OntoUML diagrams we introduce some conventions:

- A COMPOSITION relationship may be used even there is only one part;
- An INSTANCE OF (SUBTYPE OF) relationship is not shown if a type and the corresponding instance (type) is associated with an event that instantiates (subsumes) that type.
- OntoUML diagrams represent Types. When we add TYPE to the name of a concept, that means that it is a higher-order or order-less type (and INSTANCE OF relationship between them) in a sense of Multi-Level Type Theory (MLT) [21].
- A particular MIXIN OBJECT TYPE pattern, in analogy to the one in [15], is used, that combines object types with higher-order types. Such a combination is used in situations when either a type or an instance is specified (see Fig. 2). An example is a contract of buying a (yet to be produced) car of a specified model or an existing car.
- The diagrams contain four types of entities: Economic Relators, depicted in green; Economic Events – events that create and change Economic Relators - depicted in blue and having BEGIN and END points as properties, Market Participants (Economic Agents) depicted in yellow, and other Objects depicted in beige or as properties.

3.3   Market Information System

MARKETS are institutions in which human or institutional agents exchange valued ECONOMIC RESOURCES. The concept of MARKETS, however, is wider than the concept of exchange because it includes the structural macro-effects that result from a large number of exchanges, for example changes in the overall price level[1]. Market IS *facilitate* exchanges, and large number of exchanges and their dispositions aggregate in market experience – types and instances of offerings, contracts, economic exchanges, products, resources, and underlying objects as well as their valuation and risk.

The ultimate location of the Market IS is the net.

For instance, Airbnb®[2] provides a platform and rules for hosts to accommodate guests with short-term lodging and tourism-related activities. It publishes the offerings of the hosts, controls booking and payments, maintains a shared ledger of transactions, assists solving cancelation and breach situations, enforces international law, withholds service fees of Market IS and possibly taxes, and most importantly – aggregates (typifies resources) and publishes Market Prices assessed by the Aerosolve application, that optimizes the exchange for all participants.

---

[1] https://plato.stanford.edu/entries/markets/.

[2] https://www.airbnb.com/ and http://airbnb.io/aerosolve/.

The market valuation ascribed to particular (type of) lodging can be used not only for publishing an offering but also for assessing the fair value or impairment adjustment of a resource for financial reporting. Such fair value could be more objective than the one assessed by the holder due to limited information, method or subjective intentions of a participant. The Market IS has an interest in determining the most objective price to facilitate exchange.

The product - lodging services, that mainly consist of the provided facility and the services of the host, is exchanged for the payment and usage habits of the guest. Exchangeable resources are mutually described ex ante and reviewed ex post. These descriptions and reviews form the history of exchanges, products and participants, create and maintain the resource type, risk and valuation. Based on the history or other circumstances, the offering can be accepted/rejected by either party. Again, the Market IS is interested to maintain objective, symmetric information.

This Market IS application aggregates and typifies transaction participant (economic agent and resource) properties and *local*, *cumulative*, *contextual*, *modal* properties of transaction events that happen in this market scene.

Following [7] we define MARKET PARTICIPANTS (or Economic agents) as social agents – persons and policy regulated enterprises, contractual groups of people and enterprises, rule regulated markets, or the society at large, regulated by law.

All institutional Market Participants are identified, and their history maintained in the Market IS[3]. Market Participants hold economic resources, against and toward other Market Participants.

ECONOMIC RESOURCE (TYPE), a sub-kind of Economic Relator, represents (a) a BUNDLE OF RIGHTS within a spatiotemporal region and in a PRINCIPAL MARKET, over (b) an OBJECT (TYPE), that have a disposition to be transferred in exchange for (c) a VALUE ACCRUAL.

Besides valued property rights of usage and transfer over an object, economic resource can represent consensual rights to receive (resp., correlative transfer obligations of a converse party):

(1) conditional right to receive a resource, product, or contract fulfillment (resp., obligation to transfer, performance, or contract obligation) of a specified type in exchange for value accrual;
(2) right to accrued value for transferred resources (transfer value, revenue, or contract consideration);
(3) unconditional right to receive a product of a specified type, for exchanged value (transfer, performance, or contract claim).

An Economic Resource IS HELD by a Market Participant AGAINST another Market Participant – a Debtor, Society, or Any who has a Correlative Obligation to the Holder.

Underlying OBJECT, denotes a physical or social UFO::OBJECT. Note that an INTELLECTUAL PROPERTY, EXCHANGE TYPE and CONTRACT itself can also be an underlying OBJECT. Qualities and Functionality of the OBJECT prescribe the allowed activities and the allowed Roles that are physically and socially possible.

---

[3] Legal Entity Identification: see https://www.gleif.org.

BUNDLE OF RIGHTS (and correlative Obligations) prescribe legally empowered and permissible (resp, obliged) activities and roles, and should be fulfillment able.

VALUATION of Value Accrual TOWARD Principal Market Participant Type should be financially feasible, realizable, and settlement able.

PRODUCT OR PERFORMANCE RIGHT and correlative PERFORMANCE OBLIGATION comprises a coherent collection of several Rights to receive (Transfer obligations) offered or contracted as a whole aimed at creating a Product useful for the Target Customer.

The reciprocal performance obligations of parties – market participants are combined into EXCHANGE TYPES. Exchange types are instantiated into EXCHANGE OFFERINGS by a particular OFFEROR, for specified product types, and addressed toward TARGET parties in the market. The AGREEMENT of an offering by two parties creates an EXCHANGE CONTRACT that is to be fulfilled by mutual transfers of bound parties.

The market is a truth-maker of a product and thus involved resources. In the Airbnb example: (a) the proof of rights of the product is not requested - their absence will be revealed in process, (b) the functionality of the lodging object is published, (c) the market valuation is established based on typification of the offering and the context, and further maintained involving particular experience. Notice that the resource, price and the target customer type are for the Principal Market, i.e., Airbnb, but not, e.g., Booking.com.

TIMING represents the time interval of rights – the begin and end date of availability and thus depicts TRANSFER due date or triggering condition. LOCATION or address refer to place where the rights are available to the Holder.

Economic Exchanges and their dispositions, and other Economic Events, i.e. those that change Economic Resources, produce MARKET EXPERIENCE that is a base for a Market assessment of VALUATION and UNCERTAINTY, and formation of EXCHANGE and PRODUCT TYPES. However not all Economic Phenomena are captured in the Information Systems and not all such Phenomena are disclosed to the Market IS or are disclosed in the aggregated form only. EXCHANGE TYPES have a rather extensive MLT [21] hierarchy, having a core ontology at a top level, that is specialized by different IFRS Standard Ontologies, such as Trade, Lease, Insurance, and Financial Instrument Contracts, further specialized by ENTERPRISE POLICIES. The latter, together with the Financial Statements and Notes, must be disclosed in FR and to the Market IS per FR Standards [1]. Within Market IS an exchange type taxonomy should be maintained and reported by the holder and the provenanced objects maintained.

Market in a most general sense contains market participant businesses as products. The financial statements form part of enterprise description and history. Transactions include business combinations and security trades. In addition, financial statements, notes, mandatory and voluntary legal disclosures, reveal rather large amount of information that could be used for accumulating exchange, product and object type and valuation information, and hence to improve financial reporting.

EXCHANGE TYPE characterizes party and counterparty market participant types of exchange, obligations taken and fulfilled, economic resource types promised and transferred, as well as object types underlying those resources. For certain types of exchanges shared instances of exchanges, obligations, resources and underlying objects are kept in public registers.

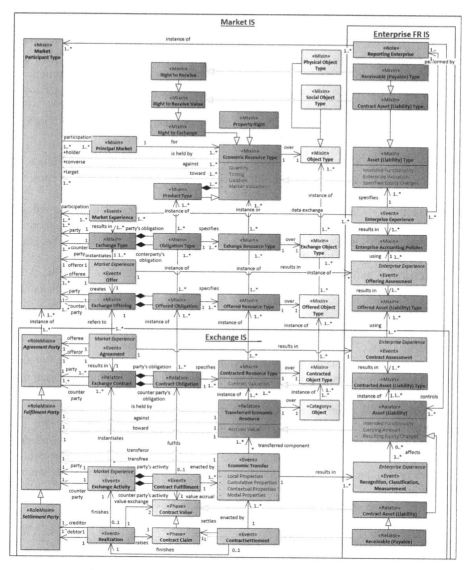

Fig. 4. COFRIS. OntoUML diagram of market, exchange, and enterprise FR IS fragment.

Individual Market Participants – OFFERORS specialize/instantiate Exchange Types and offer ECONOMIC RESOURCE TYPES for exchange in the Market to the OFFEREES via EXCHANGE OFFERINGS. Exchange Offerings form a part of Market Experience and in FR can be regarded as a source of Market based Valuation.

The PARTIES of an EXCHANGE TYPE can be non-related, related, or represent different roles of the same MARKET PARTICIPANT.

3.4   Exchange Information System

ECONOMIC EXCHANGE is conceived as a competitive OFFERING of EXCHANGE TYPE made by an OFFER of a PARTY to other PARTIES, possibly followed by AGREEMENT with the COUNTERPARTY resulting in a consensual EXCHANGE CONTRACT of mutually beneficial and correlative EXCHANGE OBLIGATIONS to TRANSFER ECONOMIC PRODUCT (OBLIGATIONS) of a SPECIFIED TYPE in exchange for agreed VALUATION.

EXCHANGE CONTRACT integrates PARTY's and COUNTERPARTY's EXCHANGE OBLIGATIONS and is instantiated by EXCHANGE ACTIVITY that consists of:

- FULFILLMENT of both Parties' Obligations by Transfer of Economic Resources (Obligations), that are instances of specified Resource (Obligation) Types, in exchange for an agreed Value Accrual for the Transfer;
- REALIZATION – CONTRACT VALUE ACCRUAL exchange among Parties, caused by complete Fulfillment of Contract Obligations by first Party who becomes CREDITOR, and resulting in raising ECONOMIC CLAIMS against the Other Party who becomes DEBTOR for its unfulfilled Obligations,
- SETTLEMENT – enforceable fulfillment of these Claims by Transfers by Debtor.
- or BREACH or SUSPENSION of the Contract by one of the Parties during Fulfillment or Settlement.

Economic TRANSFER event either conveys the Rights (Obligations) over an Object or the usage (service) of such Rights from the TRANSFEROR to the TRANSFEREE.

A TRANSFEROR under certain conditions can transfer not only its Resources, but also its Obligations – the Resources held AGAINST TRANSFEROR. For example, an Enterprise can settle income tax obligations of an Employee in exchange for the settlement of Employee's payroll claims against the Enterprise.

CONTRACT VALUATION is the agreed Transaction Price that is accrued for the Transfer, it could be (1) Fixed; (2) based on the Market Price that is the Market Valuation that could be received (paid) in the Market for similar (offered) or specific Transfer; or (3) based on disclosed Historical Cost of the Transferred Resources (Obligations).

See [7] for the specific Economic Exchange examples in COFRIS.

3.5   Enterprise Information System and Enterprise-Specific Accounts

An ENTERPRISE-SPECIFIC Exchange effects situation is depicted on the right side of Fig. 4. Market exchange events together with market other events or conditions (such as regulation, market participant, market resource and price changes), and enterprise-specific and underlying object changes, affect ENTERPRISE-SPECIFIC ECONOMIC RELATORS.

UNITS OF ACCOUNT - ASSETS (LIABILITIES) are present RIGHTS (OBLIGATIONS) for RESOURCES controlled (OBLIGATIONS indebted and unavoidable) by the ENTERPRISE, as a result of past activities which form their HISTORICAL COST [2] and ENTERPRISE EXPERIENCE. CARRYING AMOUNT represents the present VALUATION that is measured based on the MARKET and ENTERPRISE EXPERIENCE.

Changes of ASSETS (LIABILITIES) are specializations of Transfers of Resources (Obligations), extended by CONTROLLED and INTENDED FUNCTIONALITY, such as usage of the assets for enterprise activities of administration, sales of goods and rendering services and production, in specified roles, such as of raw materials, equipment and labor.

EQUITY CHANGES, including INCOME and EXPENSES, characterize performance aspects of Asset (Liability) changes and the Role performed - Nature in a Performed activity - Function.

CONTROL is a valuable capability of the ENTERPRISE "to direct the use of the Economic Resource and obtain the Economic benefits that may flow from it" [2]. Thus, Assets inhere in the ENTERPRISE. Asset's disposition, enough (*assez*) to play a role in controlling Enterprise's activities:

- is constrained by the rights, abilities, regulations, intentions of the Enterprise;
- is increased by the Enterprise's synergies in combination with other, possibly unrecognized, assets or legal rights and tax benefits;
- accumulates Enterprise's economic experience of the Asset Type or an item;
- is protected from unauthorized use or transfer by other Market Participants.

While all exchanged Resources are Enterprise Asset (Liability) changes in Financial Reporting, some are regarded as MOMENTARILY [2, 3], i.e., are transferred or consumed as received. MOMENTARILY ASSETS, such as services, increase the Carrying Amount of the affected Assets. Other Asset (Liability) changes are recognized for future recovery (Transfer) or derecognized.

CLASSIFICATION, VALUATION, and UNCERTAINTY of ASSETS (LIABILITIES) depend on the enterprise intended activities and roles, the MARKET and ENTERPRISE EXPERIENCE, and can change as a result of ASSET (LIABILITY) enhancement/impairment and MARKET and own prices and risks. The MARKET VALUATION input is either probability weighted and/or discounted at a rate that reflects risk and UNCERTAINTY for ENTERPRISE VALUATION but is not purported to be a prediction.

4 Analysis and Suggestions for a Shared Perspective in FR Conceptual Framework and Standards

In March 2018 International Accounting Standards Board (IASB) released the revised version of the Conceptual Framework (CF) for Financial Reporting. It describes the objective of, and the concepts for, general purpose financial reporting. The purpose of the CF is to [2]:

- assist the IASB to develop IFRS Standards that are based on consistent concepts;
- assist preparers to develop consistent accounting policies when no Standard applies to a particular transaction or other event, or when a Standard allows a choice of accounting policy; and
- assist all parties to understand and interpret the Standards.

Our goal is to be reasonably compliant with the framework in engineering COFRIS. Another goal is to see where the CF could benefit from our ontological analysis. Here are some preliminary suggestions for a framework in a shared environment.

1. Types of Economic Phenomena. We argue that a FR system should base on a shared Market, Exchange, and Enterprise Information System that captures interrelated Economic phenomena relevant for FR. The automatically provided Market IS and Exchange IS information is preferred because access to the history of market transactions, participants and objects, that allows for objective and symmetrical typification and valuation. This doesn't exclude the Enterprise from augmenting the Market and Exchange IS information. The Standards should determine which kinds of Market IS Sources, Exchange Types and Provenance Registers can be used for specialization/instantiation, recognition, classification and valuation.

2. Lifecycles of Economic Phenomena. The Information System should cover full Exchange lifecycles and Object provenance histories. The Enterprise FR IS should capture Offering, Contract and Exchange Activity information in related and systematic way, including types and phases of OFFERED, LAPSED, CONTRACTED, BREACHED and SUSPENDED in addition to RECOGNIZED Units of Account.

3. Capturing Economic Event Qualities. Financial Reporting can aggregate transaction-centric plus Enterprise-Specific, instead of exclusively Enterprise effect-centric information. Aggregation of consensual transactions for Financial Reporting, instead of accounts, provides additional opportunities for creating Exchange Types and Provenance Registers, comparability among market participant and among different period processes, possibilities of application of process mining methods, disclosure of event-specific information [18] and insights into the processes of value co-creation.

Object and Economic Resource QUANTITY is a fundamental feature of Economic Events [4]. However, it is not defined in CF for Assets, Liabilities and Equity Changes.

The event information makes the MOMENTARILY ASSETS concept redundant.

4. Correlative and Consensual Standards and Information. Consensuality – meaning that among parties there is an agreed shared ledger of Contracts and their Fulfillment, including Resources (Obligations) and required Asset (Liability) information – can be a quality aspect, even within the old context of audit reconciliations. Consensuality can be added to comparability, verifiability, timeliness, and understandability as a qualitative characteristic that enhances the usefulness of information that both is relevant and provides a faithful representation of what it purports to represent and reduces reporting uncertainty. When correlativeness and consensus are not regarded as a standard-setting principle, deficiencies emerge in standards already discussed by us elsewhere, such as those concerning Leases, Contract Assets and Revenue [7].

The consensual information about related Market Participants, the information of whether one Enterprise is a subsidiary of another, or one Enterprise's CEO is a board member of another company, must be deducible from the Market IS or declared and agreed by the involved parties.

5. Avoidance of Enterprise-Sensitive Information Disclosure. Providing information to Market IS or Exchange IS may disclose sensitive information (i.e. information whose disclosure could result in commercial loss to an enterprise). A similar problem exists now within FR. The IASB does not currently have a general approach to information sensitivity. Widening the amount of disclosed information requires a specialization of FR ontology for sensitive information. The immediate conclusions from our ontology is that in Exchange IS, a disclosure of one party's information leads to automatic disclosure of the counterparty's information. The disclosure in one phase of economic exchange leads to possible disclosures in other phases, and the disclosure in one provenance event leads to possible disclosures in other events. The Market experience should be based rather on type than instance information, which lowers the sensitiveness of information.

6. Increase of the FR User Scope. Regarding the Objective of the FR (Sect. 1), we argue that the users of the FR are not only "the existing and potential investors or creditors" but any Market Participant who wants to make Offerings, conclude and execute Contracts with the Enterprise. Moreover, in a Market IS all participants that want to use Exchange Type and Provenance Register information are users of FR. In addition, the focus of the FR moves from Shareholders to Stakeholders.

7. Transfer of Economic Resources. The CF defines Liability and other obligations as "a duty and responsibility to transfer Economic Resources", while TYPES of Economic Resources are implied.

8. "Transfer" of Assets and Liabilities. Assets and Liabilities cannot be transferred as metaphorically stated in some Standards [1], because they inhere in the Enterprise, but the rights that an Enterprise is capable to transfer or to use are the Resources of the Asset.

9. Exchange and Transfer of Obligations. Per CF [2], "An executory contract establishes a combined right and obligation to exchange economic resources [of the reporting entity and the other party]. The right and obligation are interdependent and cannot be separated". We argue that a contract can establish an exchange of economic resources and/or economic obligations of an enterprise.

10. Different Rights to Receive: Contracts, Products, Resources. Further, regarding Contracts, CF States that "If the reporting entity performs first under the contract, that performance is the event that changes the reporting entity's right and obligation to exchange economic resources into a right to receive, an economic resource. That right is an asset. If the other party performs first, that performance is the event that changes the reporting entity's right and obligation to exchange economic resources into an obligation to transfer an economic resource. That obligation is a liability".

We argue that different classes of rights to receive and obligations to transfer exist and are common to all contracts and thus standards, and are first-class candidates for becoming concepts in CF. Primarily, a transfer of an Economic Resource (or Obligation) leads to *a Right to receive Value* for the transferred Resource, that Right is *a Contract Asset*. Secondarily, it can be *a Right to receive Revenue*, if a Product is transferred, so it can be different - *a Contract Performance Asset*. And thirdly, it is an *Unconditional Right for Consideration*, if the Contract is fulfilled, that Right is *a Receivable Asset*. These concepts are missing in CF, the Contract Asset and Receivable are present in other IFRS Standards, but they do not differentiate among Contract and Performance Assets.

5   Conclusions

The specific contribution of this paper is the introduction of the concept of Market IS, in addition to the Exchange IS (shared ledger) and the Enterprise-Specific IS, and a corresponding partitioning of the accounting ontology. We expect Market IS and shared ledger IS to become more and more important, but if these are being built as ad-hoc extensions of Enterprise-Specific IS, or just stand-alone applications, a sound ontological basis is missing. This would hinder future integration and interoperability.

With regards to our research questions, we have argued that the shared information system is more objective (neutral), doesn't need audit (or much less), accumulates experience, context and history from events, participants, resources and objects, and so increases the quality of the information system. The UFO-compliant ontology is worked out in Sect. 3. In Sect. 2, we have given an overview of available ontologies and frameworks from which we have made use. In Sect. 4, we have indicated some deficiencies in the current FR framework on the basis of our ontology.

Within the limits of this article, we have not been able to work out an extensive example to see concretely how the different IS parts materialize and where they connect. This is a topic for future research. Apart from an example, there is also a need to work out a system architecture to integrate the different IS. Standard bodies may have a role in implementing system architecture requirements.

References

1. IASB homepage. IASB (2019). http://www.ifrs.org/issued-standards/list-of-standards
2. IASB Conceptual Framework for Financial Reporting. IASB (2018)
3. FASB Conceptual Framework for Financial Reporting. FASB (2016)
4. Ijiri, Y.: Theory of accounting measurement. american accounting association (1975)
5. Blums, I., Weigand, H.: Towards a reference ontology of complex economic exchanges for accounting information systems. In: EDOC 2016, pp. 119–128 (2016)
6. Blums, I., Weigand, H.: Towards a core ontology for financial reporting information systems (COFRIS). In: Debruyne, C., Panetto, H., Weichhart, G., Bollen, P., Ciuciu, I., Vidal, M.-E., Meersman, R. (eds.) OTM 2017. LNCS, vol. 10697, pp. 302–306. Springer, Cham (2018). https://doi.org/10.1007/978-3-319-73805-5_34
7. Weigand, H., Blums, I., de Kruijff, J.: Shared ledger accounting - implementing the economic exchange pattern in DL technology. In: Krogstie, J., Reijers, H.A. (eds.) CAiSE 2018. LNCS, vol. 10816, pp. 342–356. Springer, Cham (2018). https://doi.org/10.1007/978-3-319-91563-0_21
8. The PROV Ontology. W3C Recommendation. https://www.w3.org/TR/prov-o/
9. Weigand, H., Elsas, Ph.: Auditability as a design problem. In: IEEE CBI 2019, pp. 11–20 (2019)
10. Weigand, H.: The e3value ontology for value networks: current state and future directions. AIS J. Inform. Syst. **30**, 113–133 (2016)
11. Wieringa, R.J., Engelsman, W., Gordijn, J., Ionita, D.: A business ecosystem architecture modeling framework. In: CBI 2019, pp. 1–10 (2019)
12. Guizzardi, G.: Ontological foundations for structural conceptual models. Ph.D. thesis, CTIT, Centre for Telematics and Information Technology, Enschede (2005)

13. Guizzardi, G., et al.: Endurant types in ontology-driven conceptual modeling: towards OntoUML 2.0. In: ER 2018, Xi'an, China (2018)
14. Nardi, J.C., et al.: A commitment-based reference Ontology for services. Inform. Syst. **54**, 263–288 (2015)
15. Sales, T., et al.: Towards and ontology of competition. In: VMBO 2018, Amsterdam (2018)
16. Criffo, C., Almeida, J.P.A., Guizzardi, G., From an ontology of service contracts to contract modeling in enterprise architecture. In: EDOC (2017)
17. Almeida, J.P.A., Falbo, R.A., Guizzardi, G.: Events as entities in ontology-driven conceptual modeling. In: ER 2019, pp. 1–14 (2019)
18. Guarino, N.: On the semantics of ongoing and future occurrence identifiers. In: Mayr, H.C., Guizzardi, G., Ma, H., Pastor, O. (eds.) ER 2017. LNCS, vol. 10650, pp. 477–490. Springer, Cham (2017). https://doi.org/10.1007/978-3-319-69904-2_36
19. Guarino, N., Guizzardi, G.: Relationships and events: towards a general theory of reification and truthmaking. In: Adorni, G., Cagnoni, S., Gori, M., Maratea, M. (eds.) AI*IA 2016. LNCS (LNAI), vol. 10037, pp. 237–249. Springer, Cham (2016). https://doi.org/10.1007/978-3-319-49130-1_18
20. Azevedo, C.L.B., et al.: Modeling resources and capabilities in enterprise architecture: a well-founded ontology-based proposal for ArchiMate. Inform. Syst. **54**, 235–262 (2015)
21. Almeida, J.P.A., et al.: Multi-level conceptual modeling. In: ONTOBRAS 2018, pp. 26–41 (2018)
22. Melse, E.: The financial accounting model from a system dynamics' perspective. mpra.ub.uni-muenchen.de (2006)
23. Appelbaum, D., Nehmer, R.: Designing and auditing accounting systems based on blockchain and distributed ledger principles. Feliciano School of Business (2017)
24. Dai, J., Vasarhelyi, M.: Toward blockchain-based accounting and assurance. J. Inform. Syst. **31**(3), 5–21 (2017)
25. The Open Group: Archimate 3.0 specification. Standard (2016)
26. ISO/IEC FDIS 15944-4: Information technology—business operational view—part 4: business transactions scenarios—accounting and economic ontology. ISO 2015 (2015)
27. Financial Industry Business Ontology: Foundations Version 1.2. OMG (2017)
28. Fischer-Pauzenberger, C., Schwaiger, W.S.A.: The OntoREA accounting model: ontology-based modeling of the accounting domain. CSIMQ **11**, 20–37 (2017)

Reference Architectures and Patterns

Towards a Cross-Border Reference Architecture for the Once-Only Principle in Europe: An Enterprise Modelling Approach

Jaak Tepandi[1(✉)], Eric Grandry[2,3], Sander Fieten[4], Carmen Rotuna[5], Giovanni Paolo Sellitto[6], Dimitris Zeginis[7,8], Dirk Draheim[1], Gunnar Piho[1], Efthimios Tambouris[7,8], and Konstantinos Tarabanis[7,8]

[1] Information Systems Group, Tallinn University of Technology, Tallinn, Estonia
{jaak.tepandi,dirk.draheim,gunnar.piho}@taltech.ee
[2] Luxembourg Institute of Science and Technology, Luxembourg City, Luxembourg
[3] Ministry of Mobility and Public Works, Luxembourg City, Luxembourg
eric.grandry@tr.etat.lu
[4] Holodeck B2B, Leiden, The Netherlands
[5] ICI Bucharest, Bucharest, Romania
[6] ANAC, Rome, Italy
[7] Centre for Research and Technology Hellas, Thessaloniki, Greece
[8] University of Macedonia, Thessaloniki, Greece
{zeginis,tambouris,kat}@uom.edu.gr
http://is.taltech.ee

Abstract. The *Once-Only Principle* states that citizens and businesses provide data only once in contact with public administrations. So far, many European countries have started to implement the Once-Only Principle at national level, but its cross-border implementation is still fragmented and limited. This paper presents the development of a Reference Architecture for the Once-Only Principle in Europe. The case study, stemming from the EU-funded Once-Only Principle project (TOOP) highlights the challenges faced by the architecture team when developing the Reference Architecture that tackles the Once-Only Principle across different countries and policy domains. The architecture is not built from scratch, but re-uses and enhances already available building blocks in order to seamlessly preserve interoperability and to comply with regulations and existing technical standards, leaving at the same time enough space for vendors and open source developers to propose their compliant solutions, whatever is their business model.

Keywords: Once-Only Principle · EU Single Digital Gateway · Reference Architecture · TOOP · EU Building Blocks · TOOPRA

© IFIP International Federation for Information Processing 2019
Published by Springer Nature Switzerland AG 2019
J. Gordijn et al. (Eds.): PoEM 2019, LNBIP 369, pp. 103–117, 2019.
https://doi.org/10.1007/978-3-030-35151-9_7

1   Introduction

The Once-Only Principle (OOP) states that "public administrations should ensure that citizens and businesses supply the same information only once to a public administration. Public administration offices take action if permitted to internally re-use this data, in due respect of data protection rules, so that no additional burden falls on citizens and businesses" [5]. So far, many European countries have started to implement the OOP at national level, but its cross-border implementation is still limited. This paper presents the development of a Reference Architecture for the OOP in Europe, as well as lessons learned in this process.

Development of reference architectures is currently often focused on some specific concern, which acts both as a reference source for Business Requirements and a canvas to compose existing Solution Building Blocks. This is increasingly becoming part of a wider evidence based policy-making cycle[1]. Pilot sociotechnical systems are used to prove the viability and the feasibility of some policy objective that requires the usage of Information and Communication Technologies (ICT) platforms in order to be attained. In this context, the development of Large Scale Pilot systems along with a Reference Architecture can support decision-makers with quantitative results about the effectiveness of the devised regulations. Often the Reference Architecture itself later becomes part of a Regulation Act, as long as it does not hamper the market restraining the implementation possibilities to a single solution.

The OOP Reference Architecture (TOOPRA) development cycle within the EU-funded Once-Only Principle project (TOOP[2]) is representative of such a process, as the overarching policy objective is part of a wider European strategy, aimed at fostering competitiveness reducing duplicated work for the citizens, businesses, and government officers. This objective can only be attained through the use of an ICT platform. The architecture development cycle in this case does not start from scratch, but from a gap-analysis activity based on the assessment of the existing relevant building blocks (Core Components) aimed at deciding whether and how they can be composed or evolved to attain the OOP while complying with other legal and technological constraints. Moreover, architecture had not to be a bottleneck for the developers of OOP Pilot Solutions. Thus the development of TOOPRA proceeded with a continuous consultation with legal and domain experts working on concrete piloting use cases and with the developers taking care of the governance of the Building Blocks.

---

[1] Cf. "Better Regulation" and Regulatory Impact Analysis (RIA), which is a systemic approach to critically assessing the positive and negative effects of proposed and existing regulations and non-regulatory alternatives.

[2] http://toop.eu/.

To complement the experience, during the development of the architecture (2017–2019), a new EU Single Digital Gateway Regulation[3] (SDGR) was issued by the European Commission that mandates the cross-border application of the OOP in a number of procedures and foresees a technical system based on OOP. Furthermore, the European Interoperability Reference Architecture (EIRA), the Open Group Architecture Framework and the Archimate Modeling Language underwent significant changes. All of the above mentioned items had an impact on the TOOPRA and on the project, leading to a continuous shifting of the objectives backed by the availability of new tools and frameworks to support the work of the Enterprise Architects.

The rest of this paper presents how the OOP Reference Architecture was designed to comply with a new regulation and integrate standard building blocks, explains the usage of various modelling techniques and tools, analyses layers and concepts in each layer needed to customize enterprise modelling to the needs of OOP architecture, and discusses benefits, difficulties and lessons learned using the enterprise modelling approach in OOP.

2   Motivation and Approach

2.1   Why Designing a Reference Architecture?

The general concepts of software, systems and enterprise architecture have been widely studied, have a long history and diverse content [2, 8, 15].

In the case of the TOOP, a reference architecture is intended as a multi-stakeholder frame of reference with the specific goal of supporting OOP in a cross-domain and cross-border environment. Cross-domain means that it is intended to facilitate the creation of systems that connect multiple independent organizations having different field of business, managing heterogeneous ICT platforms and subject to different policy domains. Cross-border means that the actors come from different countries and therefore they are subject to different legal and regulatory framework - translations will be needed not only for the language, but also at the level of the semantics of the data and documents that they exchange. The reference architecture [2] must address the main OOP concern by providing a common and standardized definition of the problem domain and of the solution blueprint, without hampering interoperability between the different organizations and without compromising security, privacy and flexibility, which are qualities that come from the architectural solutions adopted by the constituent Building Blocks [10].

The specific concern of TOOPRA is the Once Only Principle: motivation elements include relevant material coming from regulations and legislation, but

---

[3] Regulation (EU) 2018/1724 of the European Parliament and of the Council of 2 October 2018 establishing a single digital gateway to provide access to information, to procedures and to assistance and problem-solving services and amending Regulation (EU) No 1024/2012Text with EEA relevance, https://eur-lex.europa.eu/legal-content/EN/TXT/?qid=1549716594539&uri=CELEX:32018R1724.

the approach to interoperability shall encompass all of the architecture layers from Strategy to Technical Implementation, since the TOOPRA is intended as a multi-domain and cross-border tool to develop OOP compliant systems. At the very early phase of the project, various practical aspects of OOP, such as its expected benefits, drivers, barriers, citizen perceptions, support, initiatives, legislative measures, costs and benefits, and perspectives, have been analysed in [1,9,16]. There are however no defined architecture of OOP systems. The current paper aims to provide this, extending and generalizing the TOOP deliverables [7,13], as well as taking into account the European Interoperability Framework (EIF) [4], the European Interoperability Reference Architecture [6], the Connecting Europe Facility Digital Service Infrastructures, and the ISA2 Study on functional, technical and semantic interoperability requirements for the Single Digital Gateway (SDG) implementation[4,5].

The attainment of the OOP in an EU-wide and cross-border mode entails a re-adjustment and the re-engineering of the administrative processes and the development of an infrastructure that purposely supports the interoperability between Administrations at various levels [LOST - Legal, Organizational, Semantic, Technical] and the exchange of information in the respect of data protection rules. Part of this infrastructure is an architecture for OOP related projects presented in the current paper.

TOOPRA improves understanding of how to achieve interoperability between domains with diverse legislation, organisations, applications, technology. It provides architecture for large-scale cross-border OOP implementation, uses EU Building Blocks to implement OOP, and contributes to implementation guidelines for SDGR. It provides support for developers of OOP projects and is based on the Connecting Europe Facility (CEF) Digital Service Infrastructures (DSIs), on the Building Blocks consolidated by the e-SENS project, and in justified cases, on new building blocks.

Organisations can benefit from TOOPRA, as it enables to select solutions without reference to a vendor - the architectural model can be included in the technical specifications of a call to reduce the risk of vendor lock in. Member States can benefit from the reference architecture, since it makes the development process of OOP-compliant applications more efficient, contributing to the implementing act of the SDGR.

2.2 Why Applying Enterprise Modelling?

Selecting modelling techniques and tools for TOOPRA is based on the main drivers and decisions of the project:

- The Once-Only Principle reduces the workload of system users who need to provide only minimum information to receive a specific public service.

---

[4] https://joinup.ec.europa.eu/community/once-only-principle/home.

[5] https://www.scoop4c.eu/.

- The legal environment of the OOP, in particular the SDGR and Member State regulations, represents the legal basis that should be considered in the implementation.
- The existing frameworks, standards, and building blocks provided by CEF, e-SENS, and other initiatives, should be re-used to minimize development effort and improve interoperability. Examples of frameworks that need to be taken into account are the European Interoperability Framework [4] and the European Interoperability Reference Architecture [6]. Examples of building blocks are the CEF DSIs, including the CEF eDelivery, eID, and eSignature.
- TOOPRA is developed in interaction with the three TOOP pilot projects. These pilot projects develop and implement the TOOP Common Pilot Solution Architecture which is a specific instantiation of TOOPRA.
- The architecture must take into account and be consistent with the user requirements from the EU Member States elicited during development of the TOOP pilots.

This list demonstrates the need for the following modelling techniques and tools, among others:

- Describing the architecture from the viewpoints of multiple users and their concerns, as well as showing the conflicts and trade-offs made.
- Managing continuous changes in legislation and technology.
- Providing interoperability with the existing frameworks, standards, and building blocks, to minimize development effort.
- Enabling cooperation and mutual support between development of the TOOPRA and the TOOP pilot projects.
- Facilitating consistent user requirements engineering from different EU Member States.

These techniques and tools are best covered by enterprise modelling. A comparison of enterprise architecture frameworks is given in [15]. From the list of available frameworks, TOGAF was selected because it satisfies all the needs highlighted above and is openly accessible. TOGAF 9.2 considers an "enterprise" to be any collection of organizations that have common goals. As the architecture attempts to connect and simplify different governmental services from different Member States, the enterprise in consideration is a group of weakly linked independent governmental entities that cooperate to achieve common goals defined by OOP principles.

ArchiMate[6] was selected as the architecture description language (ADL), since it supports multiple views' modelling and, moreover, it is the modelling language adopted in the development of the EIRA.

3   Enterprise Modelling of the OOP Architecture

Development of the OOP architecture starts from the Once-Only Principle and the selected enterprise modelling framework (TOGAF), takes into account legal

---

[6] http://pubs.opengroup.org/architecture/archimate3-doc/.

and regulatory requirements, makes use of the existing building blocks, and interacts with OOP piloting.

Based on these foundations, the business, information system and technology layers of the architecture were designed. Cross-cutting concerns include security and trust, as well as semantics. TOOPRA is aligned with EIRA, which has the primary objective to facilitate interoperability of public services while reusing existing Building Blocks (BB) at the EU level. The Building Blocks are basic digital service infrastructures - key enablers to be reused in more complex digital services. They are described as a set of technical specifications and standards that the implementation of a BB has to comply with.

3.1 Business Architecture

The business layer of TOOPRA represents a coherent set of business concepts: capabilities, end-to-end value delivery, information, as well as organizational structure and the relationships among the business elements, strategies, policies, initiatives, and stakeholders (the term "business" is here understood in a wide sense, involving also public sector organisations) [14]. TOOPRA Business Architecture is concerned with the description of the business operations conducted by the business actors involved in OOP, and describes core business assets such as business roles relevant for TOOP, business data exchanged between TOOP participants, business services provided by each of the roles to meet the business goals and business processes depicting the interactions amongst roles.

The process model describes the end-to-end scenario of executing OOP in the context of a public service delivery (see Fig. 1): a Competent Authority delivers a public service to a legal entity. In its role of Data Consumer, that Competent Authority executes the OOP, and retrieves required information (Evidence

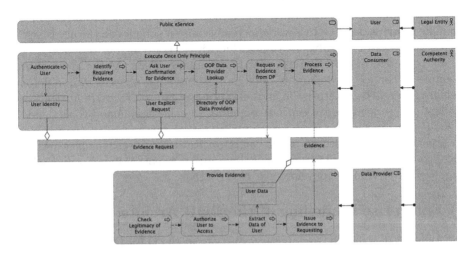

Fig. 1. TOOPRA business architecture process model

according to SDGR) from another Competent Authority in its role of Data Provider.

Architecturally Significant Requirements (ASR) and Architecture Principles guided the design of the Business Architecture, which realizes the business requirements expressed in the process model. TOOPRA Business Architecture addresses two main business concerns: the Business Interactions, which show the collaboration between the actors involved in OOP, and the Capability Map, which specifies the responsibilities of each actor participating in a cross-border Evidence exchange.

The Business Interactions view identifies five main interactions: Evidence Request Exchange, Evidence exchange, Competent Authority Information Exchange, Service Offering Exchange and Identity Exchange. The identification of Business Information exchanges between entities in TOOP business network enables the stakeholders to recognize the interoperability related aspects and to address them.

The Capability Map view enables the participants to accurately identify the business capabilities required for the role they intend to play in TOOP business network. Four roles were identified: Data Consumer, Data provider, Evidence Service Broker and Identity provider. The entity in an Identity Provider role operates a business service to provide identity information of the user to the data consumer. The entity in an Evidence Service Broker role operates a business service to provide functionality to competent authorities to update their metadata on the service offered by the authorities.

3.2 IS Architecture

The Information Systems Architecture focuses on designing Data and Application Architectures and describes how the Business Architecture is realized through Information Systems. A first step in designing the IS Architecture was a thorough assessment of the available BBs to understand what potential resources are available for OOP applications development. CEF eDelivery, eSignature, eIDAS eID and PePPOL Directory were identified as relevant technical capabilities in the context of TOOPRA. The second step consisted in assessing the technical requirements from pilots and mapping them to existing BBs. Therefore, the ASRs were analyzed, the capabilities needed to fulfill these requirements were identified and the BBs that provide the capabilities were mapped to ASRs. As a result, the IS Architecture design mixes a top-down approach, starting from ASRs and Business Architecture, together with a bottom-up approach by injecting the common pilot's solution architecture.

The IS Architecture description is composed of 2 layers: the existing generic BBs and a TOOP specific layer, leveraging the generic BBs to realize the TOOP functionalities. The Data Consumer components of the IS architecture are provided on Fig. 2, where a specific colour code is used to separate the TOOP specific elements (usual Archimate blue of application layer) from the generic BBs reused from the existing catalogue of solutions (coloured in purple). The architecture describes the TOOP Connector and the eID Component as the major components concerned with the realization of the business operations. The IS Architecture describes also the technical specifications and standards prescribing the implementation of the components.

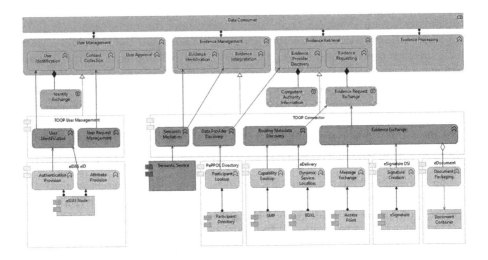

Fig. 2. TOOPRA information system architecture: data consumer

The TOOP Connector is a complex architecture component that enables the cross-border exchange of Evidences. This core component fulfills some specific functions such as: Semantic Mediation, which transforms the data input into a TOOP message and also performs the reverse process, Data Provider Discovery handling dynamic participant lookup, Routing Metadata Discovery which enables the discovery of the endpoint address used for delivery, and Evidence Exchange handling cross-border data exchange. TOOP Connector relies on BBs that were already used in other projects and new components that were developed to meet TOOP business requirements.

The aim of the eID component (identification/authentication) is to authenticate the user/Data Subject over the eIDAS network and to establish trust between the Public Authorities that are exchanging Evidence. In agreement with eIDAS recommendations, a minimum data set for eIDAS natural person identification attributes must be provided.

3.3   Technology Architecture

The Technology layer of the architecture provides technology components in a way that support the deployment of the logical components described in the IS Architecture. The components can be deployed either at central European level or at Member State level. The latter can be: (i) components deployed at the national level (i.e. shared between competent authorities) by an authority or a private business entity and (ii) components deployed at the competent authority level. Due to the many different types of deployment, there are several topologies beneficial in different contexts.

Within TOOP project a topology that enables Member States to share common services is identified as beneficial. In this topology (Fig. 3) the Semantic Server, the TOOP Directory Server and the Business Document Exchange Network Location (BDXL) implementations (BDXL Server and DNS Server) are implemented as central European components; the eIDAS Node, the SMP and Access Point are deployed at national level. The Data Consumer Competent Authority operates and maintains its own TOOP Connector. This topology simplifies business organization for Competent Authorities, since they do not need to maintain the SMP and Access Point. Additional effort is required at the Member State level, but if many different Competent Authorities use the same deployed components, then this variation is beneficial. A similar topology is used by the Data Provider Member State and Competent Authority.

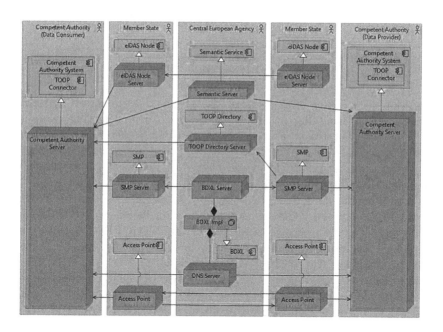

Fig. 3. Technology architecture variation 1

Although the above variation is beneficial within the context of the TOOP project, other topologies could also be envisaged under different context, such as: (i) the Data Consumer Competent Authority deploys locally the SMP, Access Point and TOOP Connector - for example, in the initial introduction of the architecture, where the Member State infrastructure is lacking and some advanced Competent Authorities want to participate, or (ii) a national OOP

Layer Provider offers the components needed to on-board to the architecture (TOOP Connector, SMP and Access Point) with an additional cost.

Solutions accepted for TOOPRA were often results of thorough choices made between several options. The length of the article does not allow for a detailed presentation of the choices and decisions made, but here are two examples.

As the first example, it would have been in principle possible to present TOOPRA just as a collection of standards and interfaces specifying the central European components of the OOP infrastructure and leave implementation of the Member State components to the Member States. Although this approach has its advantages, it was not selected for the following reasons: valuable experience gained from the pilot implementations would have been lost; usage of common solutions on MS level allows to reduce costs; and certain Building Blocks for the MS level are already available.

The second example concerns a variation introduced by one of the TOOP pilots. In this pilot, there is no need for the Data Provider discovery, as the Data Consumer already knows which Data Provider has the requested data. As both variations are valid in specific situations, they both have been included in TOOPRA.

4   Evaluation of the Architecture

This section provides an evaluation of the proposed architecture in terms of feasibility and applicability at EU level, but also demonstrating compliance between members states at a cross-border setting. Numerous approaches for architecture evaluation have been proposed [11]. For the TOOPRA evaluation, two approaches are adopted: (i) Scenario based evaluation [3] - the architecture is implemented and evaluated within the TOOP project through five pilot scenarios in real conditions proving its feasibility at the EU level and (ii) Provision of a model to deploy an OOP solution architecture based on TOOPRA. Existence of such a model indicates feasibility of using TOOPRA on a wide scale and provides an inexpensive evaluation in the spirit of the ideas of the Tiny Architectural Review Approach (TARA) technique [17].

The evaluation presented in this section provided valuable feedback for the improvement of the architecture. Final evaluation will be done with the intended end users of OOP services and the stakeholders of the reference architecture. This evaluation will take time and need significant resources.

4.1   Scenario Based Evaluation

Five pilot scenarios have been tested that focus on the exchange of company data in the context of cross-border services (e.g. a foreign citizen wants to expand his business in a country abroad, and his application form is automatically pre-filled with data from his national business register). The scenarios have been tested in real setting i.e. by EU public services and public authorities serving either as data consumers or data providers. The tested scenarios are:

- *eProcurement:* demonstrates the automatic retrieval of necessary evidences during an eTendering procedure.
- *Licenses & Permissions:* demonstrates the registration of cross-border services. The required evidences are provided by the competent authority of the origin country to the registration service of the destination country.
- *Company data & mandates:* demonstrates the way a service from a foreign country can derive data and mandate information about a company directly by the business registry of the home country of the company.
- *Business Register Data Provision:* demonstrates the exchange of information between the home business register of a company and a foreign public authority in order to authorize access to a service.
- *Business Register Interconnection:* demonstrates the exchange of information between business registers of different countries for the collaborative administration of a company and its foreign branches.

In order to evaluate the scenarios, TOOPRA has been implemented and used by the EU members states and public administrations. Specifically, three types of components have been implemented: (i) central European components, namely the Semantic Service, the TOOP Directory Service and the BDXL service, (ii) member state components, namely the Service Metadata Publisher service and the eIDAS node and (iii) competent authority components, namely TOOP connector and TOOP interface that both facilitate the connection of the competent authority's back-end system with TOOP solution.

The implementation has been tested through the "TOOP Playground" - a virtual environment implemented as a Ganeti VM Cluster that emulates a virtual Europe (with multiple virtual member states) for a more realistic deployment environment. In order to facilitate testing, "TOOP commander" has been created that is a simple Java command line app which creates data consumer and data provider endpoints for receiving messages from the TOOP connector. It also provides means for sending requests from command line between the data consumer and the data provider.

Two types of testing activities have been performed: (i) testing within the member states in order to ensure that a certain member state implementation has been installed and integrated appropriately and (ii) testing across member states in order to ensure that different member state implementations communicate as expected. The later included 20 different end-to-end connectivity tests that cover all the five scenarios presented at the begining of this section (e.g. receive a valid and complete result according to the eID values entered, or receive an appropriate error message). The connectivity tests were performed between the systems of 8 different member states (Greece, Romania, Italy, Austria, Slovakia, Poland, Sweden and Norway). Some of the member states act as data consumers (Greece, Poland, Norway) other as data providers (Italy, Romania, Slovakia) and other both (Sweden, Austria). The end-to-end tests were performed at 10 organized online "Connectathons" that test the connection between a data consumer in one member state and a data provider in another member state. The success rate of the end-to-end test reached 77% (77% of the 20 test succeeded between all the different combinations of member states).

4.2 From TOOPRA to OOP Solution Architecture

In order to successfully deploy a specific OOP project based on TOOPRA, the stakeholders need to fulfill certain organisational, semantic, and technical preconditions. In particular, the reference architecture given by TOOPRA must be used to define the solution architecture for the project under development. Due to space limitations the summary below focuses on semantic and technical preconditions.

As for the semantic processing according to TOOPRA, the stakeholders must have their data described in machine-readable formats together with metadata. The data must be accessible, standard vocabularies must be available. It should be also possible to implement necessary semantic mapping services.

A technical precondition is that the infrastructure of all stakeholders must be sufficient to initiate the project. Especially, the data and public services required by TOOPRA must exist, and data needs to be available, discoverable, and accessible. The stakeholder security and trust levels, data quality, and other characteristics must be adequate.

During design, it is necessary to decide on a deployment topology as indicated in TOOPRA - whether it is Member State shared services, local deployment, or a national OOP layer. The topology determines to a great extent the components to be deployed on a national and Competent Authority level.

During the component selection, deployment, and operation phases a decision is needed whether to use open source software, purchase proprietary software, or develop a custom solution. The stakeholders must provide integration with data providers and infrastructure components (eg, the Access Points). In general, activities on these phases are of a more generic type and less specific to TOOPRA.

5   Lessons Learnt and Discussion

The enterprise modelling approach has given many benefits, but also entailed issues and difficulties to be encountered. The subsequent discussion highlights some of the lessons learnt.

In the first version of the architecture, the component-based software engineering methodology [12] was followed based on the assumption that the existing Building Blocks were sufficient to develop the solution. In the further versions of the architecture, the needs for designing more detailed content, demonstrating compliance, as well as presenting views from various stakeholders became evident. Therefore enterprise modelling approach was switched to. Association with the TOGAF standard has given an overall methodology and framework of views and artefacts to rely upon. Usage of the enterprise modelling approach was not intended as a TOGAF application exercise, but rather as a methodology to improve the overall quality of the result. For this reason, the selected TOGAF phases have been broadly followed in the architecture development process.

One issue encountered has been related to the notion of Enterprise Architecture (EA). Initially EA was proposed in the context of organizations. When the enterprise modelling approach is used for TOOPRA, it may be not clear where is the "Enterprise" - the OOP landscape includes multiple organizations and stakeholders. However, the notion of EA has evolved and for TOGAF, an enterprise will often span multiple organizations.

As an architecture description language (ADL), Archimate 3.0 has been used starting from the very first version. There have been discussions on whether it is too stringent for TOOPRA, but these discussions have resulted in conclusion that the benefits of Archimate outweigh its drawbacks. We however faced specific issues related to the very nature of designing a reference architecture.

When defining a reference architecture, we put a specific effort in the standardization and reuse of existing components and technologies. According to TOGAF and as illustrated, we use the concept of building block to capture this unit of standardized architecture component. Archimate however does not directly support the concepts of building block and technological standards: we therefore needed to develop some kind of Archimate dialect, reusing existing modelling elements of the language to support the concepts required in the description of our reference architecture (mainly the application function and the application component). We also used a colour code to visually distinguish the generic building blocks from the specific TOOP components and functions. This solution works locally, but we could think about specializing the language and create additional modelling elements.

By definition, a reference architecture is a blueprint to a (set of) solution architecture. Those TOOPRA instances can also be described with Archimate; however, there is currently no way to relate elements of the solution architecture to elements of the reference architecture (such as realization or instance-of). This problem can obviously be solved by specific Archimate editors, however it would be valuable to define the concept of reference element as part of the language specifications. This could also solve the previous issue, as reusing a building block from a catalogue of solutions could also be seen as introducing elements of another reference architecture.

We used Archimate to describe the usual layers of an enterprise (business, IS, technology). There is however a specific concern to be addressed in the reference architecture, namely the interoperability aspect of TOOP. We introduced a specific modelling pattern in Archimate to actually capture the needs for interoperability at the business level: this allows to easily pinpoint the interaction points amongst the business partners that require interoperability solutions. We then modelled the realization of those interactions through the use of building blocks (including technical standards). The approach is compatible with the EIRA and goes further with the ability to isolate the interoperability concerns in the overall architecture.

Besides the usual views of the enterprise, we also developed specific views to describe cross-cutting concerns, and especially trust and security. The experience here is that insofar as the reference architecture requires specific building blocks to enforce trust and security, Archimate is a suitable tool to model these blocks of the trust and security framework. However, modelling the security architecture based on the ISO/IEC 27000-series of standards involves policies, procedures, guidelines, and associated resources and activities. In our opinion, these are very detailed and representing them in Archimate would give little additional value.

Experience gained in the development of the architecture, as summarized in Sect. 3, leads to the conclusion that a continuous architecture development approach is necessary, especially when new requirements coming from pilots are frequently incorporated.

One of the lessons learnt was the usefulness of evaluation in providing feedback and stimulating improvements for the architecture development as shown in Sect. 4.

During our reference architecture design, we identified variations in the way the individual process steps can be executed (e.g., in the discovery of the Data Provider that can supply the required Evidence and the actual Evidence exchange), as well as variations in terms of deployment topology. An Archimate view was designed for each of them. We were however not able to express that they are linked by a variation relationship. Such a relationship might be a useful additional concept in Archimate.

6   Conclusion

This paper presents experience and lessons learnt in designing the Reference Architecture for implementing the Once-Only principle to share data legally, securely, and efficiently. The architecture is designed to comply with a new EU Single Digital Gateway Regulation and to integrate standard building blocks.

The need for applying enterprise modelling techniques and tools stems from the architecture drivers and decisions as well as from the demand for multiple views, concerns from various stakeholders, compliance, reuse of building blocks and standards, etc.

Customization of an enterprise modelling framework to the needs of the current development is presented, together with illustrations and model excerpts. The architecture comprises business, information systems, technology, semantics, security, and trust components.

Evaluation of the architecture is based on tested use cases and on a model deployment an OOP solution architecture based on TOOPRA.

The benefits and difficulties of using the enterprise modelling approach in OOP are discussed, allowing the reader to apply lessons learnt in similar projects.

Plans for the future work include elaboration of the content of the architecture on a more detailed level together with further refinement of special issues such as semantics and security aspects.

Acknowledgements. This work was supported by the European Union Horizon 2020 research and innovation program (The Once-Only Principle Project, grant agreement no 737460). The authors would like to thank the three anonymous reviewers for their suggestions and comments.

References

1. Akkaya, C., Krcmar, H.: Towards the implementation of the EU-wide "once-only principle": perceptions of citizens in the DACH-region. In: Parycek, P., et al. (eds.) EGOV 2018. LNCS, vol. 11020, pp. 155–166. Springer, Cham (2018). https://doi.org/10.1007/978-3-319-98690-6_14
2. Cloutier, R., Muller, G., Verma, D., Nilchiani, R., Hole, E., Bone, M.: The concept of reference architectures. Syst. Eng. **13**(1), 14–27 (2010)
3. Dobrica, L., Ovaska, E.: A survey on software architecture analysis methods. IEEE Trans. Softw. Eng. **28**, 638–653 (2002). https://doi.org/10.1109/TSE.2002.1019479
4. EC: European Interoperability Framework - Implementation Strategy. Communication from the Commission to the European Parliament, the Council, the European Economic and Social Committee and the Committee of the Regions, no. COM (2017) 134 final:9
5. EC: EU eGovernment Action Plan 2016–2020 - Accelerating the Digital Transformation of Government. Communication from the Commission to the European Parliament, the Council, the European Economic and Social Committee and the Committee of the Regions 2016, no. 179, pp. 1–11 (2016)
6. EC: European Interoperability Reference Architecture (EIRA) release v3.0.0 (2019)
7. Grandry, E., et al.: Generic Federated OOP Architecture (3rd version). Deliverable D2.3 of the TOOP project. European Commission (2018)
8. ISO/IEC/IEEE: ISO/IEC/IEEE 42010:2011. Systems and Software Engineering - Architecture Description. International Organization for Standardization (2011)
9. Krimmer, R., Kalvet, T., Toots, M., Cepilovs, A., Tambouris, E.: Exploring and demonstrating the once-only principle: a European perspective. In: Proceedings of dg.o 2017, pp. 546–551. ACM, New York (2017). https://doi.org/10.1145/3085228.3085235
10. Proper, H.A., Lankhorst, M.M.: Enterprise architecture - towards essential sense-making. Enterp. Model. Inf. Syst. Architect. **9**, 5–21 (2014)
11. Shanmugapriya, P., Suresh, R.M.: Software architecture evaluation methods – a survey. Int. J. Comput. Appl. **49**, 19–26 (2012). https://www.ijcaonline.org/archives/volume49/number16/7711-1107
12. Sommerville, I.: Software Engineering, 9th edn. Addison-Wesley Publishing Company, Boston (2010)
13. Tepandi, J., et al.: Generic Federated OOP Architecture (1st version). Deliverable D2.1 of the TOOP project. European Commission (2017)
14. The Open Group Architecture Forum: TOGAF Version 9.2. The Open Group (2018)
15. Urbaczewski, L., Mrdalj, S.: A comparison of enterprise architecture frameworks. Issues Inf. Syst. **7**(2), 18–23 (2006)
16. Wimmer, M.A., Tambouris, E., Krimmer, R., Gil-Garcia, J.R., Chatfield, A.T.: Once only principle: benefits, barriers and next steps. In: Proceedings of dg.o 2017, pp. 602–603. ACM, New York (2017). https://doi.org/10.1145/3085228.3085296
17. Woods, E.: Industrial architectural assessment using TARA. J. Syst. Softw. **85** (2011). https://doi.org/10.1109/WICSA.2011.17

Identifying HCI Patterns for the Support of Participatory Enterprise Modeling on Multi-touch Tables

Anne Gutschmidt[1(✉)], Valentina Sauer[1], Kurt Sandkuhl[1], and Alexey Kashevnik[2]

[1] Computer Science Department, University of Rostock, Rostock, Germany
`anne.gutschmidt@uni-rostock.de`
[2] Information Technology and Programming Faculty, ITMO University, Saint Petersburg, Russia

Abstract. This paper deals with the question of how software enabling participatory enterprise modeling on a multi-touch table should be designed. We will present a pre-selection of existing HCI patterns addressing the requirements which come along with collaboratively creating enterprise models on a shared workspace. Moreover, we examined a software prototype based on a task model and video analysis. The videos show participatory modeling sessions and give hint on frequent activities and deficiencies of the prototype. Based on our results, we will give recommendations of HCI patterns which should be applied when designing software tools for participatory enterprise modeling on multi-touch tables.

Keywords: HCI patterns · Participatory enterprise modeling · Multi-touch table · Task analysis · Video analysis

1 Introduction

Enterprise models are supposed to capture and represent the situation in an enterprise, either in terms of the current state of affairs or of the planned future situation [1]. In this context, a precondition for high quality enterprise models is to fully and correctly elicit the relevant knowledge from within the enterprise under consideration for the defined scope and purpose of modeling. Participatory enterprise modeling (PEM) is an elicitation technique considered as in particular valuable, when an agreement and a joint view of different stakeholders on the current or future situation are important [2]. Various methods, techniques and tools have been proposed by the scientific community to support PEM (cf. Sect. 2.1). However, constantly emerging new technologies make more and more new tools possible. We argue that with an increased use of multi-touch tables (MTT) and large touch screens, more attention should be paid on adapting or specifically

© IFIP International Federation for Information Processing 2019
Published by Springer Nature Switzerland AG 2019
J. Gordijn et al. (Eds.): PoEM 2019, LNBIP 369, pp. 118–133, 2019.
https://doi.org/10.1007/978-3-030-35151-9_8

designing tools for participatory, facilitated and collaborative EM. More concretely, the paper addresses the design of user interface and human computer interaction (HCI) for MTT in the context of PEM. This may also contribute to light-weight modelling tools and the research agenda for extending the reach of enterprise modeling [3]. Our conjecture is that HCI patterns from software engineering (cf. Sect. 2.2) provide relevant and reusable knowledge for the design of PEM tools. Based on a general task analysis for goal modeling as selected part of EM and using the results of a video analysis revealing problems and challenges in PEM on a multi-touch table, we aim at contributing to an understanding of specific requirements in PEM tool design. The main contributions of the paper are (1) a list of HCI patterns supporting participation and enterprise modeling, (2) a task analysis of typical EM activities and (3) results of evaluating the HCI patterns for improving a modeling tool on a multi-touch table. The remainder of the paper is structured as follows: Sect. 2 will present the theoretical background dealing with the areas of PEM (Sect. 2.1) and HCI patterns (Sect. 2.2). In Sect. 3 we will present our selection of HCI patterns where we list patterns we found most fitting for PEM on a MTT. We examined a software prototype to determine which of the previously selected HCI patterns have already been applied (Sect. 4). Furthermore, we documented basic user interactions enabled by the prototype in a task model (Sect. 5) and, based on video recordings of thirteen PEM sessions, we analyzed the interactions with the aim of identifying potentials of improvement (Sect. 6). The paper closes with a general discussion in Sect. 7.

2 Theoretical Background

2.1 Participatory and Collaborative Enterprise Modelling

A General Background. In general terms, EM addresses the systematic analysis and modelling of processes, organization structures, product structures, IT-systems or any other perspective relevant for the modelling purpose [4]. A detailed account of EM approaches is provided in [5]. PEM and involving different stakeholder groups in EM has a long tradition (see, e.g., [5]). Since several stakeholder groups are involved in the modelling process and have to work together on one model, this process calls for participation of everyone involved. In this PEM process the methodology experts and domain experts work together on the model [6]. By working together right from the beginning, it is more likely that the final model will be accepted by the participants and they will commit to it. Furthermore, the stakeholders will agree with the model, after all, they worked on it, too. Another advantage of PEM sessions is that they can increase the quality of the model, by introducing people into the process who hold valuable knowledge of the enterprise and its processes. Domain-specific modelling languages (DSML) [7] are supposed to support these various stakeholders in model creation and use. The scientific literature on EM offers several views as its constituents (see, e.g., [8,9]), like the modelling procedure or modelling method, the result of modelling (i.e. the model), the tool support, and the organizational structures establishing modelling within an organization. However, not all researchers in EM agree on the above EM constituents. Some researchers emphasize the importance of meta-models and modelling languages for capturing different perspectives [8]. Tool support is often seen as inseparable manifestation of modelling approaches and notations [10], but in other research work as aid to support modelling [11]. Organizational structures and role descriptions are often neglected in EM approaches.

Participatory Enterprise Modeling Sessions. When an enterprise decides to start an enterprise modeling project with actively involving stakeholder representatives, they will have to invest resources into that project: Most obviously, they will have to exempt employees from work to let them take part in modeling sessions. The participants should come from different parts of the company, and have adequate domain knowledge which is why they are called domain experts. They should also have the authority to suggest organizational changes contained in the final models [2]. Stirna and Persson [2] propose a number of 4–8 participants per session. In addition to domain experts, a company should recruit so-called method experts. Their purpose is to support the domain experts in creating enterprise models based on their knowledge of modeling notation and method. Usually, a facilitator leads the discussion and modeling process while being completely neutral about the content. A tool operator assists the domain experts in creating the actual models. He or she helps handling the modeling tool and generating syntactically correct models. Optionally, a secretary may take additional notes to document the rationale of the creation process [1,2]. An enterprise modeling project may comprise multiple modeling sessions lasting several hours and possibly involving different domain experts who create and refine models [2].

Modeling Language. Enterprise models are usually represented by diagrams containing geometric shapes such as rectangles or circles. These shapes reflect concepts and are usually connected by lines or arrows representing relationships. All model elements may be labeled, giving further information. In a formal language both syntactical and semantic rules have to be followed when drawing the actual model [2]. A goal model in the 4EM notation, for example, consists of differently colored rectangles, e.g., a green rectangle represents a goal, an orange rectangle represents a problem. The rectangles usually contain an expressive description and a number. To show that a certain problem hinders a goal, a relationship between these components must be added including the respective label [1].

2.2   HCI Patterns

HCI patterns, also called HCI design patterns, describe successful best practice solutions for reoccurring User Interface (UI) design problems, therefore also affecting implicitly the usability of software tools [12]. These patterns should support the designers and keep them from reinventing the same solutions over and over again. Their advantage is that useful design solutions can be captured and generalized in the form of a pattern to solve similar problems with them [13]. The development of UIs is complex, therefore, reusing knowledge, already gained by previous design processes, helps the designers and developers to work more efficiently and improve their productivity [14–17]. A pattern is the relationship between a certain context, problem and solution [18]. It describes the context within which the patterns can be used, the problem that has to be solved by the pattern and its solution [17]. Initially, this idea of patterns was developed by Christopher Alexander for architectural designs [18]. The "Gang of Four" adopted the pattern concept for the design of object-oriented software [19]. Eventually, patterns were also adopted by the HCI community. While the Gang of Four gives instructions about how to implement a pattern, HCI patterns are about the general design of an interface and its purpose for the user. The pattern concept not only included the patterns themselves, but also a pattern language. A pattern language consists of patterns and their relationships, i.e. a network of patterns. High-level patterns in this network may be solved by low-level patterns [16]. Since the patterns of one language are connected to each other, it is apparent that a pattern language combines patterns for a given family of design problems in a specific domain [15,20]. Successor and predecessor relationships between patterns are a key concept when working with pattern languages, since they enable finding closely related patterns [15].

3   Selecting HCI Patterns for Participatory Enterprise Modeling on MTTs

We have scanned existing lists of patterns [21–25] and further works presenting HCI patterns [26,27] which covered concepts that could be applied to MTT. While the lists of Tidwell [22,23] and van Welie [21] are most often cited, Remy et al. [24] created a pattern list specifically for the MTT. We particularly looked for HCI patterns that fit the requirements of the special context of PEM with a multi-touch table. We formulated major concepts which helped us selecting and categorizing fitting patterns, and also reflected the above-mentioned requirements. Figure 1 shows these concepts in bold letters with thick frames at the top of the diagram. The remaining elements represent existing HCI patterns we have found in the above-mentioned sources. The arrows represent relationships among the elements, e.g. space may be saved using collapsible panels. A pattern may also serve several concepts. Moreover, patterns may be related.

Usually, enterprise models become very big and complex. So, space for interactions will become more and more scarce as a model is growing. To **save space**, several patterns may be used, such as *collapsible panels* or *hover tools* [23]. Tidwell introduced the pattern *hover tools* for mouse-based applications [23], where elements are displayed only when hovering the mouse icon over an object. For touch devices, there is not yet an equivalent to hovering, but only touching.

Tidwell is of the opinion that touching may cause precipitate commitment. Nevertheless, it may ensure that the displayed model is not cluttered by displaying editing options which are not needed at the moment. Different *views* [21] may be used as an alternative, where users may switch between editing view and "final" view that is showing just the model.

Depending on the size of the table and of the model elements, it may be difficult to see/read or reach certain objects. As mentioned before, there should be 4–8 domain experts plus at least one method expert present at a modeling session. Thus, the software must present the model in a way that is visually and physically available to several persons at a time. Patterns such as *zooming* [23,24] and *extending reachability* [24] support **physical and visual reachability**.

As mentioned above, the modeling tool is mainly handled by the tool operator. However, Stirna and Persson suggest that domain experts should be involved by e.g. letting them write down their ideas on colored cards, present them to the group, discuss them and then cluster related cards [2]. Thus, the editing software for the MTT should not be tailored to only the tool operator. It should also offer domain experts an easy way of capturing their ideas in their own words with the MTT. A third party like the tool operator may accidentally change the meaning of statements. Still, the tool operator may then assist in composing a syntactically correct model. Furthermore, the software should not be designed in a way that one person may take over a whole modeling session. Remy et al. [24] introduced a pattern called ***balanced participation***. This implies that there must not be any conflict about or restricted access to resources, especially input devices. An *overlay menu* [21], possibly with multiple instances, instead of a single fixed menu could support this. When providing a horizontal work surface, different perspectives must be provided for users possibly standing at all sides of the table. This is addressed by the pattern *desktop orientation* [24] meaning that the orientation of the interface can be changed. Balanced participation could also be promoted by *user identification* [24]. In *private spaces* participants may take notes of their own ideas, possibly with *embedded electronic devices* such as tablets [24], before sharing them with the group analogous to the above mentioned card writing. However, the content produced in private space should be meant to be shared, otherwise it might undermine collaboration.

The **modeling** task itself brings some special requirements with it. As mentioned before, models can become very complex. So, the table should be large enough to both display the model and let all participants have access to the model (*large collaboration table* [24]). According to [2], domain experts should not be burdened with details of the modeling notation. Consequently, at best, the software should make obvious what can be done (e.g. with *input hints* [23]), and it should not allow what should not be done (e.g. with *constraint input* [21]), possibly already considering notation rules.

As domain experts should not be expected to be experts on digital touch devices such as tabletops either, the software must be very **intuitive** and **easy to handle**. An intuitive interface may be implemented based on patterns such as *input hints*, *good defaults* [23] and *constraint input* [21] such that users know

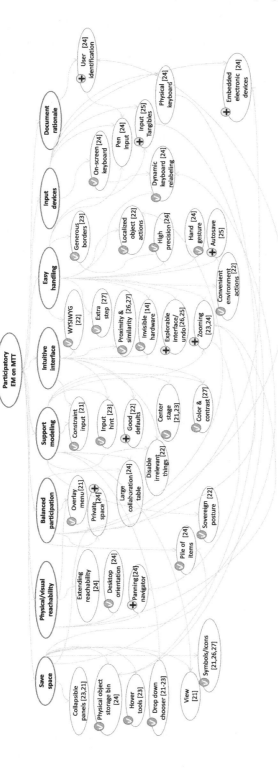

Fig. 1. Selection of HCI patterns suitable for PEM on a MTT. Please note that HCI patterns may have different names in the pattern catalogues. A check mark means, the pattern has been found in the software, a plus mark means, the pattern should be added.

what to do. With easy handling, we mean that it should not be difficult or effortful to see content on the table or to perform an interaction on the MTT. E.g., the "fat-finger" problem may be prevented by applying a pattern such as *generous borders* applied to the components of a model or buttons and keys [23]. The pattern *WYSIWYG* (what you see is what you get) [22] should make interactions quicker, as immediate feedback of one's action is given.

With the MTT, different **input devices** are available. While the *physical keyboard* is often felt as more convenient, but occupying space on the work surface, *on-screen keyboards* may be instantiated for every user at each required spot and easily dismissed if no longer needed [24]. *Input tangibles* may be used as an alternative [24], although there must be some additional space where these objects can be stored beyond the work surface (*physical object storage bin* [24]).

In an enterprise modeling session, it is also of interest how ideas evolved. The **rationale** may be documented by a secretary [1]. *User identification* may add information in a way that the author information of components in the model can be saved in addition.

4   Identifying HCI Patterns in a Prototype PEM Editor

In order to confirm the suggested HCI patterns, they should actually be applied in existing software. To our knowledge, there does not yet exist a commercial enterprise modeling editor especially developed for collaborative working with a MTT. Therefore, we have examined a prototype developed at the university of Rostock, as a starting point. In previous studies, we have worked with this prototype [28,29] which allows creating goal models according to the 4EM notation on a MTT. In particular, it supports collaboration by enabling simultaneous input by several users. We wanted to know whether some of our selected HCI patterns from Sect. 3 have already been applied in the software and present their concrete implementation. Due to space limitations, we can only describe a small selection. In Fig. 1 we have marked the patterns we have found in the prototype with a check mark.

In the editor, *localized actions* [22] in terms of buttons directly accompanying components and relations, simplify the handling and support *balanced participation*, i.e. users can manipulate all the objects they can reach without having to access a menu possibly situated somewhere else. E.g., each component has a button to set it to an editing mode and to generate a new relation starting from this component. Moreover, when the user touches one of the text fields of a component which is in editing mode, an *on-screen keyboard* [24] is attached right below the component. This keyboard belongs only to this component (*localized object actions*), every component may have its own keyboard. Thus, the keyboard is not a resource to be shared which should also promote *balanced participation*. Thus, actions referring to an object are situated in its close proximity as can be seen in Fig. 2a.

These buttons, however, are hidden by default in order to save space and keep an uncluttered view. Only when a user touches the component, the buttons

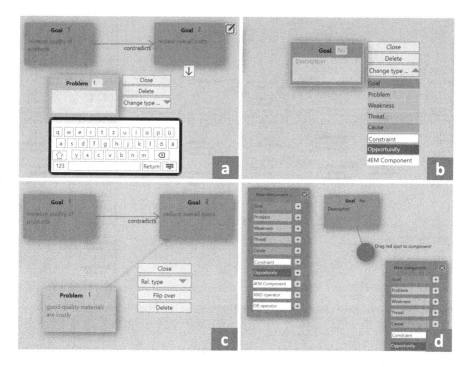

Fig. 2. Example screenshots of the prototype showing (a) localized object actions, on-screen keyboard and hover tools, (b) drop-down chooser for selecting a component type, (c) a relation in editing mode with drop-down chooser, and (d) overlay menus and a newly created relation with tool tip/input hint.

appear. After a few seconds, the buttons slowly fade out following the pattern *hover tools* [23] (see Fig. 2a).

By offering the possibility to rotate components, the pattern *desktop orientation* [24] is partly implemented. Only single elements, but not the whole model can be rotated to a participant's respective orientation.

When a user wants to create a new component, a menu (see Fig. 2d) must be opened by *hand gesture* [24], namely tap and hold. The same gesture is also used to set a relation into editing mode, e.g. for setting a label or deleting it. There is no fixed menu, but the menu can be opened at any point on the work surface as described in the pattern *overlay menu* [21]. The pattern *balanced participation* [24] is implemented by allowing several instances of the menu. That way, participants do not have to share this resource. For the creation of the actual component from the menu, the pattern *constrained input* was used. The menu allows the creation of only those elements that are included in the modeling language. There is no free drawing.

WYSIWYG [23] is applied when drawing a relation and moving elements. E.g., components may be moved and rotated, and the effect of these actions can be seen immediately. Moreover, if a relation is connected to a component in

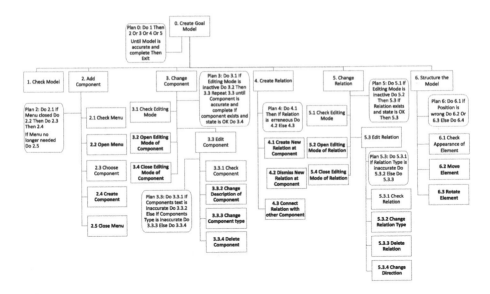

Fig. 3. Task model with basic user interactions with the prototype modeling editor.

movement, the relation's orientation and length is adapted automatically like a physical rubber band.

Although the physical conditions do not belong to the software, we want to add some more patterns which may also have an influence on using it. The multi-touch device is embedded in a wooden table making the *hardware invisible* [14] and offering some space on the table's wooden frame and below the table to store physical objects such as a physical keyboard or handouts (*physical object storage bin* [24]). Due to this setting, we are dealing with a horizontal work surface which cannot be *tilted* [24]. It was technically not possible to use *tangible objects* nor *user identification* [24] with the concrete device (cf. Sect. 6.1).

5   Task Analysis

In order to further examine the software prototype and find potentials of improvement, we wanted to create an overview of user interactions with the software necessary to generate a model. We decided to use Hierarchical Task Analysis (HTA) to attain a graphical representation of theses interactions we could then examine. HTA may help discovering those parts of a task which may cause a user to eventually fail or to succeed [30]. The basic idea of HTA is that there is a general task at the highest level which consists of an operation. Each operation is connected with a goal whose accomplishment can be measured. Goals can be decomposed into sub-goals, thus, the connected goals are decomposed into sub-goals. So-called plans determine the order in which (sub-)operations should be executed, including the formulation of conditions and circumstances by which operations are triggered [30,31]. Examining the software prototype, we considered creating a goal model as main operation which we decomposed into sub-operations. We furthermore defined plans indicating when each operation is triggered. The resulting task model (see Fig. 3) will lead us later in the observation study presented in Sect. 6.

When creating a goal model with the prototype editor, the user may repeatedly check the model before deciding on an action. When the user decides to add a new component, a menu must be opened offering the possibility to create as many components as desired. When the user wants to change the description or type of a component, or wants to delete the component, the editing mode of the component has to be started. Relations between components may be created starting from one component, drawing the relation to the target component. If a relation was created erroneously, it may be deleted right away. Relations may be labeled with a type by first starting an editing mode. The editing mode is also necessary if the relation is to be deleted. The general appearance of the model may be changed by moving and rotating components.

6   Video Analysis

From a previous study, we used secondary data to find out which of the interactions contained in the task model occur most frequently. We examined video recordings of thirteen modeling sessions performed with the software prototype without interventions of a tool operator. This might give hint on critical points that should be improved or supported in a better way by HCI patterns. For the same purpose, we examined what caused the most difficulties for its users. We also recommend additional patterns, marked with a plus sign in Fig. 1.

6.1   Method and Sample

Thirteen teams of three persons performed an enterprise modeling task on an MTT (3M Multi-Touch Display C5567PW, size: 1210×680 mm) in a study conducted in 2018 at the University of Rostock [32]. The teams had to create a goal model for a fictitious company within half an hour. 27 of the 39 participants were students, among them students of psychology, business information systems, pedagogy, biology, physics, chemistry, economics, engineering and computer science. On a scale from 1 (novice) to 5 (expert) the participants reported to be quite inexperienced in the modeling notation ($\mu = 1.3, \sigma = 0.8$) and with MTT ($\mu = 1.2, \sigma = 0.5$).

The modeling sessions were video recorded from two perspectives, one showing the table from above, another one capturing the front view on the team. We analyzed the video recordings looking for specific difficulties the participants had during the modeling. Sometimes, participants commented on their problems during the critical incident. At other times, clearly identifying problems with the use of the software turned out to be difficult and is dependent on the observer's interpretation. Moreover, we counted the interactions introduced in our task model (Fig. 3).

6.2   Results and Recommendations

The difficulty which occurred most often ($\mu = 11.2$ times over all sessions) was that menus were opened accidentally. When movements, such as dragging a component, were performed too slowly, this was misinterpreted by the software as tap-and-hold gesture, and unwanted menus were opened. The challenge is to choose hand gestures which are easy enough for the user to perform but clear enough for the system to be distinguished from other actions. We suggest a double tap as a substitute since more complex gestures might make the software less intuitive [24]. Hand gestures have to be thoroughly tested.

Three types of negative incidents were often caused by a lack of space: the editing mode was opened accidentally ($\mu = 3$), a new relation was created by accident ($\mu = 2.6$), and the wrong component was moved ($\mu = 2.3$). As the models grew in complexity, more and more elements were overlapping. To save space, hidden buttons were used. Although the buttons were no longer visible they were still active. This caused users to accidentally press hidden buttons of closely situated components creating new relations etc. To solve this problem, we could disable buttons when they are not visible. Putting buttons inside the components bears the danger of accidentally triggering actions where components should only be moved. A hand gesture could be used to replace one button, possibly mitigating the problem. Close proximity of model elements was, however, only one reason for these negative incidents. Accidental actions were also triggered by participants leaning or putting sheets of paper on the table. Remy et al. [24] suggested *physical object storage bin* for storing items such as keyboard or tangible objects, but no surface to actually lean on or put down sheets of paper is mentioned. In the future, additional frames around the MTT might turn out as a pattern. Nevertheless, such a frame can be in conflict with reachability of all elements on the MTT depending on the size of table and frame.

Considering the interactions to be performed with the goal of **creating an enterprise model**, **opening a component's editing mode** was performed most frequently ($\mu = 31.4$ times over all sessions), followed by **closing a component's editing mode** ($\mu = 30.1$) and **editing a component's description** ($\mu = 29.8$). This frequency might encourage to believe that these interactions should be additionally supported. E.g., one could think about simplifying the access to editing functions as we have already described above. Another option could be to automatically set a component into editing mode after having created it. This, however, could be in conflict with creating a *pile of items* where participants create a kind of repository similar to a stack of cards.

Creating a new relation is the next most frequently performed interaction ($\mu = 25.8$). It is performed by tapping on the component resulting in the display of an arrow button. When the button is pressed a new relation arrow is generated pointing to a red circle that must be drawn to the target component (see Fig. 2b). We observed that some users wanted to draw the arrow button to the target component right away. It seems that this button implies this functionality. Either the button symbol has to be changed or, better because reducing the number of steps, the expected behavior should be implemented. The latter would also make dismissing new relations obsolete and simplify the creation process.

Drawing a relation occurred 20.8 times on average over all sessions. It seems to work well for the participants, probably being very intuitive. **Opening the editing mode** of the relation was performed equally often ($\mu = 19.8$). The low occurrence of editing interactions such as **changing the relation type** ($\mu = 11.4$) and changing a relation arrow's direction might be explained by the way they had to be accessed (see Fig. 2c for illustration of the editing mode). We observed that some participants did not expect a tap-and-hold gesture but simply tapped once on the relation. The latter would, however, increase the danger of triggering unwanted actions. Nevertheless, it should be taken care that hand gestures are consistent for similar functions. Moreover, *good defaults* could be provided for new relations taking into consideration syntactic rules.

Creating components occurred with an average frequency of 18.8 times. We see the possibility of opening multiple menus for the creation of components at every spot as a major advantage when supporting this interaction. It also enables the creation of a pile of components compared to a participant grabbing a pile of cards he or she can write on.

Closing a menu ($\mu = 14.8$) and **closing the relation editing mode** ($\mu = 14.5$) occurred with a similar frequency. They could be made obsolete by closing them automatically after an interaction was performed. It must be investigated and compared how useful users find each feature.

Deleting a relation ($\mu = 4.6$), **deleting a component** ($\mu = 2.5$), **dismissing a new relation** ($\mu = 2.5$) and **changing a component's type** ($\mu = 2.4$) occurred rarely. Participants did not seem to experiment with model elements after they had created them. Nevertheless, an *undo function* is fundamentally advisable with inexperienced users. **Opening a menu** was also a rare interaction ($\mu = 4.4$). Menus remained open although they took a lot of space. Either users prefer a constantly present menu or the actions necessary to open (tap-and-hold) and close a menu are considered as too effortful.

We also observed how much participants **moved and rotated components**. For the interactions, we measured the average overall amount of time over all sessions. As some users tended to perform one big movement in several small steps, frequencies would have given a distorted impression of the actual movement behavior. We noted that rotation was rarely used ($\mu = 4.6$ s). One reason might be that rotating components is too difficult. Secondly, rotating single elements might not be seen as beneficial when the remaining model keeps its original orientation. Remy et al. [24] suggest a generally adaptable desktop orientation. This would be a global function requiring the awareness and approval of all users such that no one will be disturbed while working. 5.8 s were spent on average on handing over components to another person, and 13.8 s were spent on average on moving components to oneself. Due to space problems and layered objects, users often moved components to a place where they could interact with them more conveniently ($\mu = 17.5$ s). Movement that we could not assign to any of the above categories made about 179.1 s on average. We often observed that participants repeatedly rearranged components to minimal extend, similar to fidgeting with a pen.

In one of the modeling sessions, a software bug made the system crash. As there was no *autosave*, the model had to be recreated quickly. Although the bug has been removed, *autosave* is fundamentally advisable.

The space problem caused several difficulties. It could generally be mitigated by a *zoom* function. A global zoom is again a function whose activation must be agreed on by all active users. A *panning navigator* should additionally be used to give users some orientation about what part of the model they are currently viewing. Another option would be to make all elements smaller by default, but still recognizable, and offer a zooming function for a single component for further examination and editing. Furthermore, the menus are very big in relation to the work surface and the other model elements. To save space, the menu could be replaced by simply creating default components, set into editing mode from the beginning. This would, however, make creating a pile of components difficult. The work surface could be extended using *embedded electronic devices* which may also serve as *private spaces*. Finally, one could also consider buying a bigger table, however a *large collaboration table* could undermine reachability.

7   General Discussion

New digital devices such as MTT appear very attractive in the context of PEM. They can be a useful tool for collaboratively gathering knowledge and ideas. The intent of this paper was to present experiences and give inspiration on how to design software for MTT serving PEM. HCI patterns provide proven solutions to frequent design problems which may be reused by interface designers. We have searched existing lists of HCI patterns, many of them do not originally refer to touch applications. We presented a selection of HCI patterns we assume to be suitable for PEM on MTT. However, a pattern is really a pattern when it is repeatedly used. To our knowledge, there is no commercial PEM software which is originally made for MTT. So, as a starting point, we investigated a software prototype to check whether we would find some of the previously selected patterns and we showed what kind of interactions are required to create an enterprise model on an MTT with this prototype. Our task and video analysis have shown that the number of interactions may actually be reduced in the prototype. The results of the video analysis also revealed shortcomings of the prototype which might be overcome by using additional HCI patterns from our selection.

One of our major findings is that certain patterns may be in conflict. E.g., in the prototype, multiple instances of menus and on-screen keyboards were used. On the one hand, this supports balanced participation. On the other hand it takes a lot of space. The lack of space is a severe challenge, yet, a large collaboration table could make it difficult for users to recognize and reach all elements. A zoom function could also help solving the space problem, however, as a global function it might disturb users in their work. Thus, we recommend to use global functions with care. Hand gestures are a beneficial means for saving space. Nevertheless, we recommend to test which gestures users find intuitive and convenient. Furthermore, there must be consistent gestures for similar functions.

We observed modeling sessions where participants were usually standing. We found that some persons tended to lean on the table or put down paper on it. Thus, we would recommend to use a frame around the table, but thoroughly considering that this will not restrict reachability.

Eventually, our selection of HCI patterns can certainly not be considered as complete or final. We hope to be able to investigate more applications in this area in the future to further test, confirm and adapt our selection of HCI patterns.

Acknowledgements. Part of the research has been developed in scope of a project financed by Government of Russian Federation (Grant 08-08).

References

1. Sandkuhl, K., Stirna, J., Persson, A., Wißotzki, M.: Enterprise modeling. The Enterprise Engineering Series. Springer, Heidelberg (2014). https://doi.org/10.1007/978-3-662-43725-4

2. Stirna, J., Persson, A.: Enterprise Modeling - Facilitating the Process and the People. Springer, Heidelberg (2018). https://doi.org/10.1007/978-3-319-94857-7

3. Sandkuhl, K., et al.: From expert discipline to common practice: a vision and research agenda for extending the reach of enterprise modeling. Bus. Inf. Syst. Eng. **60**(1), 69–80 (2018)

4. Vernadat, F.: Enterprise modeling and integration (EMI): current status and research perspectives. Ann. Rev. Control **26**(1), 15–25 (2002)

5. Stirna, J., Persson, A., Sandkuhl, K.: Participative enterprise modeling: experiences and recommendations. In: Krogstie, J., Opdahl, A., Sindre, G. (eds.) CAiSE 2007. LNCS, vol. 4495, pp. 546–560. Springer, Heidelberg (2007). https://doi.org/10.1007/978-3-540-72988-4_38

6. Gutschmidt, A., Sandkuhl, K., Borchardt, U.: Multi-touch table or plastic wall? Design of a study for the comparison of media in modeling. In: Abramowicz, W., Alt, R., Franczyk, B. (eds.) BIS 2016. LNBIP, vol. 263, pp. 123–135. Springer, Cham (2017). https://doi.org/10.1007/978-3-319-52464-1_12

7. Van Deursen, A., Klint, P., Visser, J.: Domain-specific languages: an annotated bibliography. ACM Sigplan Not. **35**(6), 26–36 (2000)

8. Frank, U.: Multilevel modeling. Bus. Inf. Syst. Eng. **6**(6), 319–337 (2014)

9. Henderson-Sellers, B., Ralyté, J., Ågerfalk, P.J., Rossi, M.: Situational Method Engineering. Springer, Heidelberg (2014). https://doi.org/10.1007/978-3-642-41467-1

10. Gonzalez-Perez, C., Henderson-Sellers, B.: Metamodelling for Software Engineering. Wiley, Hoboken (2008)

11. Dietz, J.: Enterprise Ontology: Theory and Methodology. Springer, Heidelberg (2006). https://doi.org/10.1007/3-540-33149-2

12. Specker, M., Wentzlaff, I.: Exploring usability needs by human-computer interaction patterns. In: Winckler, M., Johnson, H., Palanque, P. (eds.) TAMODIA 2007. LNCS, vol. 4849, pp. 254–260. Springer, Heidelberg (2007). https://doi.org/10.1007/978-3-540-77222-4_20

13. Wurhofer, D., Obrist, M., Beck, E., Tscheligi, M.: Introducing a comprehensive quality criteria framework for validating patterns. In: Dini, P., (ed.) Computation world, pp. 242–247. IEEE (2009)

14. Borchers, J.O.: A pattern approach to interaction design. In: Boyarski, D., Kellogg, W.A. (eds.) Proceedings of the 3rd Conference on Designing Interactive Systems: Processes, Practices, Methods, and Techniques (DIS 2000), pp. 369–378. ACM, New York (2000)

15. Hitz, M., Kruschitz, C.: Human-computer interaction design patterns: structure, methods, and tool. Int. J. Adv. Softw. **3**(1&2) (2010)

16. Kruschitz, C., Hitz, M.: Analyzing the HCI design pattern variety. In: Hanyuda, E., (ed.) Proceedings of the 1st Asian Conference on Pattern Languages of Programs, p. 1. ACM (2010)

17. Guerrero-García, J., González-Calleros, J.M., González-Monfil, A., Pinto, D.: A method to align user interface to workflow allocation patterns. In: González Calleros, J.M., Collazos Ordoñez, C.A., Guerrero-García, J., (eds.) Proceedings of the XVIII International Conference on Human Computer Interaction. ICPS, pp. 1–8. ACM (2007)

18. Alexander, C.: A Pattern Language. Center for Environmental Structure Series, vol. 2. Oxford University Press, Oxford (1977)

19. Gamma, E., Helm, R., Johnson, R., Vlissides, J.: Design Patterns, Addison-Wesley Professional Computing Series, 39 Printing edn. Addison-Wesley, Boston (2011)

20. Lukosch, S., Schümmer, T.: Communicating design knowledge with groupware technology patterns. In: de Vreede, G.-J., Guerrero, L.A., Marín Raventós, G. (eds.) CRIWG 2004. LNCS, vol. 3198, pp. 223–237. Springer, Heidelberg (2004). https://doi.org/10.1007/978-3-540-30112-7_19

21. van Welie, M.: Welie.com: Patterns in interaction design. http://www.welie.com/patterns/index.php (2008). Accessed 30 July 2019

22. Tidwell, J.: Common ground (1999). http://www.mit.edu/~jtidwell/common_ground_onefile.html. Accessed 02 May 2019

23. Tidwell, J.: Designing Interfaces, 2nd edn. Safari Tech Books Online, O'Reilly (2011)

24. Remy, C., Weiss, M., Ziefle, M., Borchers, J.: A pattern language for interactive tabletops in collaborative workspaces. In: Proceedings of the 15th European Conference on Pattern Languages of Programs, EuroPLoP 2010, pp. 9:1–9:48 (2010)

25. Laakso, S.A.: User interface design patterns (2003). https://www.cs.helsinki.fi/u/salaakso/patterns/index.html. Accessed 02 May 2019

26. Coram, T., Lee, J.: Experiences - a pattern language for user interface design (2016). http://www.maplefish.com/todd/papers/Experiences.html#Interaction

27. Lockton, D., Harrison, D., Stanton, N.A.: Exploring design patterns for sustainable behaviour. Des. J. **16**(4), 431–459 (2013)

28. Gutschmidt, A.: Empirical insights into the appraisal of tool support for participative enterprise modeling. In: Proceedings of the 9th International Workshop on Enterprise Modeling and Information Systems Architectures, Rostock, Germany, 24th–25th May 2018, pp. 70–74 (2018)

29. Gutschmidt, A.: On the influence of tools on collaboration in participative enterprise modeling—an experimental comparison between whiteboard and multi-touch table. In: Andersson, B., Johansson, B., Barry, C., Lang, M., Linger, H., Schneider, C. (eds.) Advances in Information Systems Development. LNISO, vol. 34, pp. 151–168. Springer, Cham (2019). https://doi.org/10.1007/978-3-030-22993-1_9

30. Stanton, N.A.: Hierarchical task analysis: developments, applications, and extensions. Appl. Ergon. **37**(1), 55–79 (2006)

31. Annett, J.: Hierarchical task analysis. In: The Handbook of Task Analysis for Human-Computer Interaction, pp. 83–98. CRC Press (2003)
32. Gutschmidt, A., Sauer, V., Schönwälder, M., Szilagyi, T.: Researching participatory modeling sessions: an experimental study on the influence of evaluation potential and the opportunity to draw oneself. In: Pańkowska, M., Sandkuhl, K. (eds.) BIR 2019. LNBIP, vol. 365, pp. 44–58. Springer, Cham (2019). https://doi.org/10.1007/978-3-030-31143-8_4

Assessing the Adoption Level of Agile Development Within Software Product Lines: The AgiPL-AM Model

Hassan Haidar[1]([✉]), Manuel Kolp[1], and Yves Wautelet[2]

[1] LouRIM-CEMIS, UCLouvain, Louvain-la-Neuve, Belgium
{hassan.haidar,manuel.kolp}@uclouvain.be
[2] Faculty of Economics and Business, KULeuven, Brussels, Belgium
yves.wautelet@kuleuven.be

Abstract. Agile Product Lines are combinations of agile and product-line techniques. Introducing agile software development methods into software product lines makes the development processes evolve from predictive to iterative and incremental and offers flexibility to react on customers' changing requirements and market demand and deliver high quality software [1]. However, this combination is still challenging and the maturity of an agile adoption is often hard to determine. Assessing the current situation regarding the combination is thus an essential step towards a successful integration of agile methods into software product lines. Following a specific research approach, we have built an assessment model called AgiPL-AM allowing self-evaluations within the team in order to determine the current state of agile software development in combination with software product lines. AgiPL-AM, our model for assessing organizational agility of Agile Product Line approaches, is comprised of six categories (five are related to agile principles and one to product line architecture) and five levels of maturity. The assessment results demonstrate that AgiPL-AM has the ability to reveal and pinpoint agile product-line approach strengths and weaknesses. It makes recommendations to improve the status and may give a guideline for this improvement.

Keywords: Agile Product Line Engineering · Agile software development · Process maturity model · Agile assessment model

1 Introduction

To deal with the growing complexity of information systems and to handle the competitive and changing needs of the IT production industry, practitioners and researchers have proposed several approaches with the intention to combine agile and product lines techniques [1]. The goal was to make software product-line methodologies evolve from predictive to iterative and incremental, and to agile approaches.

Many questions could be asked about the conducted combinations, their results, and their effectiveness. If "agility" is considered as a "quality attribute" of the development process, two crucial research questions arise: *"how to combine agile practices*

© IFIP International Federation for Information Processing 2019
Published by Springer Nature Switzerland AG 2019
J. Gordijn et al. (Eds.): PoEM 2019, LNBIP 369, pp. 134–148, 2019.
https://doi.org/10.1007/978-3-030-35151-9_9

*with product-line techniques?".*and *"how to assess the agility attribute of an agile product line method?".*

This paper focuses on the second one and proposes an assessment model to determine the current state of agile development in combination with software product lines. In fact, assessing the status of the development is a crucial step for a successful combination of agile methods and software product lines. Thus, through this paper we propose an assessment model called AgiPL-AM that allows self-assessments within the "*domain* and *application* teams" in order to determine the current state of agile software development in the context of software product lines.

To develop our targeted assessment model we followed a research process of three phases. The first phase reviews the literature on maturity models that concern *Software Product Line Engineering*, *Agile Product Lines*, and *Agile Software Development*. The desired assessment model is built in the second phase. Finally, the third phase applies and evaluates the proposed model.

The obtained model (i.e. AgiPL-AM) is an agility assessment model for assessing agility of Agile Product Line approaches that comprises six categories (i.e. five categories are related to agile principles and one category is related to product line architecture) and five levels of maturity. To build the assessment model, we took an existing agile maturity model (SAMI model [14]) as a basis.

2   Background

This section consists of three parts. The first part introduces the combination of agile software development and software product lines. The second one presents existing assessment models that focus on software reuse strategies. The third part presents existing assessment models that focus on agile practices adoption.

2.1   Agile Software Product Lines

Research works such as [2–5] have demonstrated the difficulty of integrating agile methods with product line engineering due to the plan-driven and sequential nature of product line approaches versus the iterative and flexible nature of agile frameworks. However, they have highlighted that adding agility to product line engineering is not only possible but can also be highly beneficial [2].

Due to their actual benefits, agile methods could help product line teams to deal with the highlighted issue and thus being agile. According to [6], combining agile with Software Product Lines is not trivial, and thus, Agile Software Product Line Engineering has been identified as driven by an assumed improvement of customer collaboration and software development. It promises to deliver high-quality software at the required faster pace.

In practice, companies who intend to adopt an agile software product-line approach, assume that the development could benefit from both a working reuse strategy and an increased flexibility with the adopted agile practices. Note that this flexibility is necessary to react on customer needs and changing requirements during the development process [6, 7].

Generally, in most cases, Software Product Line approaches are already used and companies target to transform towards agile [7]. Therefore, companies need approaches that integrate the agility while preserving the software product lines. Many already proposed models and approaches ensure the agility integration within software product lines and consequently help teams and companies to achieve their aim of being agile.

In the literature, several concrete approaches and methods that combine agile with product line concepts are available. For example, Tian and Cooper [2] mention two possible approaches: one approach is to take an existing SPL process and introduce agility; the other approach starts with an agile process and tailors it for SPLs. They identify the way to end up with a combination of Agility and Software Product Line Engineering. However, they do not give any recommendations on how to reach this state. In addition, dos Santos and Lucena [8], introduce the ScrumPL approach, which supports iterative domain and application engineering based on Scrum.

The review of the relevant agile software product line approaches shows that most of these approaches present only benefits after a successful agility integration and give a combination model. However, some of these approaches do not give any recommendations on how to reach the presented state. In addition, some of the reviewed approaches require suitable tools and appropriate infrastructure as a precondition to the successful integration of agile. Moreover, some approaches impediment during early phases of the agile adoption that are related to project management, coordination, and communication [7].

2.2   Assessment Models for Software Reuse Strategies

Over the past years, different assessment models were proposed to assess software reuse. Hereafter, we present three of them. The CMMI-DEV model [9] provides a collection of best practices that support organizations to improve their processes. It focuses on activities for developing products to meet needs of customers and a well-known standard that defines methods to evaluate complete process models and organizations.

Based on CMMI, Jasmine and Vasantha [10] have defined the Reuse Capability Maturity Model (RCMM). RCMM model focuses on a well-planned and controlled reuse oriented software development. This model comprises maturity levels that denote an achieved level in the evolution to a mature reuse process.

The "VDA QMC Working Group" has proposed the Automotive SPICE model [11]. that is a process assessment model that contains a set of indicators to be considered when interpreting the intent of the Automotive SPICE process reference model. These indicators may also be used when implementing a process improvement program subsequent to an assessment.

2.3   Assessment Models for Agile Development

In practice, organizations are unable to fully adopt agile development practices immediately or over a short period since it requires a socio-technical transformation/migration process [12]. Accordingly, maturity models can help and guide organizations in providing the directions concerning the practices and the manner that they can be introduced and established in the organization.

Schweigert et al. [13] have identified several maturity models for agile development. They use a set of assessment criteria to assess each identified maturity model in term of their fitness of purpose, completeness, definition of agile levels, objectivity, correctness, and consistency. With these assessment criteria, they surveyed the related issues (e.g. *Whether the emphasis of the model is on assessing agile practices or not (i.e. Fitness of purpose)*). Following these criteria, they have concluded that the SAMI model (Sidky Agile Measurement Index) proposed by Sidky et al. [14] has the highest scores among the studied models. SAMI consists of two components. The first one is *an agile measurement index* and the second one is *a four-stage process*. Together, these two components guide and assist the agile adoption efforts of organizations.

SAMI is structured into four main parts: agile levels, agile principles, agile practices and concepts, and indicators. Driven from the values and principles of the "Agile Manifesto" [15], the model defines five agile levels:

- **Level 1:** is dedicated for the *Collaboration* which is one of the essential values and qualities of agile;
- **Level 2:** represents the objective of *"Developing software through an evolutionary approach"*;
- **Level 3:** represents the objective of *"Effectiveness and efficiency in developing high quality software"*;
- **Level 4:** is depicted for the objective of *"gaining the capability to respond to change through multiple levels of feedback"*;
- **Level 5:** represents the objective of *"Establishing a vibrant and all-encompassing environment to sustain agility"*.

In addition, the SAMI model has clustered the 12 agile principles into five categories that group the agile practices. These categories are: (1) Embracing change to deliver customer value; (2) Plan and deliver software frequently; (3) Human-centricity; (4) Technical excellence; (5) Customer collaboration. In total, SAMI incorporates 40 agile practices. Organization should start adopting agile practices on lower levels first, because the agile practices on a higher level are dependent on the practices introduced at the lower levels [14]. Moreover, Sidky et al. [14] have proposed a range of indicators that are used to assess certain characteristics of an organization or project, such as people, culture, and environment, in order to ascertain the readiness of the organization or project to adopt an agile practice [13]. The SAMI model contains about 300 different indicators for the 40 agile practices [17].

3 Research Approach

To reach the main target of this paper, we have inspired our research procedure from the work of Hevner et al. [18]. Since our primary objective is to propose an assessment artifact that could be used to assess the adoption level of agile development within Agile Software Product Lines, the followed research method involves mainly the three phases. The first phase is dedicated for the definition of the problem and the objectives of the assessment artifact. The second phase is devoted for the design and the development of the targeted assessment artifact. The third phase illustrates the applicability of the proposed model.

Figure 1 depicts a detailed view on the procedure that we followed in order to develop, apply, and evaluate the Agility Assessment Model (i.e. AgiPL-AM) proposed in this paper. The first phase starts by a review of literature on maturity models that concern Software Product Line Engineering, Agile Product Lines, and Agile Software Development. The second phase involves the construction of the proposed "agile assessment model". After defining the main objectives of the required assessment model, the AgiPL-AM was designed and developed in an iterative way. In the third phase, the model was applied and evaluated. At this stage, the model was reviewed and refined in order to optimize and finalize AgiPL-AM.

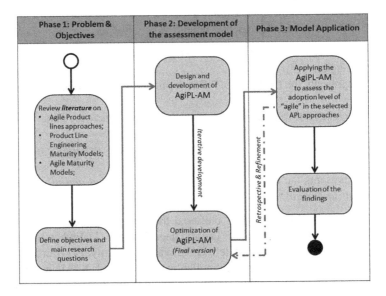

Fig. 1. Research procedure

4   Assessment Model for Agile Product Lines: AgiPL-AM

In order to attempt our target, we started by performing an extensive review of agile product line approaches, relevant case studies, and software process oriented-maturity models with emphasis on the agile software development approaches and on the agile product line approaches. It was identified that seven important areas need to be considered in an assessment for the combination of agile development and software product lines. According to Hohl et al. [22], these areas are the following:

1. *Product Line Architecture:* the objective of this area is to provide a suitable software architecture to enable the implementation of several software variants for different products with a high degree of software reuse;

2. *Domain Requirements Engineering:* behind this area, the purpose is to identify the reuse assets that should be developed in a software product line. This includes the identification of products and features that should be part of the product line and the definition of common and variable features;
3. *Agile Software Development:* the main target of this area is to react faster on customer needs and legal constraints to reduce the time-to-market for innovative feature upon a simultaneous increase of the quality of software;
4. *Continuous Execution:* the objective of this area is to continuously execute tasks that lead to a more stable, compliant, and better products;
5. *Continuous Model Improvement:* the purpose of this area is to continuously reflect on the assessment model and improve the interaction of assessment results and the suggested improvement for the software development process;
6. *Test Strategy:* the main purpose of this area is to provide an environment that allow the verification of the correct behavior and ensure the software quality for various software variants that are developed in a fast development pace within the software development;
7. *Communication:* the objective of the Communication Area is to verify the communication of all participating roles to avoid knowledge silos and to react on customer requirements faster.

Considering these areas, the review has led us to take the SAMI agile maturity model [14, 17] as a basis to develop our proposed model. Ozcan-Top and Demirörs [19] have confirmed that the SAMI model is comprehensive and well-organized structure, an argument confirmed also in [16]. By reviewing the agile practices offered by the SAMI model and evaluating their applicability, SAMI can be viewed as providing agile practices that the Agile Product Lines (APL) require at several levels. Therefore, we have adopted these agile practices as the basis for the targeted maturity model to address the "APL team level practices". In fact, we have adopted the 40 original SAMI agile practices. Then we have adapted and extended the SAMI model in accordance with the Agile Product Line principles and practices defined in the main sources of Agile Product Line Engineering such as [1, 20, 21].

4.1   Development of AgiPL-AM

In addition to the 38 original SAMI agile practices, we defined 49 Agile Product Line practices that are incorporated in the final version of the AgiPL-AM model. Precisely, both the SAMI agile practices and the APL practices went through a review and refinement by using the phase two of our research approach. These refinements and changes were applied with respect to the original agile practices of the SAMI model.

Considering the areas presented above, it was identified that the SAMI model covers mainly the area 3 (i.e. Agile Software Development) and partially the area 2, area 4, area 5, and area 6. In our proposed model we have defined a new cate-gory called "Category 6 – Product line Architecture". Moreover, in our proposed assessment model we have conserved the five agile levels of SAMI model. Here-after we presented the different added practices. Due to lack of space, we have presented the new defined agile practices for each category separately.

Category 1 – Embrace Change to Deliver Customer Value. Table 1 presents the practices of each level that belong "Category 1". We have held back 5 practices from SAMI model and defined 5 new practices, namely L2.C1.2, L2.C1.3, L2.C1.4, L3. C1.1, L3.C1.2, and L4.C1.3.

For example, the description of the practice "L1.C1.1 – Reflect and tune process" is the following:

Holding retrospectives at regular intervals of the development process. The objective of this practice is to overcome process challenges that have been faced thus far [1].

In addition, the practice "L2.C1.2 – Domain requirements" is an APL practice and the description of this practice is the following:

Domain requirements encompass requirements that are common to all applications of the software product line as well as variable requirements that enable the derivation of customized requirements for different applications [2].

Table 1. Practices of "Category 1" of AgiPL-AM model

Levels	Practices
Level 1	L1.C1.1 – Reflect and tune process [14]
Level 2	L2.C1.1 – Evolutionary requirements [14, 17]
	L2.C1.2 – Domain Requirements [24]
	L2.C1.3 – Smaller, more frequent release [23]
	L2.C1.4 – Requirements discovery [23]
Level 3	L3.C1.1 – Regular reflection and adaptation [13]
	L3.C1.2 – Customer feedback is accessed for new features and ideas [6]
Level 4	L4.C1.1 – Client driven iterations [14]
	L4.C1.2 – Continuous customer satisfaction feedback [14]
	L4.C1.3 – Lean requirements at scale [23]
Level 5	L5.C1.1 – Low process ceremony [14]

Category 2 – Plan and Deliver Software Frequently. Table 2 presents the practices of the "Category 2". In this category, 7 agile practices were held back from SAMI model and 10 APL practices were adopted. The adopted practices are L2.C2.2, L2. C2.3, L2.C2.4, L2.C2.5, L2.C2.6, L3.C2.3, L3.C2.4, L3.C2.5, L4.C2.3, and L5.C2.2.

Category 3 – Human Centricity. Table 3 presents category 3. We have adopted 5 agile practices from SAMI model and we have defined 3 new APL practices, namely, L2.C3.1, L4.C3.2, and L5.C3.2.

Category 4 – Technical Excellence. This section is dedicated to the different practices of the "Category 4" introduced in the Table 4. In fact, the Category 4 of the AgiPL-AM has 24 practices among these practices 14 practices were held back from SAMI model. Moreover, 10 new APL practices have been defined, namely, L1.C4.1, L1.C4.5, L1. C4.6, L2.C4.4, L2.C4.5, L3.C4.1, L3.C4.3, L3.C4.4, L4.C4.3, and L4.C4.4.

Table 2. Practices of "Category 2" of AgiPL-AM model

Levels	Practices
Level 1	L1.C2.1 – Collaborative planning [14]
Level 2	L2.C2.1 – Continuous delivery [14, 17]
	L2.C2.2 – Two-tier planning and tracking (i.e. Domain Engineering tier & Application Engineering tier) [24]
	L2.C2.3 – Two-level planning and tracking [23]
	L2.C2.4 – Agile Estimating and Velocity [23]
	L2.C2.5 – Release planning [23]
	L2.C2.6 – Work product list [6]
Level 3	L3.C2.1 – Risk driven Iterations [14]
	L3.C2.2 – Plan features not tasks [14]
	L3.C2.3 – Mastering the iteration [23]
	L3.C2.4 – DoD after each software release [23]
	L3.C2.5 – Backlogs and Kanban Systems [23]
Level 4	L4.C2.1 – Smaller and more frequent releases [14]
	L4.C2.2 – Adaptive planning [14]
	L4.C2.3 – Measuring business performance (Project measure; Quality measure; Risk measure; Delivery record) [6, 23]
Level 5	L5.C2.1 – Agile project estimation [14]
	L5.C2.2 – Audit activities [6]

Table 3. Practices of "Category 3" of AgiPL-AM model

Levels	Practices
Level 1	L1.C3.1 – Empowered and motivated teams [14]
	L1.C3.2 – Collaborative Teams [14]
Level 2	L2.C3.1 – The Define/Build/Test teams of each tier: Domain Engineering tier & Application Engineering tier [23]
Level 3	L3.C3.1 – Self-organizing teams [14]
	L3.C3.2 – Frequent face-to-face communication [14]
Level 4	L4.C3.1 – Managing highly distributed teams [23]
Level 5	L5.C3.1 – Ideal agile physical setup [14]
	L5.C3.2 – Changing the organizations [16]

Category 5 – Customer Collaboration. This category has 15 agile practices. According to the proposed assessment model, 8 APL practices were defined and 7 practices were adopted from SAMI model. Table 5 presents the practices of the "Category 5" of AgiPL-AM. Precisely, L1.C5.2, L1.C5.3, L1.C5.4, L3.C5.1, L3.C5.2, L4.C5.3, L4.C5.4, L4.C5.5, and L5.C5.2.

Table 4. Practices of "Category 4" of AgiPL-AM model

Levels	Practices
Level 1	L1.C4.1 – Product Backlog [16, 23]
	L1.C4.2 – Coding standards [16]
	L1.C4.3 – Knowledge sharing [14]
	L1.C4.4 – Task volunteering [14]
	L1.C4.5 – Continuous and automated tasks [6]
	L1.C4.6 – Acceptance testing [16]
Level 2	L2.C4.1 – Software configuration management [14]
	L2.C4.2 – Tracking iteration progress [14]
	L2.C4.3 – No big design up front [14]
	L2.C4.4 – Automated testing [6]
	L2.C4.5 – Bidirectional traceability record [6]
Level 3	L3.C4.1 – Continuous deployment [6]
	L3.C4.2 – Continuous integrating [14]
	L3.C4.3 – Scalable and Continuous tests [6]
	L3.C4.4 – Continuous compliance [6]
	L3.C4.5 – Continuous improvement (refactoring) [14]
	L3.C4.6 – 30% of "level 2" and "level 3" people [14]
	L3.C4.7 – Unit tests [14]
Level 4	L4.C4.1 – Daily progress tracking meetings [14]
	L4.C4.2 – User stories [14, 23]
	L4.C4.3 – Adaptive test strategy [6]
	L4.C4.4 – Improvement opportunity and plan [6]
Level 5	L5.C4.1 – Test driven development [1]
	L5.C4.2 – no or minimal number of Cockburn Level "1B" or "−1" [14]

Category 6 – Product-Line Architecture. This category is a new category added to the 5 five categories of SAMI model. In this category, the product line principles related to Agile Product Lines architecture are gathered. Here, 13 APL practices were defined. These new practices of the "Category 6" of AgiPL-AM model are presented in Table 6.

4.2   The AgiPL-AM

Based on the iteration development and the retrospective of followed approach, several adjustments were done in order to optimize the AgiPL-AM model, which involves both agile practices adopted from the SAMI model and APL practices that were defined to address the main objective. The main changes that are performed on the agile practices adopted from the SAMI model are the following:

- The agile practices "Paired programming" and "Agile documentation" were removed as their purposes are covered by "L2.C3.1 – Define/Build/Test teams of

Table 5. Practices of "Category 5" of AgiPL-AM model

Levels	Practices
Level 1	L1.C5.1 – Customer commitment to work with development team [6, 14]
	L1.C5.2 – Destructed "Knowledge silos" [6]
	L1.C5.3 – Fast feedback channels [6]
	L1.C5.4 – Common understanding for the SPL [6]
Level 2	L2.C5.1 – Customer contract reflective of evolutionary development [14]
Level 3	L3.C5.1 – Direct communication channels [6]
	L3.C5.2 – Vertical commitment [6, 24]
Level 4	L4.C5.1 – "CRACK" Customer immediately accessible [14]
	L4.C5.2 – Customer contact revolve around commitment of collaboration [14]
	L4.C5.3 – DevOps (Integrated Development and Operations) [16]
	L4.C5.4 – Vision, features [4]
	L4.C5.5 – Impact on customers and operations [16, 23]
Level 5	L5.C5.1 – Frequent Face-to-face interaction between develops and users [14]
	L5.C5.2 – Concurrent testing [16]

Table 6. Practices of "Category 6" of AgiPL-AM model

Levels	Practices
Level 1	L1.C6.1 – Software Product Line architecture [6]
	L1.C6.2 – Reuse strategy [24]
	L1.C6.3 – Modular software architecture [6]
Level 2	L2.C6.1 – Distributed development [6, 23]
	L2.C6.2 – Modularity of software components [6]
	L2.C6.3 – Reusable software units [6]
Level 3	L3.C6.1 – SPL architecture is open to changes and refactoring is possible [6]
	L3.C6.2 – Collaboration with supplier is improved [6]
Level 4	L4.C6.1 – Fast changes in requirements [6, 24]
	L4.C6.2 – Adequate scoping process [24]
	L4.C6.3 – Intentional architecture [23]
Level 5	L5.C6.1 – Standardized interfaces for software units [6]
	L5.C6.2 – Continuously evaluation of the architecture [6]

each tier: Domain Engineering tier & Application Engineering tier" and "L2.C1.2 – Domain Requirements";

- The agile practices "Backlog" was renamed into "Product Backlog" in order to match more the actual agile terminology and thus provide a better representation;
- The practice "Product Backlog" was moved to the "level 1 – Collaborative" since it is considered to provide the basis for other practices at higher maturity levels.

When the agile/APL practices were defined and refined, a set of governing rules were applied in order to populate these practices in the appropriate maturity level and principle. These rules are the followings:

- The *first rule* states that each practice has to contribute to the achievement of the maturity level objective in which it is positioned. For example, the practice "L1. C3.2 – Collaborative Teams" should addresses directly the "collaboration" objective of maturity Level 1 (i.e. Collaborative);
- The *second rule* is followed to ensure the relevancy of the practice with respect to the agile principle that it is associated. The practice L1.C3.2 is related to the principle for "Human-centricity";
- The *third rule* states that the relation between the practices in such a way that practices positioned at higher levels depend on the achievements of the practices at lower levels. For example, the APL practice of "L2.C2.2 – Two-tier planning and tracking (i.e. Domain Engineering tier & Application Engineering tier)" at level 2 depends on achieving some of "Level 1" practices, such as "L1.C3.2 – Collaborative Teams" and "L1.C2.1 – Collaborative planning".

The final version of the AgiPL-AM model was optimized and its adopted practices are presented above in Sect. 4.2. AgiPL-AM is considered as a descriptive model (i.e. as opposed to prescriptive) since it describes only the essential practices that an organization that adopt an APL approach should possess at a particular level of maturity.

In our proposed model, on the one hand, the agile practices adopted from SAMI model are assessed by using the original indicators of SAMI model. On the other hand, the APL practices are assessed by using AgiPL-AM indicators (i.e. as set of defined indicators related to the APL practices defined as part of AgiPL-AM). These indicators are not listed in this paper due to the lack of space. For example, in order to assess the practice "L3.C2.3 – Mastering the iteration", the following indicator is used: *"L3.C2.3. ind – the development team has effective iterations consisting of sprint planning, tracking, execution, and retrospectives"*.

Furthermore, based on the practices of AgiPL-AM, all the indicators are rated by using an achievement scale. From the ISO/IEC 15504 assessment standard [27], the rating scheme was adopted. This rating scheme is the following:

i. (N) – **"Not achieved (0%–35%)"** represents little or no evidence of achievement of the practice;
ii. (P) – **"Partially achieved (35%–65%)"** denotes some evidence of an approach to, and some achievement of the practice. Some aspects of achievement may be unpredictable;
iii. (L) – **"Largely achieved (65%–85%)"** indicates that there is evidence of a systematic approach to, and significant achievement of the practice; despite some weaknesses;
iv. (F) – **"Fully achieved (85%–100%)"** indicates strong evidence of a complete and systematic approach to, and full achievement of the practice without any significant weaknesses.

The assessment process requires going through all practices and corresponding indicators to assess the entire set of practices in AgiPL-AM. In order to provide confirmation regarding the results of the assessment, an assessment report should compiled to present the results to relevant parties.

5   Application of AgiPL-AM

In this section, we apply the AgiPL-AM model to assess the adoption level of agile development within an Agile Software Product Line approach, namely, the ScrumPL approach [8].

According to Santos and Lucena [8], the ScrumPL process is intended to develop agile software product lines (APLs) by combining engineering activities from Software Product Line Engineering with the Scrum method. ScrumPL is composed on the one hand, by the Scrum lifecycle phases, namely, Planning, Staging, Development, and Release. On the other hand, by the Software Product Line Engineering (SPLE) stages, that is, Domain Engineering and Application Engineering. The Scrum phases and the SPLE sub-processes are combined to form ScrumPL.

By repeating the rules applied in developing the proposed model, AgiPL-AM has been developed in such a way that each practice contributes to the founda-tion required for the practices that are at higher maturity levels. For example, the agile practice of level 2 "L2.C2.5 – Release planning" provides necessary basis for the practice of level 4, which is "L4.C2.2 – Adaptive planning". Thus, focus-ing the attention on 'Level 3' practices without satisfying the 'Level 2' ones will be ineffective. Therefore, it is expected during the assessment process to have more practices satisfied at lower levels than at higher levels.

Figure 2 summarizes the results of assessing the approach ScrumPL by applying our proposed model AgiPL-AM. It is clear that the level of achievement tends to decrease towards higher maturity levels. However, the practices that are "Not Achieved" are spread over all levels. ScrumPL achieves only "6.9%" of the practices. "28.7%" of the practices are not achieved at all. Moreover, 33.4% (i.e. 29 practices) of the practices are largely achieved whereas, 31% of the practices are partially achieved.

Level 1 represents the collaborative level and has 17 practices. Among these practices one practice is 'not achieved', six practices are 'partially achieved', and three practices are APL practices. Thus, just seven practices are 'largely achieved' and 'Fully achieved'.

Accordingly, the collaboration issue is not strongly ensured by ScrumPL approach. At level 3, which represents the effectiveness level, only five practices (i.e. 5 out of 20) are 'largely achieved' the other practices either 'partially achieved' or 'not achieved' at all. This means that the ScrumPL approach lacks practices that ensure its effectiveness.

By using the AgiPL-AM approach, the strengths and the weakness of the ScrumPL method were identified. In fact, the model has highlighted all the agile and APL practices that are not covered by ScrumPL. Thus, the results of the assessment could be used to improve ScrumPL or even to define a new APL approach. For example, at "Level 3" three practices are not achieved. These are the "L3.C1.2 – Customer feed-back is accessed for new features and ideas", "L3.C3.2 – Frequent face-to-face

Level 1 Collaborative	L1.C1.1 (L)	L1.C2.1 (P)	L1.C3.1 (P)	L1.C3.2 (L)	L1.C4.1 (F)	L1.C4.2 (L)	L1.C4.3 (L)	L1.C4.4 (N)	L1.C4.5 (P)	L1.C4.6 (L)	L1.C5.1 (P)	L1.C5.2 (P)	L1.C5.3 (P)	L1.C5.4 (L)	L1.C6.1 (F)	L1.C6.2 (L)	L1.C6.3 (L)			
Level 2 Evolutionary	L2.C1.1 (P)	L2.C1.2 (F)	L2.C1.3 (L)	L2.C1.4 (P)	L2.C2.1 (L)	L2.C2.2 (F)	L2.C2.3 (F)	L2.C2.4 (N)	L2.C2.5 (L)	L2.C2.6 (L)	L2.C3.1 (P)	L2.C4.1 (L)	L2.C4.2 (P)	L2.C4.3 (N)	L2.C4.4 (N)	L2.C4.5 (P)	L2.C5.1 (P)	L2.C6.1 (N)	L2.C6.2 (L)	L2.C6.3 (L)
Level 3 Effective	L3.C1.1 (N)	L3.C1.2 (N)	L3.C2.1 (N)	L3.C2.2 (P)	L3.C2.3 (L)	L3.C2.4 (P)	L3.C2.5 (P)	L3.C3.1 (P)	L3.C3.2 (N)	L3.C4.1 (P)	L3.C4.2 (L)	L3.C4.3 (L)	L3.C4.4 (L)	L3.C4.5 (N)	L3.C4.6 (P)	L3.C4.7 (L)	L3.C5.1 (N)	L3.C5.2 (N)	L3.C6.1 (P)	L3.C6.2 (N)
Level 4 Adaptive	L4.C1.1 (P)	L4.C1.2 (N)	L4.C1.3 (N)	L4.C2.1 (L)	L4.C2.2 (P)	L4.C2.3 (N)	L4.C3.1 (N)	L4.C4.1 (F)	L4.C4.2 (L)	L4.C4.3 (L)	L4.C4.4 (N)	L4.C5.1 (N)	L4.C5.2 (N)	L4.C5.3 (N)	L4.C5.4 (N)	L4.C5.5 (P)	L4.C6.1 (P)	L4.C6.2 (L)	L4.C6.3 (L)	
Level 5 Encompassing	L5.C1.1 (L)	L5.C2.1 (P)	L5.C2.2 (N)	L5.C3.1 (L)	L5.C3.2 (P)	L5.C4.1 (L)	L5.C4.2 (P)	L5.C5.1 (P)	L5.C5.2 (L)	L5.C6.1 (N)	L5.C6.2 (N)									

Achievement scale	Color	# Achieved Practices	%
Fully Achieved (F)		6	6.9 %
Largely Achieved (L)		29	33.4 %
Partially Achieved (P)		27	31 %
Not Achieved (N)		25	28.7 %

Fig. 2. Results of the assessment of ScrumPL using AgiPL-AM model

communication", and "L3.C5.1 – Direct communication channels". At this level, a special situation is manifested as a communication barrier between the user representatives and the development team members, which prevented them to establish a close integration of development and operations. These subjects of weaknesses in the lower maturity levels were indicated as the most prominent points on which any company should direct its attention when adopting ScrumPL.

6 Conclusion

The combination of agile software development and software product lines is a promising approach. The current status on the agile adoption within agile soft-ware product line approaches is hard to define [6], thus, it was identified the need for a specific assessment model for assessing the situation of agile adoption with-in agile product line approaches.

The research objective of this paper is to design an assessment model that can be used as a guideline by organizations to adopt agile product line methodologies and assess the success level of agile practices adoption. Through the review of the literature it was identified that known of the studied assessment models focus simultaneity on agile and APL practices in detail within APL approaches. Comparing to these approaches, AgiPL is considered as a structured approach that increases the chances of success in agile and APL practices within agile software product lines. In addition, AgiPL serves as an evolutionary path that increases organization's agile maturity. Also, the proposed model prioritizes the improvement actions in adopting agile and APL practices. The illustrated example in this paper shows the applicability of the assessment model.

The proposed work is an ongoing work. For future work, we plan to further evaluate the AgiPL-AM model in order to improve AgiPL-AM model. As next step, we will validate AgiPL-AM empirically and we will involve a number of members of companies in the evaluation of the applicability of AgiPL-AM, in assessing the level of agility of their companies, and in evaluating the overall findings of the assessment model.

References

1. da Silva, I.F., Neto, P., O'Leary, P., de Almeida, E., de Lemos Meira, S.R.: Agile software product lines: a systematic mapping study. Soft. Prac. Exp. **41**(8), 899–920 (2011)
2. Tian, K., Cooper, K.: Agile and software product line methods: are they so different? In: 1st international Workshop on Agile Software Product Line Engineering, pp. 1–8 (2006)
3. Carbon, R., Lindvall, M., Muthig, D., Costa, P.: Integrating product line engineering and agile methods: flexible design up-front vs. incremental design. In: 1st International Workshop on Agile Product Line Engineering (2006)
4. Boehm, B.W.: Get ready for agile methods, with care. Computer **35**(1), 64–69 (2002)
5. Navarrete, F., Botella, P., Franch, X.: How agile COTS selection methods are (and can be). In: Proceedings of the 31st EUROMICRO Conference on Software Engineering and Advanced Applications, pp. 160–167 (2005)

6. Hohl, P., Münch, J., Schneider, K., Stupperich, M.: Real-life challenges on agile software product lines in automotive. In: Felderer, M., Méndez Fernández, D., Turhan, B., Kalinowski, M., Sarro, F., Winkler, D. (eds.) PROFES 2017. LNCS, vol. 10611, pp. 28–36. Springer, Cham (2017). https://doi.org/10.1007/978-3-319-69926-4_3

7. Klünder, J., Hohl, P., Schneider, K.: Becoming agile while preserving software product lines: an agile transformation model for large companies. In: ICSSP 2018, pp. 1–10 (2018)

8. dos Santos Jr., A. F., Lucena Jr, V.F.: SCRUMPL - Software Product Line Engineering with Scrum. In: Proceedings of ENASE 2010, pp. 239-244 (2010)

9. CMMI Product Team: CMMI for development, Version 1.3: improving processes for developing better products and services. Technical report (2010)

10. Jasmine, K.S., Vasantha, R.: A new capability maturity model for reuse based software development process. Int. J. Eng. Technol. 2(1), 112–116 (2010)

11. VDA QMC Working Group 13/Automotive SIG. Automotive spice process assessment/reference model (2017)

12. Qumer, A., Henderson-Sellers, B.: A framework to support the evaluation, adoption and improvement of agile methods in practice. J. Syst. Soft. 81(11), 1899–1919 (2008)

13. Schweigert, T., Vohwinkel, D., Korsaa, M., Nevalainen, R., Biro, M.: Agile maturity model: a synopsis as a first step to synthesis. In: McCaffery, F., O'Connor, R.V., Messnarz, R. (eds.) EuroSPI 2013. CCIS, vol. 364, pp. 214–227. Springer, Heidelberg (2013). https://doi.org/10.1007/978-3-642-39179-8_19

14. Sidky, A., Arthur, J., Bohner, S.: A disciplined approach to adopting agile practices: the agile adoption framework. Inno. Syst. Soft. Eng. 3(3), 203–216 (2007)

15. ManifestoAgile: Manifesto for Agile Software Development (2001)

16. Turetken, O., Stojanov, I., Trienekens, J.J.M.: Assessing the adoption level of scaled agile development: a maturity model for Scaled Agile Framework. JSEP 29(6), e1796 (2017)

17. Sidky, A., Arthur, J.: Agile adoption process framework - indicators document (2006)

18. Hevner, A.R., March, S., Park, J., Ram, S.: Design science in information systems research. MIS Q. 28(1), 75–105 (2004)

19. Ozcan-Top, O., Demirörs, O.: Assessment of agile maturity models: a multiple case study. In: Woronowicz, T., Rout, T., O'Connor, R.V., Dorling, A. (eds.) SPICE 2013. CCIS, vol. 349, pp. 130–141. Springer, Heidelberg (2013). https://doi.org/10.1007/978-3-642-38833-0_12

20. Díaz, J., Pérez, J., Alarcón, P.P., Garbajosa, J.: Agile product line engineering—a systematic literature review. Soft. Pract. Exp. 41(8), 921–941 (2011)

21. Farahani, F.F., Ramsin, R.: Methodologies for agile product line engineering: a survey and evaluation. In: SoMeT_14, pp. 545–564. IOS Press BV, Amsterdam (2014)

22. Hohl, P., Stupperich, M., Münch, J., Schneider, K.: An assessment model to foster the adoption of agile software product lines in the automotive domain. In: ICE/ITMC, pp. 1–9 (2018)

23. Leffingwell, D.: Agile Software Requirements: Lean Requirements Practices for Teams, Programs, and the Enterprise. Addison-Wesley Professional, Boston (2011)

24. Apel, S., Batory, D., Kästner, C., Saake, G.: Feature-oriented Software Product Lines: Concepts and Implementation. Springer, Berlin (2013). https://doi.org/10.1007/978-3-642-37521-7

Methods for Architectures and Models

Developing a Structured Approach to Converging Business Process Management and Customer Experience Management Initiatives

Dino Pavlić(✉) and Maja Ćukušić

Faculty of Economics, Business and Tourism, University of Split, Split, Croatia
{dpavlic,mcukusic}@efst.hr

Abstract. Both in theory and practice, a lack of a formulated structure to facilitate integrated modeling and analysis of internal business processes and customer experiences external to the organization has been identified by many authors. Tackling this issue, a convergent approach aligning Business Process Management (BPM) and Customer eXperience Management (CXM) initiatives, is proposed in the paper, along with a full set of top-down BPM-CXM models varying in the level of detail. To validate the proposed models, a focus group study with experts in BPM and CXM domains was organized, and the findings are reported and further operationalized using a tool widely used in the EMEA region.

Keywords: Focus group · BPM · CXM · Customer journey

1 Introduction

In practice, in the context of Business Process Management (BPM) initiatives, customer orientation often remains a mantra, while process optimization efforts are observed through "inside-out" perspective only, disregarding the customers' perspective. The innovative "outside-in" approach to BPM (by actively involving the customer as in [1]) poses a significant challenge for BPM researchers and experts who are usually focused on process modeling and analysis, as well as for the existing BPM tools and methodologies [2]. Recent research studies stress out the importance of involving customers in internal BP analysis and optimization, as well as in business transformation programs [3–10]. However, there are still a number of problems that lead to BPM and Customer eXperience Management (CXM) initiatives not being aligned in practice, for example [11]: BPM is too oriented on cost reduction and efficiency improvements while ignoring customer interactions; Customer Journey Mapping (CJM) as a part of CXM initiatives is too oriented on customer interactions while ignoring the internal processes of the organization; connections between customer journeys and business processes are not well identified; customer journey maps are not standardized; functional silos are not cooperating well; and the key performance indicators (KPIs) between departments are misaligned. One of the reasons for this

© IFIP International Federation for Information Processing 2019
Published by Springer Nature Switzerland AG 2019
J. Gordijn et al. (Eds.): PoEM 2019, LNBIP 369, pp. 151–166, 2019.
https://doi.org/10.1007/978-3-030-35151-9_10

misalignment is a lack of a model or a structure for integrated modeling and analyzing of internal business processes and customer experiences external to the organization [12–15], a topic that this paper addresses directly. The concept of BPM-CXM convergence has been presented earlier (in [16]) while this paper develops it further and presents the results of its evaluation by experts.

The second section of the paper describes the approach to designing BPM-CXM convergence, taking into account the "outside-in" approach to BPM [1] and building around a well-established BPM lifecycle [17]. It also outlines the feedback from a focus group study that was conducted with the view to demonstrate the feasibility of the concept with experts from the EMEA region. The third section of the paper provides an operationalized top-down view of the convergent approach following the same structure, manifested in several models developed using a tool widely popular in the region. The fourth section of the paper provides plans for further work and concludes the paper.

2   Designing BPM-CXM Convergence

2.1   State-of-Art in BPM-CXM Convergence

The convergence of BPM-CXM presents a new concept addressed by several authors and papers that point out the need for research in this field, in particular [8, 11, 13, 15, 18]. The general idea is that the identification, discovery, analysis, redesign, and control of processes should be performed in convergence with identification, discovery, analysis, redesign, and control of customer experience, and not independently [19]. On the one hand, Gloppen et al. [8] promote the strategic use of customer journeys for innovation and business transformation in particular, while on the other, Kumar et al. [20] emphasize BPM as a key factor in achieving customer satisfaction. To overcome this and change the "traditional" end-to-end approach to business transformation, Richardson (in [1]) proposes using a specific type of targeted modeling of customer touchpoints with the organization, and their analysis and optimization in the context of internal organization. This particular standpoint is favored by the authors of the paper, as demonstrated further in the proposed operationalized, prototyped solution in Sect. 3. By incorporating elements of CXM in the proposed solution, customer journey mapping, in particular, a new "outside-in" modern approach to BPM is implemented.

Apart from identifying the need for a structured approach for BPM-CXM convergence in the available literature, related issues (listed as in, e.g. [11]) were observed by authors of the paper in several business transformation projects in large companies. Consequently, the operationalization and evaluation of BPM-CXM convergence model constitute the main contribution of this research study.

2.2   BPM-CXM Convergence Concept

To formulate and structure the BPM-CXM convergence, design science approach is used [21] as a research framework. Standard phases were followed (identification of the problem and motivation, definition of the objectives of a solution, design and development, demonstration, evaluation, and communication) during several workshop events during 2018 when there were multiple iterations of literature analysis, objectives definition, and model formulation with BPM experts resulting in a high-level concept (presented in [16]) structured around BPM lifecycle and related descriptions and top-down models. BPM-CXM convergence concept (Fig. 1) was the main starting point for discussions as it is structured in a way that would facilitate integrated analysis of customer experience and internal business processes. In general, customer experience is designed and analyzed by using customer journey mapping (as suggested by [22]), which is used as an input for BPM initiatives – from strategic identification of processes for initiating BPM initiatives, to analysis and optimization of processes [19, 23–27]. BPM-CXM convergence approach should reflect the way customer experience can be perceived and analyzed through the whole BPM lifecycle [28]. That is why the proposed concept lays precisely on those foundations – it is based on standard BPM lifecycle [17], and is developed further and operationalized (as in Sect. 3). It reflects the focus on the analysis of touchpoints between the internal organization and the customer external to the organization combining best practices from BPM and CXM.

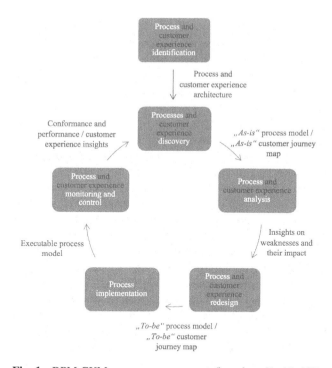

Fig. 1. BPM-CXM convergence concept (based on [1, 17, 28])

2.3   Evaluation of BPM-CXM Convergence Concept with Experts

A focus group workshop was organized in March 2019 with the purpose to collect target audience (experts') opinions and attitudes about the proposed convergence concept, related issues and model prototypes. As such, it constitutes an integral part of the design process. Since the required knowledge and experience is very specific, the criteria for expert selection were: at least 10 years of work experience in BPM or CXM projects combined, at least two years of experience in each discipline (BPM and CXM projects), regional experience (conducted BPM or CXM projects in at least three countries), and experience in at least three different industries.

Within the network, there were six experts that fit the profile. As all the experts have worked on projects in the EMEA region (primarily in Croatia, Serbia, Bosnia and Herzegovina, and Montenegro), the results of the study reflect their understanding and experience that cannot be easily generalized to other regions. However, in terms of the industries, they have worked in various industries, including finance, gas and oil, local government, transport, logistics, trade, telecommunications, and IT. Basic sociode-mographic data about the experts are presented in Table 1.

Table 1. General characteristics of the six experts that participated in the focus group

	Gender	Education	Role	Work experience
Expert 1	Female	MBA	Head of project management department	20 years
Expert 2	Male	MCS	BPM consultant	10 years
Expert 3	Male	MCS	Management consultant	13 years
Expert 4	Female	MCS	Head of organization department	12 years
Expert 5	Male	MCS	Management consultant	11 years
Expert 6	Female	MBA	Management consultant	22 years

Although the structure of the session was preset, the format was kept flexible, to allow the conversation to develop naturally and to elicit views and opinions. Over the course of three hours, the participants were asked 40 questions split into three parts (Expert background, Current state of BPM & CXM initiatives, and BPM-CXM convergence approach discussion & design). The participants were first presented with the focus group purpose and protocol and then were given an overview of the BPM-CXM convergence approach, which included the high-level introduction to the proposed method, as well as all of the operational details (e.g. phases, models, objects, attributes etc.). They were given a short introduction for each question (question examples: Would you adjust the proposed mathematical formula? Would you adjust, edit, or remove any of the elements of the proposed customer journey map?) and enough time to discuss it with other participants and note their individual and consolidated answers. After the focus group, written transcripts by the moderator as well as the participant's notes were analyzed and synthesized in a presentable form.

Within the following paragraphs, consolidated views of the group are presented following the same structure used during the session. Generally, in terms of the problem and motivation of the study, there was a strong consensus, and in terms of the suggestions, all experts contributed considerably and helped to formulate the top-down model prototypes that are presented in Sect. 3. The choice to present the prototypes in a separate section was made due to two different reasons: to differentiate between the elicited feedback from the experts presented in Sect. 2 and additional (technical) commentary provided by the authors of the paper that accompanies the prototypes in Sect. 3; and to provide an operational view on the concept in its entirety. However, the two sections are strongly interrelated with references where appropriate.

Current State of BPM and CXM Initiatives

BPM Initiatives as Enablers of Amazing CX. All experts agree that at the moment, BPM initiatives do not put enough focus on CX. They are missing information about the actual CX and CX KPIs. There is no proper way of getting the real data about the CX and pairing them with the internal process models. BPM experts are too focused on internal business processes, while communication with CX departments and customers is something that is missing within BPM initiatives. Internal processes are only considered in the context of CXM if a customer is complaining – this is too late since the negative experience already occurred. Overall, there is a consensus that BPM initiatives are not set up as enablers of an amazing CX.

Focus of BPM Initiatives on CX. There is agreement that BPM initiatives are only sometimes focused on achieving customer's satisfaction. There is a lack of involvement of the CX departments and customers within BPM initiatives. At this point, BPM initiatives are focused on the internal processes and achieving process excellence without actually considering the external/customer perspective. From a theoretical perspective, BPM initiatives are almost always focused on customer satisfaction; however – in real life, this focus often does not exist.

Customer Focus within Business/IT Transformations. Similarly, experts report that as a part of business/IT transformations, customer focus often remains just a phrase since no CX departments or customers are involved. Customer focus often is the main driver for business/IT transformations however when it comes actually to perform the transformation, the real link between "classic" BPM, CXM, process execution, and performance management is missing. Customers are often a trigger to start an internal process or IT transformation; however, they are not given enough attention during the transformation process itself.

Alignment of BPM and CXM Initiatives. Experts also agree that BPM and CXM initiatives are not aligned and well-coordinated, and this should be improved. It is mainly due to management vision not being defined in a way to support and encourage the alignment. One of the challenges is in getting the real data from the process execution as well as real data about the customer experience and performing consolidated analysis with internal process data.

Alignment of Goals and KPIs of BPM and CXM Departments. Furthermore, BPM and CXM departments are considered as not aligned by experts. BPM and CXM departments usually have a completely different strategy, goals, and KPIs.

Communication Between BPM and CXM Departments. Another issue regularly observed by the experts is that BPM and CXM departments do not communicate regularly, and they see this would need large improvement. Quality of communication between BPM and CXM departments should be improved as well.

BPM-CXM Convergence Approach Discussion and Design

Structure of BPM and CXM Lifecycle. Experts find that the proposed BPM-CXM concept (presented Fig. 1) is well structured to support the BPM and CXM convergence considering that CX is introduced as a part of BPM lifecycle.

CX Landscape Positioning Within the Virtual Organization Model. As a part of the "virtual organization" (a term used to denote entry-level models in BP repositories), business process landscape and CX landscape provide a clear entry point to the more detailed models (top-down approach). It was agreed that Customer experience should be placed within a new, separate quadrant of a virtual organization (as further operationalized in entry-level model prototype in Sect. 3).

Scoring the Overall Customer Experience of Customer Journey. Experts suggest that the overall customer experience of a customer journey should be calculated as an average of overall customer experiences on each touchpoint, which is a part of the individual journey. They propose to build a script for automatic calculation within a BPM tool.

Elements, Attributes, and Color Coding of a Customer Journey Landscape. Attribute naming and color-coding of a customer journey landscape model (presented in Sect. 3) were evaluated as clear and appropriate. Elements and attributes of customer journey landscape were also assessed as well structured. It was proposed and agreed that the overall customer experience of a customer journey landscape should be calculated as an average of overall customer experiences on each customer journey, which is a part of the customer journey landscape.

Elements, Attributes, and Color Coding of a Customer Journey Map. Attribute naming and color-coding of a customer journey map (model presented in Sect. 3) were also evaluated as clear and appropriate. Elements and attributes of a customer journey map were assessed as well-structured. As an addition to the proposed elements of the customer journey maps, input/output data/cluster were suggested to be added. Within customer journey maps, it was suggested that color indication of the overall experience should be visible on individual touchpoints, as well as customer journey steps. Touchpoints are the "real" connection between the internal organization and the customer external to the organization, and therefore are more relevant for scoring representation.

Customer Journey Landscape and Customer Journey Map Ownership. The experts suggested that customer journey owners and business process owners should be separated, like front-end and back–end in software development, however, that they should communicate regularly to make sure their goals are aligned. Also, there could be separate ownership roles for customer journeys and customer journey landscapes. Considering that the customer journey owner should enforce the will of the customer within the internal business processes, customer journey owner and business process owner should not be the same person and should align and communicate regularly.

Elements, Attributes, and Color Coding of a Customer Touchpoint Allocation Diagram. Elements and attributes of customer touchpoint allocation diagrams were assessed as well-structured. Attribute naming and color-coding of a customer touch-point allocation diagram are also considered clear and appropriate. Out of 2 proposed options, option 2 of the proposed touchpoint allocation diagram was selected as preferred one by experts and is presented in Sect. 3. It was agreed that customer experience of the individual touchpoint should be calculated by considering the customer feeling and adding a weighting factor/ponder (importance to the customer).

Setting Up an Indication of Customer Experience Related to Certain Internal Business Processes. Overall customer experience linked to an internal business process was agreed to be calculated as an average of customer experience of each touchpoint that is a part of the individual internal business process. Also, the script for automatic calculation would be then necessary to be developed and implemented within a BPM tool in order to represent the impact that certain internal business processes have on positive or negative customer experience. The script could be triggered on an hourly basis.

Establishing a Link Between the BPM and CXM Initiatives by Indicating the Customer Experience Levels on Value Added Chain Diagrams. Proposed value-added chain diagram which includes customer experience layers and indication (as in Sect. 3), experts agree, would bring various benefits in terms of BPM-CXM alignment compared to the standard value-added chain diagram. By using the proposed method, they agree that there would be a clear link established between the BPM & CXM initiatives, BPM initiatives would be more focused on the customer, and internal resources would be spent more optimally. Also, by using the proposed method and formula within the value-added chain diagrams indicating the associated customer experience, focus on the experience while analyzing the internal business process would be achieved. An internal business process model, value-added chain, which includes the information and indication on the status of customer experience, is found to be the most beneficial part of the proposed BPM-CXM approach.

Benefits of the Proposed BPM-CXM Convergence Approach. Here, experts confirmed and found multiple benefits of including customer touchpoints within both high level and detailed internal business process models. They believe that the proposed methodology ensures better process optimization as it would combine both internal and external views on the process. Furthermore, it would ensure better alignment between the classical BPM and CXM approaches. BPM-CXM convergence would ultimately lead to focusing BPM initiatives on those business processes which would have the greatest impact on CX improvement. It would point out that everything that a company or its resources do affect the customer. Internally, the customer would "become alive" as experts state. The proposed approach would enable customer-experience-driven internal business process optimizations as well as achieving true customer focus. It would ensure better alignment between the internal and external view on the processes, thus helping to optimize the processes that would ultimately serve customers in a better way.

Indicators to Measure the Effectiveness of BPM-CXM Approach. The effectiveness of the proposed BPM-CXM approach was suggested to be measured through the improvement of customer satisfaction. Also, another way to measure would be through the number of detected pain points related to internal business process, number of detected positive experiences related to internal business process, number of eliminated pain points due to the internal business process optimization.

Pitfalls of the Proposed Convergence Approach. No significant pitfalls of the proposed approach were detected. However, one potential shortcoming was identified – the experts emphasized that the ownership roles are not clear enough. It could lead to inadequate governance of BPM-CXM convergent approach. Another aspect that was emphasized as important in considering and implementing the proposed structure was the frequency of the processes that should be considered within the analysis.

3   Proposing the Set of Models for BPM-CXM Convergence

To demonstrate and operationalize the concepts presented above, and to provide a functioning and structured convergent approach that could be used in practice, a number of model prototypes were developed and evaluated with experts during the course of the focus group, and are presented in this section. These model prototypes are mapped to ARIS Value Engineering (AVE) methodology and ARIS platform [29] due to the popularity of the methodology and tool in the region.

3.1   Structuring the Models Around the BPM Lifecycle

The models are structured around the lifecycle [17] phases (as already illustrated in Fig. 1): (1) Internal business processes and customer experience are *identified* by defining process and CX landscapes within the "virtual organization". They are mapped on a high level; the top-down approach is used. (2) *Discovery* phase includes mapping of as-is business process models and customer journey maps. It also includes setting up customer touchpoints as a part of customer journey maps, as well as internal business processes. (3) *Analysis* phase includes analysis of internal business processes and customer journeys, with a focus on the analysis of customer touchpoints. The analysis phase is greatly impacted by the new approach since it includes an indication on the level of overall customer experience being positive or negative concerning the internal processes. (4) According to these findings and the analysis performed, processes and customer journeys *redesign* is performed. (5) Process *implementation* and (6) processes and customer journeys *monitoring* close the (iterative) model lifecycle.

3.2   Overview of Top-Down BPM-CXM Convergent Models in BP Repository

Entry-Level Model. Entry-level model (Fig. 2) (also called "start model" or "overview model" [30]), in addition to five "standard" virtual organization elements as proposed by AVE methodology (organizational view, data view and other), now contains CX landscape included in a separate quadrant.

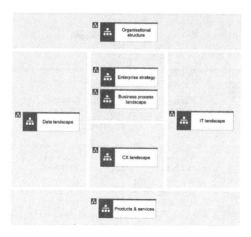

Fig. 2. A prototype of the new entry-level model

This way, a virtual organization or entry-level model includes the same level of details for both internal business processes and customer experience. On this (top) level of detail, both internal business processes and customer experience are represented as a landscape. When clicked on any of the two landscapes, more detailed models are opened.

Customer Journey Landscape. In a more detailed representation, customer lifecycle stage, and customer journeys, which are a part of the specific lifecycle are represented (Fig. 3). *Overall customer experience (CX)* attribute of a Customer lifecycle stage is proposed to be calculated as an average of Overall customer experience (CX) of all customer journeys connected to it. Overall customer experience (CX) attribute of both Customer lifecycle stage and Customer journey objects are used as a basis for color-coding of those objects. The proposed method to calculate a value of a customer experience for a single customer journey is described in the next section. The Overall customer experience (CX) falls into ranges unanimously agreed by the experts: 6 to 10 (Very good, i.e. 5), 2 to 5.99 (Good, i.e. 4), −2 to 1.99 (Neutral, i.e. 3), −6 to −1.99 (Bad, i.e. 2), −10 to −5.99 (Very bad, i.e. 1) while the respective stage/journey color-coding is green for very good (5), yellow for good (4), grey for neutral (3), orange for bad (2) and red for very bad (1). On the customer lifecycle stage level, Customer lifecycle stage owners can be defined as an object attribute. Descriptions can be added as a model/object attribute.

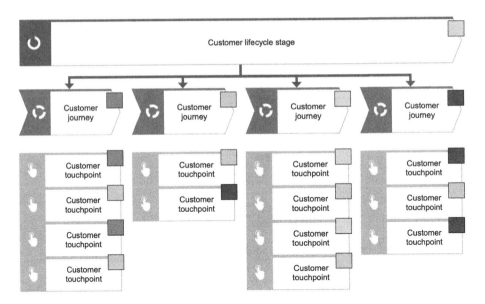

Fig. 3. A prototype of the new customer lifecycle stage model

Customer Journey Map. The model (Fig. 4) is composed of various elements describing the journey: customer journey steps, customer touchpoints, channels, inputs, outputs, risks, KPIs, initiatives, ownership, internal process step. Each touchpoint contains a description and customer journey owners are defined as a model attribute.

To calculate the *Overall customer experience (CX)* attribute of Customer journey object, each touchpoint within the journey (Fig. 4) is taken into consideration. The overall customer experience (CX) of a Customer journey is calculated as an average of Overall customer experience (CX) attributes of all touchpoints within the journey. Attributes which are relevant for calculation within the touchpoints are *Importance to customer (CX)* (5 - very high, 4 - high, 3 - neutral, 2 - low, and 1 - very low) and *Customer feeling (CX)* (2 - very good, 1 - good, 0 - neutral, -1 - bad, -2 - very bad). The data is based on existing KPIs, or comes from different systems, and research.

Overall customer experience (CX) of each individual touchpoint is calculated in a following way: *Customer feeling (CX)* on Touchpoint X * *Importance to customer (CX)* on Touchpoint X. *Overall customer experience (CX)* and *Overall customer experience (CX)* attributes are used for grading and color-coding in the same way as explained earlier. Each touchpoint can be (optional) a pain point, moment of truth, and best practice. Those three are represented with icons below touchpoints. Customer touchpoints which are also pain points are expected to have *Customer feeling (CX)* of Very bad (1), while Customer touchpoints which are also moments of truth are expected to have *Importance to customer (CX)* of Very high (5).

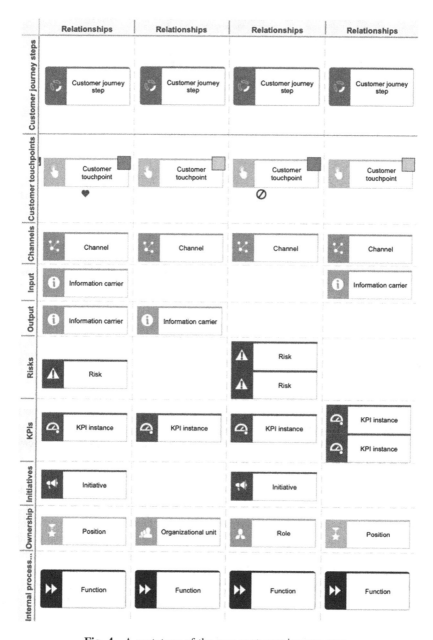

Fig. 4. A prototype of the new customer journey map

Customer Touchpoint Allocation Diagram. Customer touchpoints are analyzed in detail by using the Customer touchpoints allocation diagram, containing various standard elements presented in Fig. 5. Elements which describe a certain touchpoint include: customer journey steps, channels, inputs, outputs, ownership, risks, KPIs, initiatives, and internal process step.

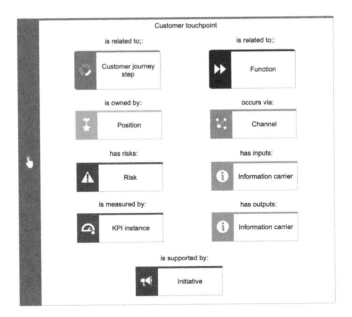

Fig. 5. A prototype of the new customer touchpoint allocation diagram

Value-added Chain Diagram. From the internal business process perspective, high-level business processes are represented by using the value-added chain diagrams (Fig. 6). They include a color indication of the *Overall customer experience (CX)*, which is related to the individual process. They also include customer experience (touchpoints) layer. Based on the relation between the individual touchpoints (which are a part of certain Customer journey) with internal business process steps (which are a part of a certain Value-added chain diagram), the calculation is performed to determine which internal business processes (on a value-added chain level) have the best/worst customer experience. According to this, recommendations are given on which internal business processes should be modified in order to improve customer experience most effectively. The *Overall customer experience (CX)* on internal business process level is calculated as an average of *Overall customer experience (CX)* of all Customer touchpoints which are a part of the underlying internal business process model. The *Overall customer experience (CX)* of the end-to-end value-added chain (higher level internal business process) is calculated as an average of all connected underlying value-added chains. The same color-coding principle is used as presented earlier within this paper. Optionally, the number of process instantiations and/or revenue per each sub-process (value-added chain) can be added in order to add value to the analysis.

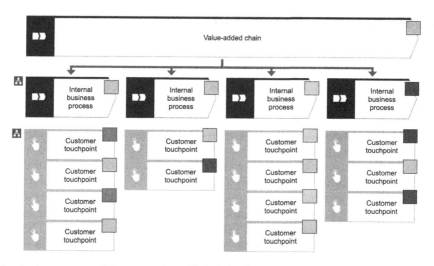

Fig. 6. A prototype of the new value-added chain diagram (with touchpoint representation)

Event-Driven Process Chain. On a detailed level, internal business processes are represented by using the event-driven process chain diagrams (EPC), Fig. 7.

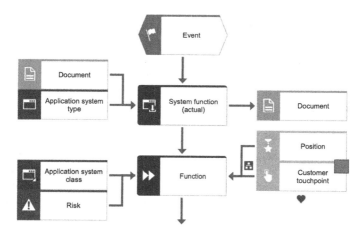

Fig. 7. A segment of the prototype of the new process model (with touchpoint representation)

Other than the "regular" elements of an internal business process model, they also contain customer touchpoints to represent the customer interactions with the internal organization as well as the with the internal process steps. Touchpoints include a color indication of the overall customer experience following the same color-coding principle as above.

4 Conclusions and Planned Work

This paper presented an effort to structure and design a BPM-CXM convergence approach. It is focused on the design itself – problem definition and solution proposal and development, which was presented and evaluated with a group of experts with substantial experience in BPM and CXM fields in the EMEA region. The main deliverable of this phase of the research is the verified and operationalized version of the BPM-CXM structured convergence approach, including the prototype models and recommendations for their use. Based on the feedback from the field received so far, it is expected that this research will influence BPM and CXM disciplines by proposing a convergence approach, but also the BPM systems used in practice to conduct BPM projects. There are specific plans by several of the experts that participated in the focus group to follow the proposed approach in delivering their future consulting projects should some preconditions be fulfilled (such as customer motivation, level of engagement of teams from both BPM and CXM departments, freedom to use the methodology of own choosing) but they are also waiting for the implementation evidence. On that note, a new phase of the evaluation of the proposed approach would include implementation in a real-life setting in order to further test the feasibility and value of the proposed convergence approach. The implementation and a follow-up evaluation through in-depth interviews with international experts in BPM and CXM fields that participate in the project are in progress. The findings would be used to adjust the proposed work if necessary, detect issues, and measure the effects of the new approach. In-depth interviews to evaluate the benefits of using the proposed approach compared to the traditional BPM and CXM approached will specifically evaluate the effects of BPM-CXM convergence approach on the internal organization, alignment of business processes of an internal organization with the needs of the customer, and the customer experience itself.

Multiple benefits from following the proposed approach are expected compared to traditional BPM approaches. The expected effects would include the following: reduction of emphasis on internal business process mapping or "modelling because of modelling" within the BPM initiatives, reduction of functional silos effect and better alignment between the organizational departments, improved coordination between the organizational departments in defining the key performance indicators, increase of innovation level in organizations, design of business processes which take the interactions with the customer into the account and enable customer expectations fulfilment, development of products and services that are really needed by the customers, rational usage of organizational resources and more.

After validating the theses in a real-life setting, it is expected that the results will influence BPM and CXM disciplines by proposing a new version of the structured convergence approach and instructions for its implementation, but also the BPM systems used in practice as these will need adjustments in terms of available models, objects and methods as demonstrated in the paper.

Acknowledgment. This work is supported by the Croatian Science Foundation [grant number HRZZ-UIP-2017-05-7625].

References

1. Schooff, P.: End of the road for end-to-end process transformation. interview with Clay Richardson. In: BPM Today blog (2016). http://bpm.com/bpm-today/blogs/1136-end-of-the-road-for-end-to-end-process-transformation. Accessed 26 July 2019
2. Van Den Bergh, J., Thijs, S., Viaene, S.: Transforming Through Processes Leading Voices on BPM, People and Technology. Springer, London (2014). https://doi.org/10.1007/978-3-319-03937-4
3. Gersch, M., Hewing, M., Schöler, B.: Business process blueprinting – an enhanced view on process performance. Bus. Process. Manag. J. **17**(5), 732–747 (2011). https://doi.org/10.1108/14637151111166169
4. Trkman, P., Mertens, W., Viaene, S., Gemmel, P.: From business process management to customer process management. Bus. Process. Manag. J. **21**(2), 250–266 (2015). https://doi.org/10.1108/BPMJ-02-2014-0010
5. Neubauer, T.: An empirical study about the status of business process management. Bus. Process. Manag. J. **15**(2), 166–183 (2009). https://doi.org/10.1108/14637150910949434
6. Schmiedel, T., Vom Brocke, J., Recker, J.: Development and validation of an instrument to measure organizational cultures' support of business process management. Inf. Manag. **51**(1), 43–56 (2014). https://doi.org/10.1016/j.im.2013.08.005
7. Johnston, R., Kong, X.: The customer experience: a road map for improvement. Man Ser. Qual. Int. J. **21**(1), 5–24 (2011). https://doi.org/10.1108/09604521111100225
8. Gloppen, J., Lindquister, B., Daae, H.-P.: The customer journey as a tool for business innovation and transformation. In: DeFillippi, R., Rieple, A., Wikström, P. (eds.) International Perspectives on Business Innovation and Disruption in Design, pp. 118–138. Edward Elgar Pub. (2016)
9. Becker, J., Niehaves, B., Malsbender, A., et al.: Taking a BPM lifecycle view on service productivity: results from a literature analysis. In: Proceedings of the XXI International RESER Conference, Germany (2011). https://www.researchgate.net/publication/267298145_Taking_a_BPM_Lifecycle_View_on_Service_Productivity_Results_from_a_Literature_Analysis Accessed 26 July 2019
10. Norton, D.W., Pine II, B.J.: Using the customer journey to road test and refine the business model. Strateg. Leadersh. **41**(2), 12–17 (2013). https://doi.org/10.1108/10878571311318196
11. Straßer, J.: Aligning customer journey management with business process management. Masters thesis, University of Amsterdam (2016)
12. Surbakti, F.P.S.: Customer process management: a systematic literature review. Eng. Manag. Res. **4**, 1–8 (2015). https://doi.org/10.5539/emr.v4n2p1
13. Følstad, A., Kvale, K., Halvorsrud, R.: Customer journeys: involving customers and internal resources in the design and management of services. In: Proceedings of the Fourth Service Design and Innovation conference, pp. 412–417 (2014). http://ep.liu.se/ecp/099/042/ecp14099042.pdf. Accessed 26 July 2019
14. Van Den Bergh, J., Thijs, S., Isik, Ö., Viaene, S.: The world is not enough: customer centricity and processes. Bus. Process. Trends 1–7 (2012). https://www.bptrends.com/the-world-is-not-enough/ Accessed 26 July 2019
15. Hewing, M.: Business Process Blueprinting: A Method for Customer-Oriented Business Process Modeling. Springer, Berlin (2014). https://doi.org/10.1007/978-3-658-03729-1
16. Pavlić, D., Ćukušić, M.: Conceptualizing the convergence model of business process management and customer experience management. In: Di Ciccio, C., et al. (eds.) BPM 2019. LNBIP, vol. 361, pp. 328–332. Springer, Cham (2019). https://doi.org/10.1007/978-3-030-30429-4_24

17. Dumas, M., La Rosa, M., Mendling, J., Reijers, H.A.: Fundamentals of business process management. Springer, Heidelberg (2018). https://doi.org/10.1007/978-3-662-56509-4
18. Rosenbaum, M.S., Otalora, M.L., Contreras Ramírez, G.: How to create a realistic customer journey map. Bus. Horiz. **60**(1), 143–150 (2017). https://doi.org/10.1016/j.bushor.2016.09.010
19. Davis, R.: It's the customer journey that counts. BPTrends Column, pp. 1–5 (2011). https://www.bptrends.com/processes-in-practice-its-the-customer-journey-that-counts/ Accessed 26 July 2019
20. Kumar, V., Smart, P.A., Maddern, H., Maull, R.S.: Alternative perspectives on service quality and customer satisfaction: the role of BPM. Int. J. Serv. Ind. Manag. **19**(2), 176–187 (2008). https://doi.org/10.1108/09564230810869720
21. Peffers, K., Tuunanen, T., Rothenberger, M.A., Chatterjee, S.: A design science research methodology for information systems research. J. Manag. Inf. Syst. **24**(3), 45–78 (2007). https://doi.org/10.2753/MIS0742-1222240302
22. Lemon, K.N., Verhoef, P.C.: Understanding customer experience throughout the customer journey. J. Mark. **80**(6), 69–96 (2016). https://doi.org/10.1509/jm.15.0420
23. Vanwersch, R.J.B., et al.: A critical evaluation and framework of business process improvement methods. Bus. Inf. Syst. Eng. **58**, 43 (2015). https://doi.org/10.1007/s12599-015-0417-x
24. Moormann, J., Palvolgyi, E.Z.: Customer-centric business modeling: setting a research agenda. In: 15th Conference on Business Informatics, pp. 173–179 (2013). https://doi.org/10.1109/cbi.2013.33
25. Flint, D.J., Larsson, E., Gammelgaard, B., Mentzer, J.T.: Logistics innovation: a customer value-oriented social process. J. Bus. Logist. **26**, 113–147 (2005). https://doi.org/10.1002/j.2158-1592.2005.tb00196.x
26. Chen, H., Daugherty, P.J., Landry, T.D.: Supply chain process integration: a theoretical framework. J. Bus. Logist. **30**, 27–46 (2009). https://doi.org/10.1002/j.2158-1592.2009.tb00110.x
27. Lee, C.-H., Huang, S.Y., Barnes, F.B., Kao, L.: Business performance and customer relationship management: the effect of IT, organisational contingency and business process on Taiwanese manufacturers. Total Qual. Manag. Bus. Excell. **21**, 43–65 (2010). https://doi.org/10.1080/14783360903492595
28. Ruland, Y.: Customer experience and its potential to extend business process management. Master thesis - UHasselt (2016). http://hdl.handle.net/1942/22258
29. Software AG product website. https://www.softwareag.com/in/products/aris_alfabet/bpa/aris_architect/default.html Accessed 26 July 2019
30. Davis, R., Brabander, E.: ARIS Design Platform: Getting Started with BPM. Springer, Heidelberg (2007). https://doi.org/10.1007/978-1-84628-613-1

A Modeling Approach for Bioinformatics Workflows

Laiz Heckmann Barbalho de Figueroa[1], Rema Salman[1], Jennifer Horkoff[1,2]([⊠]),
Soni Chauhan[1], Marcela Davila[1], Francisco Gomes de Oliveira Neto[1,2],
and Alexander Schliep[1,2]

[1] University of Gothenburg, Gothenburg, Sweden
{gushecla,gussalmre}@student.gu.se, jennifer.horkoff@gu.cse.se
[2] Chalmers University of Technology, Gothenburg, Sweden

Abstract. Bioinformaticians execute frequent, complex, manual and semi-scripted workflows to process data. There are many tools to manage and conduct these workflows, but there is no domain-specific way to textually and diagrammatically document them. Consequently, we create methods for modeling bioinformatics workflows. Specifically, we extend the Unified Modeling Language (UML) Activity Diagram to the bioinformatics domain by including domain-specific concepts and notations. Additionally, a template was created to document the same concepts in a text format. A design science methodology was followed, where four iterations with seven domain experts tailored the artefacts, extending concepts and improving usability, terminology, and notations. The UML extension received a positive evaluation from bioinformaticians. However, the written template was rejected due to the amount of text and complexity.

Keywords: UML · Activity diagram · Workflow · Bioinformatics

1 Introduction

Bioinformatics is a branch of biology, which is connected to computational methods for biological data generation. Generating data for biological analysis, such as DNA sequencing, requires several connected tools in a workflow, defined as a sequence of tasks that cover the steps of a process from initialisation to producing final results [10]. Bioinformaticians create workflows that need to be followed precisely to achieve satisfactory results [13]. To design and manage these workflows, bioinformaticians use a mixture of tools and frameworks from various sources [2,10], often interspersed with manual steps and checks.

Work in [2] reported usability challenges when using available tools, such as limitations on data visualisation and patterns for workflows. Additionally, [11] describes the lack of features, notations, or concepts, such as the absence of loops. Our experience with a local bioinformatics lab reveal that workflows are

J. Gordijn et al. (Eds.): PoEM 2019, LNBIP 369, pp. 167–183, 2019.
https://doi.org/10.1007/978-3-030-35151-9_11

incredibly complex, often implicit, and involve decisions without clear-cut criteria. These limitations hinder bioinformaticians and researchers in visualizing, sharing, replicating and improving workflows.

The literature reports languages used to describe bioinformatics workflows, e.g., Domain-Specific Languages (DSLs) can be tailored to bioinformatics [5]. UML has been adapted for bioinformatics processes (e.g., [19]). However, this work does not focus specifically on capturing manual and scripted bioinformatics workflows and does not address the issues identified above.

The purpose of this study is to create a usable modeling language for capturing and understanding bioinformatics workflows. The long-term aim is to establish a shared understanding and consistency between the activities of the involved parties; create sharable documentation to provide a clear vision of the process; support training new bioinformaticians; identify problems in the workflow design; reduce the bioinformatician's reliance on individual interpretation; increase the replication precision of the analysis; and improve traceability. To develop and evaluate our solutions, we have worked with bioinformaticians at the University of Gothenburg's Bioinformatics Core facility[1], following a Design Science Research Methodology (DSRM), to answer the main research question and its three sub-questions:

RQ1: How can we support modeling of bioinformatics workflows in an effective and usable way?

- RQ1.1: What are the defining and unique characteristics of bioinformatics workflows compared to standard workflows?
- RQ1.2: How should workflows, including the concepts discovered in RQ1.1 be visualised to be understandable by the bioinformaticians?
- RQ 1.3: How can we design a useful and understandable template to document the concepts from RQ1.1?

The rest of this document is structured as follows: Sect. 2 describes how DSRM was used to develop the artefacts. Sect. 3 presents the final artefacts and the results for each iteration, while Sect. 4 discusses the findings and limitations. Sect. 5 compares with related work, while Sect. 6 concludes the paper.

2   Methodology

This paper uses the DSRM due to its pragmatic nature and strength in solving real-world problems [9]. The DSRM procedure proposed by Peffers et al. in [17] was adapted to the needs of this research, as summarized in Fig. 1. Based on the problems identified in the 0th iteration, three artefacts were created, evaluated, and improved: the UML Activity Diagram (AD) meta-model extension, its concrete syntax, and the Workflow Description Specification Template (WDST).

---

[1] https://cf.gu.se/english/bioinformatics.

Facilities. The research was conducted with participants from three different facilities: the Bioinformatics Core Facility, part of the Sahlgrenska Academy Core Facilities at the University of Gothenburg; the Genomic Medicine Sweden (GMS); and the Translational Genomics Platform[2].

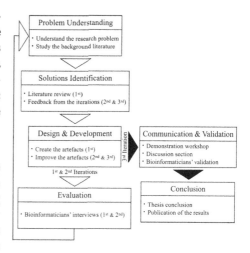

Fig. 1. The DSRM process in this study.

Participants. The head of the Bioinformatics Core Facility (the 5th author) used a purposive sampling technique to select the participants for this research. This technique aims to diminish the accidental sampling bias as the participants' selection is based on the researchers' belief that they fulfil stipulated criteria [25], in this case, workflow knowledge. The seven participants are identified as P1 to P7. The four DSRM iterations are briefly described below.

0th Iteration. In the first exploratory iteration, two of the authors (MSc. student and a modelling expert) worked iteratively with the head of the Bioinformatics Core Facility to map out 2–3 specific workflows, as initial exploratory examples. Challenges and concepts specific to bioinformatics were noted, feeding into the next rounds.

First to Third Iterations. Based on the findings from the 0th iteration, as well as ideas from the literature, we created three artefacts and evaluated them with the seven bioinformaticians (P1–P7). During the first and second iterations, we conducted semistructured interviews that lasted a maximum of, respectively, 30 and 60 min with five bioinformaticians each. The interviews were hosted at the laboratory's facility, recorded upon interviewees' agreement, with assured anonymity of the participants' answers. All interview questions and other materials for the study can be found in [6].

During the interviews for the first iteration, the created WDST, two concrete syntaxes, and two examples were presented, eliciting opinions via the pre-set questions. In the second iteration, participants were asked to draw for 15 min a workflow of their choosing using the updated notation by using a stencil in https://www.draw.io/. They were also asked to fill in a WDST template for 15 min in Google sheets. When the participants were using the artefacts, they

---

[2] https://wcmtm.gu.se/research-groups/genomics-platform.

were asked to follow the think-aloud protocol [7], while the observations were recorded in a log template by a researcher. In the end, they answered questions about language and method usability, inspired by the System Usability Scale (SUS), a widely used ten-item survey to assess usability and learnability [4].

In the final iteration, all participants from previous iterations were invited to the one-hour workshop, recorded upon their approval. In the workshop, the artefacts were described through examples and participants were paired to discuss the usability and understandability of the notations and concepts. After that, each pair explained their thoughts, and then the participants individually and anonymously validated the notations and concepts using a survey via Mentimeter[3]. All workshop material can be found in [6].

After transcribing the data we conducted thematic analysis to identify significant patterns, grouping them into themes [20]. After coding, the suggestions and problems were addressed during the *Solutions Identification* and *Design and Development* steps in each iteration. In the last iteration, the artefacts were not further refined; with the changes suggested for future work.

3   Results

In this section we will present the final artefacts and the output from each iteration. Note that, for space considerations, we present only the final artefacts, but their intermediate versions for each iteration can be found in [6]. Below, in each iteration, we describe (Fig. 1): a starting point (i.e., Solution identification); the work on the extension of the AD meta-model, concrete syntax and the WDST (Design & Development), and an Evaluation performed. Note that the evaluation reveals suggestions and solutions taken as the starting point of the upcoming phases.

3.1   Final Artefacts

We show a small example using the final version of the language, used in the evaluation workshop (Fig. 2). The final version of the developed artefacts includes a UML Activity Diagram (AD) meta-model extension for bioinformatics domain (Fig. 3); an excerpt of the final version of the WDST (Fig. 4); and the final concrete syntax (Table 1). The following sections describe the iterative results that lead to these artefacts.

---

[3] https://www.mentimeter.com.

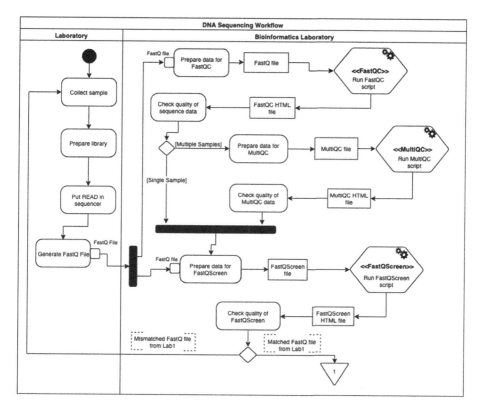

Fig. 2. A bioinformatics workflow example using the final version of the language.

3.2   0th Iteration

In the first exploratory iteration, we attempted to capture examples of workflows in several existing modeling languages, including Business Process Model and Notation (BPMN) and Data-Flow Diagrams (DFDs). We found BPMN to be too complex for our purposes, for example, we did not make use of most different types of gateways. Given that the target end users were not native modelers, we perceived AD to be simpler to build on. We also found it easier to express the flow of file inputs and outputs in AD, although this is also possible in BPMN. Finally, we made extensive use of conditional forks and joins, and we found the visual guard condition ([condition]) in AD quite convenient for this. We found that DFDs were limited in capturing the usage of tools in the workflow, a key element for bioinformaticians. In the end, we settled on UML Activity Diagrams as they: encompass an appropriate level of complexity, support extensibility, come with familiarity (for IT specialists), and the support of the UML community [16].

Our early examples revealed gaps in AD, which motivated further iterations. We found that bioinformatics workflows involve: (1) many complex and repetitive tasks; (2) many 'quality checks' of tool outputs using threshold values which

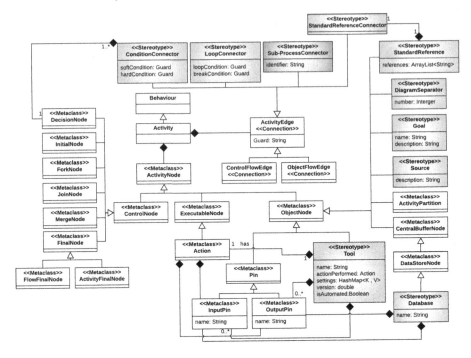

Fig. 3. The final version of the extended UML AD meta-model (white classes are from UML AD [16], while grey classes were added in this work).

Workflow Description Specification				
Workflow ID:				*the workflow name or identifier*
Date of creation:	*date on which this document was created*		Number of steps:	*amount of steps*
Workflow version:	*version of the document*	Modification date:	*date of modification*	Workflow creator:	*name*
Workflow				
Workflow goal:				*what do you want to achieve with this workflow?*
Workflow source:			*Is this workflow created locally? or it follows a reference – in that case, add link to the reference or name, the person*	
Workflow responsible:				*person who signs the final output or who uses this workflow*
First Step (Start point)			**Final Step (End point)**	
Step ID:	*The name or identifier of the start step*		Step ID:	*The name or identifier of the start step*

Fig. 4. An excerpt of the final version of the workflow description specification template - WDST.

could sometimes be subjective to interpretation; (3) constant splitting of tasks between people and tools; (4) data emphasis where files were exchanged back and forth; and (5) unclear motivation behind some tasks.

We also created a draft template aimed to help elicit and capture bioinformatics workflows. The idea was that bioinformaticians are not necessarily experts in structured modeling languages, such as UML. Therefore, they may be more comfortable capturing process details in text via a template. These findings and the first draft of the template were used as input to the next iterations.

Table 1. The final meta-model concepts and the sources of each concrete syntax with their notations and explanations.

Concept Name	Concrete Syntax Source	Notation	Explanation
Loop	UML structured nodes [23]		Follow the *Loop* semantics and syntax suggested for UML, where using arrows with guards lead to activity repetition. Helps to capture complex and repetitive tasks found in bioinformatic workflow examples.
SoftCondition	UML AD [16] & different usage of line styles from [1]		Follows the standard UML AD semantics and usage, where the guard syntax was changed to dashed lines. It is used to captures fuzzy thresholds.
HardCondition			Follow notation and concept of the guard in the standard UML AD. It captures hard thresholds as found in practice.
Source	Flowchart notations & i* visual syntax [15]		Concept identical to *Resource* in i*, using the document notation from the flowchart notations. Captures source of task or action, often a research paper or external reference.
Tool (Manual)	Flowchart notations & i* visual syntax [15]		The task concept is from i* visual syntax with an additional icon on its corner to allow a faster visualisation of the tools, depending on the mode (manual or automated). It captures tasks operated by or through tools.
Tool (Automated)			
Database	UML AD extensions in [22]		Concept identical to UML *Datastore*, but with the flowchart cylinder shape, *Database* notation. It captures storage of files.
StandardReference-Connector	UML AD notes connector [16]		Connects between the *StandardReference* notation and its *InputPin*.
StandardReference	UML AD [16]		To add standard data as input to be compared with the data being analysed, differentiating them from the ordinary input. It is used to show that this data is not part of the data flow.
DiagramSeparator			The semantic and syntax are inspired by *ActivityEdgeConnector* with a graphical modification, a triangle with a number instead of circles with letters. Helps to deal with large workflows via diagram splitting.
Sub-processConnector			Identical to the semantic and syntax of UML AD *ActivityEdgeConnector* with a different name. Help to compress parts of the workflows.
OutputPin			Follow exactly the standard notations and usage in UML AD. The standalone pin is the same file between two consecutive steps. Input and output are often file exchanges in bioinformatics workflows. Helps to show the data flow.
InputPin			
StandalonePin			

3.3   First Iteration

Solutions Identification: The 0th iteration identified *thresholds, source,* differentiation of *files, goals, sub-process,* and *repeated iterations* as needed by bioinformaticians while creating their workflows. We started by incorporating each of those concepts into our three artefacts.

AD Meta-Model Extension: Our starting point was the UML AD meta-model in [16]. Based on the nature of the UML profile, all the UML default AD syntax and semantics were kept (e.g., action, decision, join, forks). Additionally, the concepts *activityPartition* (swimlanes) and *activityEdgeConnector* from the UML AD [16] maintained the same syntax, where the former was based on [21] and the latter was used to represent sub-processes for the bioinformatics domain (a connection point instead of drawing a long process).

The implemented extensions included the added stereotypes: *tool, diagramSeparator, source,* and *goal,* which were inherited from the meta-class *objectNode* classifiers. The *tool* has a composition relationship with the meta-classes *action, inputPin,* and *outputPin.* Due to some changes on the *datastore* notation, the class was added as a stereotype. Additionally, the *loopConnector* was inspired by [23], inherited from the super-class *activityEdge,* containing *loopCondition* and *breakCondition* guards, and *thresholdConnector* inherited from the super-class *activityEdge,* containing the specified guards *softThreshold* and *hardThreshold.* The *decisionNode* composites at least one *thresholdConnector.*

Concrete Syntax: The design decisions for our concrete syntax, considered the principles for cognitive effectiveness of the visual notations, which are: symbols deficit, redundancy, overload, and excess. These principles ensure the correspondence between semantics and graphical shapes of notations [14,15], which is part of the Visual Alphabet theory and Physics of Notations theory. We followed the UML AD patterns, while avoiding to use different colours or texture to define the visual syntax of the concepts. This results in an inclusive language that can be used by any person with visual disabilities or colour blindness.

WDST: We added workflow information to the WDST, such as *workflow* and *step ID, name, creator, version number,* and *date of creation.*

Evaluation: Five bioinformaticians (P1–P5) from the three facilities were interviewed to evaluate the WDST. The diagram users should be bioinformaticians and stakeholders. The results for this first iteration included: improving the *understandability* use of the *swimlanes* and *loops* inclusion and exclusion factors; the addition of a *tool settings and parameters* field (by two participants); three participants outlined the notations usage as *system documentation,* thoughts *structuralisation,* and process overview; the current state of the workflow diagrams depends on an individuals' drawing style. Moreover, all participants said that they would draw the workflow first and then fill the WDST. However, P2 stated that "I think like there's so much here (WDST) that would be redundant when you're using this (both artefacts)".

3.4   Second Iteration

Solutions Identification: The solutions for this iteration come from the participants during the interviews in the previous iteration (i.e., the results described in the previous evaluation).

AD Meta-Model Extension: We included more attributes to the stereotypes *tool*, *standardReference*, and *threshold*. We renamed the *threshold* and the meta-classes *activityEdgeConnector* and *datastore*. We added stereotype *standardReferenceConnector* as an inheriting classifier of *activityEdge* because the *standardReference* was mentioned as missing by two participants. However, based on participant feedback, we modified the naming of *thresholdConnector* and *datastore* to *conditionConnector* and *database* respectively, as visible in the final version of the meta-model (Fig. 4).

Concrete Syntax: We only added a sub-concept for input, the *standardReference* (see Table 1 for its design sources and explanations).

WDST: Based on the participants' feedback, we added, reworded, and deleted repetitive and unnecessary fields. The goal was to decrease redundancy and increase familiarity. We added guidance for the template usage and the required input and output data for each tool, as well as more information about their version and settings. We also added 'conditions' to the 'thresholds' section. Additionally, participants requested to change the role of the WDST to become a standardised way to document workflows for stakeholders and to share knowledge, as opposed to a simple helper during the workflow elicitation process.

Evaluation: Five participants (P1, P3–P6) were interviewed and recorded. Regarding the concrete syntax, Two participants indicated that the *goal* notation was *unneeded* and two other participants pointed *vertical* and *horizontal join/fork* as *unfamiliar*. Two participants requested to *add*: (i) the parallelogram shape of pins, (ii) no database with in/output pins, and (iii) different arrow shapes. Participants indicated the provided stencil of workflow shapes would be used, but not frequently since it is time-consuming to draw workflow diagrams, usually created only for publications. Even though the notations complexity was considered low by four participants, the other two participants stated that the number of graphical shapes was high. The participants suggested a descriptive *manual* to guide the users, while others stated that *training* is necessary. Finally, the participants felt confident using the notation stencil but highlighted challenges when using draw.io as a modeling tool.

Regarding evaluation of the WDST, the participants indicated that its content flow was good. However, three of the participants stated that they would not use the template because of its complexity (i.e., the amount of information to be written) and time consumption. The participants mentioned that *training* (e.g., a user manual or usage examples) should help the users. Conversely, two participants said that the WDST grey-text is sufficient and self-explanatory.

In summary, participants' general impressions of the artefacts were that the diagram is good, useful, and provides a clear overview, whereas the WDST requires time and holds much information. Additionally, P4 stated that both artefacts "complement each other."

3.5   Third Iteration

Identify Solutions: Similarly to the second iteration, the solutions for this iteration come from the previous iteration's evaluation.

UML AD Meta-Model Extension: We added a composition association between the *database* stereotype class and the *input* and *output pins* meta-classes. Additionally, we added an attribute to the *tool* stereotype-class to identify if the tool is automatically or manually operated (Fig. 3 shows the updated meta-model).

Concrete Syntax: Improvements to the concrete syntax include: (i) changing the location of the *inputPin* on *tool* to ensure the vertical gradient of the diagram, (ii) attaching *inputPin* and *outputPin* to the *database* to represent the data flow and keep the consistency between shapes in the XML notations stencil, (iii) improving the *action* and *tool* descriptions to decrease confusion, (iv) adding a separate text field for the performed activity on the *tool* shape to remove the issue of deleting the name or performed activity when writing them, (v) adding a new notation for the manually operated *tool* to increase transparency of the automation level, (vi) removing the *goal* notation upon participants' request, and (vii) adding the *standalonePin* to the stencil to include familiar notations to the bioinformaticians. See Table 1 for the final version of the concrete syntax.

WDST: The WDST annoyed the participants because of its documentation traceability fields and its descriptive nature, which was unfamiliar to the participants. Some of the changes implemented were: further explanation for several cells by using a light grey text, format fixing on the cell *tool settings and parameters*, removal of the *workflow name* due to its interchangeable use with *workflow ID* by the participants, and the word 'process' in the sentence *process step* from the WDST, addition of a basic excel formula to linking the *workflow ID* on the first page to the second page to avoid typing the same information twice, and a conditional formatting that changes the text colour while filling cells from grey to black. The grey text fields held the explanation to help new users and were thus kept since they are vital to the WDST understandability.

Evaluation: Six participants (P1–P3, P5–P7), including the head of the Bioinformatics Core Facility, joined the workshop to evaluate the final version of the artefacts. Regarding the concrete syntax, participants' feedback revealed that the notations and concepts are understandable and simple, but they requested improvements related to better concepts definition and different software for drawing the diagrams. One participant wanted the diagrams to be automatically generated, as in Snakemake (https://snakemake.readthedocs.io). The bioinformaticians outlined *fork nodes*, *join nodes*, *swimlanes*, and *standardReference* as unnecessary notations. Additionally, they said that the diagrams would be used for final and standard documentation, after sketching, and stated that the notations would increase the time spent to draw the current workflows, which were described as having overloaded and overused *boxes*, and *notes* symbols.

Table 2. Mentimeter validation results in the third iteration.

Question	Median	Mean
How understandable are the presented concepts and notations?	3	4.3
How easy is to use the concepts and notations library?	3	3.7
How likely would you use the concepts and notations in a diagram?	3	3
How likely do you believe a stakeholder can understand the concepts and notations?	3	2.8
How understandable is the documentation for you?	3	2
How easy is to fill the documentation template?	3	1.7
How likely would you use the documentation template?	3	1.3
How likely do you believe a stakeholder can understand the documentation template?	3	1

The participants answered Likert scales and an open-ended question for each artefact using Mentimeter, see Table 2 for the results with mean and median values. Here, 1 is very unlikely, incomprehensible, or arduous, while 5 is very likely, understandable, or easy. The results show that the participants find the concepts and notations of the stencil understandable with an average of 4.3, where 3.7 reflected ease of use. The participants would likely use the concepts and notations; with an average of 3, and 2.8 is their average perception of stakeholders' understandability. Nevertheless, the open-ended question had similar results as the qualitative workshop results. However, one participant requested a further improvement to, "make it easier to add several outputs". Moreover, a participant proposed renaming the *soft-condition* to "manual-inspection or manual evaluation" and changing its concrete syntax to differentiate it even more from the *hard-condition*. A participant abstained from answering.

Regarding evaluation of the WDST, the participants *disliked* the amount of typing, identified traceability issues, and mentioned that the stakeholders could have trouble understanding the WDST because of its complexity. They also outlined that *automation* would save time when producing the written template from graphs since the WDST was indicated as time-consuming. Table 2 shows that the WDST was deemed incomprehensible by most of the participants, with an average of 2 and 1.7 regarding the ease of filling it. The participants would be very unlikely to use the WDST ($\mu = 1.3$) and they do not believe that the stakeholders would understand it ($\mu = 1$). Regarding the open-ended question, five participants agreed that it is complicated. Thus, they suggested simplifying it by removing most of its content, keeping only the *tool section*, and adding a place to input the command line commands. One participant left the question unanswered.

4   Discussion

Here, we return to answer our research questions by summarizing the main results found throughout all iterations, followed by the limitations of our study.

RQ1.1: The defining and unique characteristics of bioinformatics workflows were found mainly on the 0th iteration (e.g., complex and repetitive tasks, quality checks, thresholds splitting of tasks, many files). Additional feedback lead to *tool* and *diagramSeparators* in the first iteration; while in the second iteration we added *standardReference* concept and the attributes *tool settings and parameters* for the meta-model extension, as well as the possibility to document *concurrent steps* in the WDST. Although these concepts arose specifically for bioinformatics workflows, of course they may be useful in other contexts. Three of these concepts (namely, *diagramSeparators*, *standardReference*, and *tool*) with its attributes, were not found in any related work, but were requested by the domain experts, leading us to believe they may be more specific to bioinformatics. Generally, any individual-driven workflow with many tools, scripts and file exchanges may require similar concepts.

RQ1.2: We employed the theories, Visual Alphabet and Physics of Notations [14] to visualize the concepts from RQ1.1. In the first and second iterations, the feedback received was compatible with these theories and did not result in any deletion, while in the last iteration, four concepts and notations were seen as unnecessary. We believe that the change of heart was due to the group discussion, resulting in the participants' confidence to reject concepts.

Moreover, the UML AD extension in this paper has a high graphical complexity, measured by the size of its visual vocabulary, containing 14 standards and nine extended notations, totalising 23 shapes (Table 1). Even though the complexity is high, the participants mentioned an average understandability of 4.3. Finally, some participants mentioned that the shapes were not intuitive when validating the concrete syntax. Therefore, we recommend that future use of our concrete syntax comes with textual labels for each shape and link.

Participants' feedback reveal a preference for their current unstructured (i.e., without a meta-model or set syntax) graphical representations rather than the developed notations, because using the former requires less knowledge about the modeling language and more about the context. Overall, we see a general reluctance to use a structured modeling language with a meta-model. However, we believe the drive towards open science will make such models increasingly necessary when boxes and arrows are too inexpressive and subject to interpretation.

RQ1.3: The WDST was envisioned for elicitation when it was created; however, during the first evaluation, the participants said that they would draw a diagram first and then fill the documentation. Therefore, we changed the WDST purpose from *workflow elicitation* to *documentation*. Even after this change, the participants preferred the diagrams over the WDST. Initially, we introduced a textual version of the workflow language with the idea that non-modelers may be more comfortable with the text. However, although bioinformaticians typically do not have training in modeling, they seem to prefer diagrams over text.

Overall, the WDST was a unanimously disliked template, with only negative average scales ranging from 1 to 2. Nonetheless, three important findings were made: (i) the participants want an automatically generated documentation; (ii) it must contain the tools settings and parameters; and (iii) the amount of text and technicality should be as low as possible. We believe that an automatically generated documentation after drawing the workflow is the best solution.

4.1   Threats to Validity

Internal Validity: The lack of bioinformaticians resulted in the availability of only seven participants, considered representative and having a mixed experience level. Some of the bioinformaticians participated in more than one round; thus, there is a gradual learning effect. However, we anticipate that the resulting language would be used more than once on a long-term basis; thus learning is a reasonable evaluation context. One of the drawbacks of group activities is the possibility for individuals to avoid taking part in the discussions and follow the crowd. To mitigate that, the seven participants were paired during the discussions to stimulate participation and prevent inhibition.

The researchers observed that the participants were avoiding answering the questions related to the WDST usage, addition, and removal of fields, by providing evasive and polite answers. As a mitigation, the validation question in the final iteration was performed entirely anonymously using Mentimeter. This approach revealed the participants' real thoughts about WDST.

The participants and interviewees were not native English speakers and did not share the same domain expertise. Additionally, the three involved facilities had a divergence of concepts. However, we adopted a simple language while interacting with the participants, created discussion sections, asked follow-up questions, and provided clarifications to mitigate any misunderstandings.

Reliability: To increase the reliability of our qualitative coding, one researcher created the code frame with its description and matching statements, while the other researcher independently checked reliability looking at the correspondence between the codes and the data [8]. We believe that other authors would create nearly the same concepts of this study but give them different names depending on their origin field and other factors. These additions were justified by the findings on 0th iteration and the participants' validation.

External Validity: We have used purposive sampling in this work. To address generalizability, three facilities took part during this study, and the participants worked with different workflows or different ways of designing workflows.

5   Related Work

Requirements Elicitation and Templates. In the requirements elicitation process, information is collected from stakeholders and end-users to understand system needs. In this case, we want to understand workflows and associated issues. General, requirements templates exist in the literature, e.g., the Volere template from Robertson and Robertson [18].

There are few approaches specifically for elicitation for bioinformatics. Work in [10] aimed to document workflow specifications for genomics data analysis. The workflow specifications consisted of the prescribed steps, until reaching a particular conclusion, including information about the specific tool versions with their parameter settings. However, the authors focused on using pre-built pipelines and standardized workflow definitions, where we focused on creating a language to facilitate standardized workflow documentation to provide an understandable and shareable view among collaborating bioinformaticians in projects.

Further work used semantic web standards to improve data workflow systems allowing bioinformaticians to publish and share their workflows via the cloud, providing an open collaboration between experts for workflow reproducibility, reusability, and data provenance [11]. Although the aims are similar, our approaches are different but potentially complementary.

UML Extensibility Mechanisms and Extensions. The creation of UML stereotype profiles allows UML meta-model extension and adaptation while keeping the existing UML syntax and semantics of the elements [16]. These stereotypes can have a different abstract syntax and extend either a meta-model class or another profile in a light-weight way, e.g., [12]. However, there is still no specific profile found for bioinformatics domain.

The literature covers several attempts to extend the UML AD meta-model for fields such as context-aware systems [1], production systems [3], project management [24], and business processes [22]. Although these extensions are not aimed for bioinformatics, some of these concepts and notations are useful and align with the needs found in this work. Therefore, we have used this work as inspiration (see Table 1 for more detail).

UML has been used previously for bioinformatics workflows. For example, the authors in [19] evaluated UML use for specifying biological systems and processes, aimed for analysis, simulation, and prediction. However, this work does not focus specifically on the human-oriented workflow issues that we address.

6   Conclusion

The current state of bioinformatics workflow documentation is subjective and unstandardised. This paper presents a UML AD extension with its concrete syntax and a WDST as one of the first attempts to provide a language for a standard representation, where bioinformaticians validated the proposed concrete syntax as understandable and straightforward. According to the bioinformaticians, this extension would be used to document standard workflows, usually requested by stakeholders. The created WDST requires refinement and automation to be used for knowledge sharing and documentation by the bioinformaticians, as it was evaluated negatively. Much of the negative feedback we received was directed towards the tool (draw.io) and not the specifics of the language. We suggest further investigation, including the exploration of other modeling tools and frameworks (e.g. ADOxx or Eclipse Sirius).

We hope to validate the concepts with a broader bioinformatics community. Finally, future work should use our new language to assess and improve workflows, including making decision criteria clearer and adding more workflow automation when possible.

Acknowledgements. This work was supported by a Chalmers ICT Area of Advance SEED project and the Swedish Foundation for Strategic Research (RIF14–0081).

References

1. Al-alshuhai, A., Siewe, F.: An extension of UML activity diagram to model the behaviour of context-aware systems. In: 2015 IEEE International Conference on Computer and Information Technology; Ubiquitous Computing and Communications; Dependable, Autonomic and Secure Computing; Pervasive Intelligence and Computing, pp. 431–437. IEEE (2015)
2. Amstutz, P., et al.: Common workflow language, v1. 0 (2016)
3. Bastos, R.M., Ruiz, D.D.A.: Extending UML activity diagram for workflow modeling in production systems. In: Proceedings of the 35th Annual Hawaii International Conference on System Sciences, pp. 3786–3795. IEEE (2002)
4. Brooke, J.: SUS: a retrospective. J. Usability Stud. **8**(2), 29–40 (2013)

5. Fernando, T., Gureev, N., Matskin, M., Zwick, M., Natschläger, T.: WorkflowDSL: scalable workflow execution with provenance for data analysis applications. In: 2018 IEEE 42nd Annual Computer Software and Applications Conference (COMPSAC), vol. 1, pp. 774–779. IEEE (2018)
6. de Figueroa, L.H.B., et al.: A modeling and elicitation approach for bioinformatics workflows: supporting material (2019). http://www.cse.chalmers.se/~jenho/BioinformaticsWorkflows/
7. Güss, C.D.: What is going through your mind? Thinking aloud as a method in cross-cultural psychology. Front. Psychol. **9**, 1292 (2018)
8. Harper, D., Thompson, A.R.: Qualitative Research Methods in Mental Health and Psychotherapy: A Guide for Students and Practitioners. Wiley, Hoboken (2011)
9. Hevner, A.R.: A three cycle view of design science research. Scand. J. Inf. Syst. **19**(2), 4 (2007)
10. Kanwal, S., Lonie, A., Sinnott, R.O.: Digital reproducibility requirements of computational genomic workflows (2017)
11. Karim, M.R., Michel, A., Zappa, A., Baranov, P., Sahay, R., Rebholz-Schuhmann, D.: Improving data workflow systems with cloud services and use of open data for bioinformatics research. Brief. Bioinf. **19**(5), 1035–1050 (2017)
12. Korherr, B., List, B.: Extending the UML 2 activity diagram with business process goals and performance measures and the mapping to BPEL. In: Roddick, J.F., et al. (eds.) ER 2006. LNCS, vol. 4231, pp. 7–18. Springer, Heidelberg (2006). https://doi.org/10.1007/11908883_4
13. Krishna, R., Elisseev, V., Antao, S.: BaaS - bioinformatics as a service. In: Mencagli, G., et al. (eds.) Euro-Par 2018. LNCS, vol. 11339, pp. 601–612. Springer, Cham (2019). https://doi.org/10.1007/978-3-030-10549-5_47
14. Moody, D.: The "physics" of notations: toward a scientific basis for constructing visual notations in software engineering. IEEE Trans. Softw. Eng. **35**(6), 756–779 (2009)
15. Moody, D.L., Heymans, P., Matulevicius, R.: Improving the effectiveness of visual representations in requirements engineering: an evaluation of i* visual syntax. In: 2009 17th IEEE International RE Conference, pp. 171–180. IEEE (2009)
16. OMG: OMG Unified Modeling Language (OMG UML), Superstructure, Version 2.4.1, August 2011. http://www.omg.org/spec/UML/2.4.1
17. Peffers, K., Tuunanen, T., Rothenberger, M.A., Chatterjee, S.: A design science research methodology for information systems research. J. Manag. Inf. Syst. **24**(3), 45–77 (2007)
18. Robertson, S., Robertson, J.: Mastering the Requirements Process: Getting Requirements Right. Addison-Wesley, Boston (2012)
19. Roux-Rouquié, M., Caritey, N., Gaubert, L., Rosenthal-Sabroux, C.: Using the unified modelling language (UML) to guide the systemic description of biological processes and systems. Biosystems **75**(1–3), 3–14 (2004)
20. Smith, J.A.: Qualitative Psychology: A Practical Guide to Research Methods. Sage, Thousand Oaks (2015)
21. Spyrou, S., Bamidis, P., Pappas, K., Maglaveras, N.: Extending UML activity diagrams for workflow modelling with clinical documents in regional health information systems. In: Connecting Medical Informatics and Bioinformatics: Proceedings of the 19th Medical Informatics Europe Conference (MIE2005), pp. 1160–1165 (2005)
22. Stefanov, V., List, B., Korherr, B.: Extending UML 2 activity diagrams with business intelligence objects. In: Tjoa, A.M., Trujillo, J. (eds.) DaWaK 2005. LNCS, vol. 3589, pp. 53–63. Springer, Heidelberg (2005). https://doi.org/10.1007/11546849_6

23. Störrle, H.: Semantics of structured nodes in UML 2.0 activities. In: 2nd Nordic Workshop on UML, pp. 19–32 (2004)
24. Syriani, E., Ergin, H.: Operational semantics of UML activity diagram: an application in project management. In: 2012 Second IEEE International Workshop on Model-Driven Requirements Engineering (MoDRE), pp. 1–8. IEEE (2012)
25. Taherdoost, H.: Sampling methods in research methodology; how to choose a sampling technique for research (2016)

Process Algebra to Control Nondeterministic Behavior of Enterprise Smart IoT Systems with Probability

Junsup Song and Moonkun Lee[✉]

Chonbuk National University, 567 Baekje-daero, Deokjin-gu,
Jeonju-si, Jeonbuk 54896, Republic of Korea
moonkun@jbnu.ac.kr

Abstract. Process algebra is one of the best suitable formal methods to model enterprise Smart IoT Systems with some uncertainty of risks. However, because of choice operations in process algebra, it is necessary to control nondeterministic behaviors of the systems. The process algebra, i.e., PAROMA, PACSR, tried to control the degree of selection in the choice operations with probability, but they didn't have any notion of controlling nondeterminism in the systems, since they were based on static probability models only. In order to overcome the limitation, the paper presents a new formal method, called dTP-Calculus, extended from the existing dT-Calculus with dynamic properties on probability. Consequently, it will provide all the necessary probable features to determine the safe and secure range of the system behaviors. For implementation, the SAVE tool suite has been developed on the ADOxx Meta-Modeling Platform, including Specifier, Analyzer and Verifier.

Keywords: dTP-Calculus · Formal method · Probability · Fault-tolerance · Smart IoT systems · SAVE · ADOxx Meta-Modeling Platform

1 Introduction

Enterprise Smart IoT Systems, like Smart City, are mostly based on IoT, and are run by Big Data and AI [1–3]. Because of the complexity and intelligence of the systems, the systems must be provided with some means of controlling the uncertainty caused by the complexity and against the intelligence to handle some probable risks.

In general, it is well known that process algebra is most suitable to model enterprise IoT systems, since each IoT can be considered as a process, and its activities and properties can be represented by those of the process in the algebra [4]. For example, distributedness, mobility, interactivity, control, periodicity, real-time, etc. Further, the unpredictable behavior of the systems from uncertainty can be represented by the unconditional nondeterministic choice operations in the algebra [5], which needs to be controlled by some means. The first method to control nondeterminism was the probability in PAROMA [6] and PACSR [7], based on the static probability models. However the method did not provide some feature to control uncertainty to satisfy

© IFIP International Federation for Information Processing 2019
Published by Springer Nature Switzerland AG 2019
J. Gordijn et al. (Eds.): PoEM 2019, LNBIP 369, pp. 184–196, 2019.
https://doi.org/10.1007/978-3-030-35151-9_12

threshold to manage risks, caused by nondeterminism, since PACSR was only based on discrete model and PAROMA only on exponential distribution model.

In order to overcome limitations, this paper presents dTP-Calculus [8, 9], a probabilistic process algebra extended from dT-Calculus [10] with dynamic probability properties. The model can control nondeterministic behavior of the system with the dynamic properties determined by the various functional entities. Further the model can be used to manage risks and capability. In order to prove the feasibility of the approach, the paper presents the SAVE tool suite [11] to specify, analyze and verify such systems with dTP-Calculus, developed on ADOxx Meta-Modeling Platform [12].

The paper consists of the following sections. In Sect. 2, dTP-Calculus is described. In Sect. 3, the controlling methods for nondeterminism are presented with usage. In Sect. 4, a Smart City example is specified and analyzed using dTP-Calculus. In Sect. 5, the SAVE tool is described. In Sect. 6, conclusions and future research are made.

2 dTP-Calculus

2.1 Syntax and Semantics

dTP-Calculus is a process algebra extended from existing dT-Calculus in order to define probabilistic behavior of processes on the choice operation. Note that dT-Calculus is the process algebra originally designed by the authors of the paper in order to specify and analyze various timed movements of processes on the virtual geographical space. The syntax of dTP-calculus is shown in Fig. 1.

$P ::= A$	Action ...... (1)	$A ::= \emptyset$	Empty ...... (12)
$\mid A^{p,n}_{[r,to,e,d]}$	Timed action ...... (2)	$\mid r(\overline{msg})$	Send ...... (13)
$\mid P^{p,n}_{[r,to,e,d]}$	Timed process ...... (3)	$\mid r(msg)$	Receive ...... (13)
$\mid P_{(n)}$	Priority ...... (4)	$\mid M$	Movement action
$\mid P[Q]$	Nesting ...... (5)	$\mid C$	Control action
$\mid P\langle r\rangle$	Channel ...... (6)	$M ::= m^p(k)\ P$	Movement request ..... (14)
$\mid P + Q$	Choice ...... (7)	$\mid P\ m(k)$	Movement permission (15)
$\mid P\{c\} +_F Q\{c\}$	Probabilistic choice .... (8)	$m ::= in$	In movement
$\mid P \parallel Q$	Parallel ......(9)	$\mid out$	Out movement
$\mid P\backslash E$	Exception ...... (10)	$\mid get$	Get movement
$\mid A \cdot P$	Sequence ...... (11)	$\mid put$	Put movement
$F ::= D$	Discrete distribution	$C ::= new\ P$	Create process ...... (16)
$\mid N(\mu,\sigma)$	Normal distribution	$\mid kill\ P$	Kill process ...... (17)
$\mid E(\lambda)$	Exponential distribution	$\mid exit$	Exit process ...... (18)
$\mid U(l,u)$	Uniform distribution		

Fig. 1. Syntax of dTP-Calculus

Each part of the syntax is defined as follows:

(1) *Action*: Actions performed by a process.
(2) *Timed action*: The execution of an action with temporal restrictions. The temporal properties of [*r, to, e, d*] represent *ready time, timeout, execution time*, and *deadline*, respectively. *p* and *n* are properties for periodic action or processes: *p* for period and *n* for the number of repetition.
(3) *Timed process*: Process with temporal properties.
(4) *Priority*: The priority of the process *P* represented by a natural number. The higher number represents the higher priority. Exceptionally, 0 represents the highest priority.
(5) *Nesting*: *P* contains *Q*. The internal process is controlled by its external process. If the internal process has a higher priority than that of its external, it can move out of its external without the permission of the external.
(6) *Channel*: A channel *r* of *P* to communicate with other processes.
(7) *Choice*: Only one of *P* and *Q* will be selected nondeterministically for execution.
(8) *Probabilistic choice*: Only one of *P* and *Q* will be selected probabilistically. Selection will be made based on a probabilistic model specified with *F*, and the condition for each selection will be defined with *c*.
(9) *Parallel*: Both *P* and *Q* are running concurrently.
(10) *Exception*: *P* will be executed. But *E* will be executed in case that *P* is out of timeout or deadline.
(11) *Sequence*: *P* follows after action *A*.
(12) *Empty*: No action.
(13) *Send/Receive*: Communication between processes, exchanging a message by a channel *r*.
(14) *Movement request*: Requests for movement. *p* and *k* represent priority and key, respectively.
(15) *Movement permission*: Permissions for movement.
(16) *Create process*: Creation of a new internal process. The new process cannot have a higher priority than its creator.
(17) *Kill process*: Termination of other processes. The terminator should have the higher priority than that of the terminatee.
(18) *Exit process*: Termination of its own process. All internal processes will be terminated at the same time.

Semantics of all the operations are defined as transition rules as shown in the Table 1.

Table 1. Semantics of dTP-Calculus

Name	Transition Rules	Name	Transition Rules
In	$\dfrac{P \xrightarrow{in(k)\,Q} P',\ Q \xrightarrow{P\,in(k)} Q'}{P \parallel Q \xrightarrow{\delta} Q'[P']}$	Out	$\dfrac{P \xrightarrow{out(k)\,Q} P',\ Q \xrightarrow{P\,out(k)} Q'}{Q[P] \xrightarrow{\delta} P' \parallel Q}$
Get	$\dfrac{P \xrightarrow{get(k)\,Q} P',\ Q \xrightarrow{P\,get(k)} Q'}{P \parallel Q \xrightarrow{\delta} P'[Q']}$	Put	$\dfrac{P \xrightarrow{put(k)\,Q} P',\ Q \xrightarrow{P\,put(k)} Q'}{P[Q] \xrightarrow{\delta} P' \parallel Q}$
InP	$\dfrac{P_{(n)} \xrightarrow{in^P(k)\,Q_{(m)}} P'_{(n)}}{P_{(n)} \parallel Q_{(m)} \xrightarrow{\delta} Q_{(m)}[P_{(n)}]}\ (n \geq m)$	OutP	$\dfrac{P_{(n)} \xrightarrow{out^P(k)\,Q_{(m)}} P'_{(n)}}{Q_{(m)}[P_{(n)}] \xrightarrow{\delta} P'_{(n)} \parallel Q_{(m)}}\ (n \geq m)$
GetP	$\dfrac{P_{(n)} \xrightarrow{get^P(k)\,Q_{(m)}} P'_{(n)}}{P_{(n)} \parallel Q_{(m)} \xrightarrow{\delta} Q_{(m)}[P_{(n)}]}\ (n \geq m)$	PutP	$\dfrac{P_{(n)} \xrightarrow{put^P(k)\,Q_{(m)}} P'_{(n)}}{Q_{(m)}[P_{(n)}] \xrightarrow{\delta} P'_{(n)} \parallel Q_{(m)}}\ (n \geq m)$
InN	$\dfrac{P \xrightarrow{in(k)\,Q} P',\ Q \xrightarrow{P\,in(k)} Q'}{P \parallel Q[R] \xrightarrow{\delta} Q'[P' \parallel R]}$	GetN	$\dfrac{P \xrightarrow{get(k)\,Q} P',\ Q \xrightarrow{P\,get(k)} Q'}{P[R] \parallel Q \xrightarrow{\delta} P'[R \parallel Q']}$
Action	$\dfrac{-}{A.P \xrightarrow{A} P}$	ChoiceL ChoiceR	$\dfrac{P_{(n)} \xrightarrow{a} P'_{(n)}}{P_{(n)} + Q_{(n)} \xrightarrow{a} P'_{(n)}},\ \dfrac{Q_{(n)} \xrightarrow{a} Q'_{(n)}}{P_{(n)} + Q_{(n)} \xrightarrow{a} Q'_{(n)}}$
ChoiceP	$\dfrac{P_{(n)} \xrightarrow{a_1} P_{(n)}}{P_{(n)} + Q_{(n)} \xrightarrow{a} P'_{(n)}}$	ParlL ParlR	$\dfrac{P \xrightarrow{a} P'}{P \parallel Q \xrightarrow{a} P' \parallel Q},\ \dfrac{Q \xrightarrow{a} Q'}{P \parallel Q \xrightarrow{a} P \parallel Q'}$
ParCom	$\dfrac{P \xrightarrow{a} P',\ Q \xrightarrow{\bar{a}} Q'}{P \parallel Q \xrightarrow{\tau} P' \parallel Q'}$	NestO NestI	$\dfrac{P \xrightarrow{a} P'}{P[Q] \xrightarrow{a} P'[Q]},\ \dfrac{Q \xrightarrow{a} Q'}{P[Q] \xrightarrow{a} P[Q']}$
NestCom	$\dfrac{P \xrightarrow{a} P',\ Q \xrightarrow{\bar{a}} Q'}{P[Q] \xrightarrow{\tau} P'[Q']}$	Tick-Time R	$\dfrac{-}{A_{[r,to,e,d]} \xrightarrow{\triangleright_1} A_{[r-1,to,e,d-1]}}\ (r \geq 1)$
Tick-Time TO	$\dfrac{-}{A_{[0,to,e,d]} \xrightarrow{\triangleright_1} A_{[0,to-1,e,d-1]}}\ (to \geq 1)$	Tick-Time End	$\dfrac{-}{A_{[0,to,0,d]} \blacksquare A' \xrightarrow{\triangleright_1} A'}$
Tick-Time SyncE	$\dfrac{A\vert A' \xrightarrow{(\tau \vee \delta) \wedge \triangleright_1} A''\vert A'''}{A_{[0,to_1,e_1,d_1]}\vert A'_{[0,to_2,e_2,d_2]}\ \&\&\ \xrightarrow{(\tau \vee \delta) \wedge \triangleright_1} A_{[0,to_1,e_1-1,d_1-1]}\vert A'_{[0,to_2,e_2-1,d_2-1]}}\ (e_1 \geq 1 \wedge e_2 \geq 1)$		
Tick-Time AsyncE	$\dfrac{-}{A_{[0,to,e,d]} \xrightarrow{\triangleright_1} A_{[0,to,e-1,d-1]}}$	Tick-Time P	$\dfrac{-}{P_{[r,to,e,d]} \xrightarrow{\triangleright_1} P_{[r,to,e,d-1]}}$
Timeout	$\dfrac{-}{A_{[0,0,e,d]} \backslash P \xrightarrow{\triangleright_1} P}$	Dead-line	$\dfrac{-}{A_{[r,to,e,0]} \backslash P \xrightarrow{\triangleright_1} P}$
Period	$\dfrac{-}{A^{p,n}_{[r,to,e,d]} \xrightarrow{\triangleright_p} A^{p,n-1}_{[r,to,e,d]}}\ (n > 1)$	Period End	$\dfrac{-}{A^{p,1}_{[r,to,e,d]} \cdot A' \xrightarrow{\triangleright_p} A'}$
Probability Choice	$\dfrac{a.P \xrightarrow{a} P}{(\sum_{i \in I} a_i\{p_i\}).P \xrightarrow{a_i\{p_i\}} P'}\ (\sum_{i \in I} a_i = 1, i \in I)$		

2.2 Probability

There are 4 types of probabilistic models to specify probabilistic choice as follows. Each model may require variables to be used to define probability properties:

(1) Discrete distribution: It is a probabilistic model without variable. It simply defines specific value of probability for each branch of the choice operation. There are some restrictions. For example, the summation of the probability branches cannot be over 100%.

(2) Normal distribution: It is a probabilistic model based on the normal distribution with the mean value of μ and the standard deviation of σ, whose density function is defined by $f(x|\mu, \sigma^2) = \frac{1}{\sigma\sqrt{2\pi}}\exp\left(-\frac{(x-\mu)^2}{2\sigma^2}\right)$.

(3) Exponential distribution: This is a probabilistic model based on the exponential distribution with frequency of λ, whose density function is defined by $f(x; \lambda) = \lambda e^{-\lambda x}(x \geq 0)$.

(4) Uniform distribution: This is a probabilistic model based on the uniform distribution with the lower bound l and the upper bound u, whose density function is defined by $f(x) = \begin{cases} 0 & (x < a \vee x > b) \\ \frac{1}{u-l} & (l \leq x \leq u) \end{cases}$

2.3 Example

As an example, the PBC example is defined in dTP-Calculus as shown Fig. 2. It consists of 3 processes: P (for Producer), B (for Buffer), and C (for Consumer). Note that there are two processes, $R1$ and $R2$ (for Resource), in P. The operational requirements with probability are as follows:

(1) *Producer* produces two resources, $R1$ and $R2$.
(2) *Producer* stores the resources in *Buffer* in order.
(3) *Producer* informs *Buffer* of the order of $R1$ and $R2$, or $R2$ and $R1$.
　　　① The probability of choosing the order of $R1$ and $R2$ for *Producer* is 0.6 ; that of $R2$ and $R1$ is 0.4.
　　　② The probability of choosing the order of $R1$ and $R2$ for *Consumer* is 0.7; That of $R2$ and $R1$ is 0.3.
(4) *Consumer* consumes the resources from *Buffer* in order.
(5) *Consumer* informs *Buffer* of the order of $R1$ and $R2$, or $R2$ and $R1$.
　　　① The probability of choosing the order of $R1$ and $R2$ for *Consumer* is 0.5; That of $R2$ and $R1$ is 0.5.
　　　② The probability of choosing the order of $R1$ and R2 for *Buffer* is 0.8; That of $R2$ and $R1$ is 0.2.

```
PBC = P[R1 ∥ R2] ∥ B ∥ C;
P = (PB(Send R1){0.6}.put R1.put R2+_D PB(Send R2){0.4}.put R2.put R1).exit;
B = (PB(Send R1){0.7}.get R1.get R2+_D PB(Send R2){0.3}.get R2.get R2).
      (CB(Send R1){0.5}.put R1.put R2+_D CB(Send R2){0.5}.put R2.put R1).exit;
C = (CB(Send R1){0.8}.get R1.get R2+_D CB(Send R2){0.2}.get R2.get R1).exit;
R1 = P put.B get.B put.C get.exit;
R2 = P put.B get.B put.C get.exit;
```

Fig. 2. Code for PBC example

The pictorial system view of the example is shown in Fig. 3, where P and B are connected with a channel PB, and P and B with a channel PB. Note that the synchronous communications between P and B on PB are uncertain due to the unconditional nondeterministic choice operation, but these are controlled by probability on the choice operation, which causes 4 possible combination of the communication with the probability of 0.42, 0.28, 0.18, and 0.12 from the 0.6 vs. 0.4 of P by the 0.7 vs. 0.3 of B. Both operations are ruled by the definitions of *ParCom* and *ProbabilityChoice* in Table 1. Similarly, those between B and C on BC are 0.40, 0.40, 0.10, and 0.10 from the 0.5 vs. 0.5 of B by the 0.8 vs. 0.2 of C.

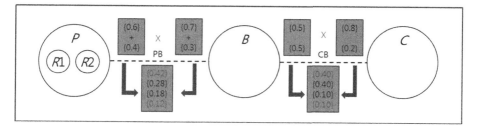

Fig. 3. System view for PBC example with probabilities

3   Control Methods and Usage

3.1   Probability Function Management

The left side of Fig. 4 shows the reachability graph of the PBC Example. The top node indicates the 4 possible compositions of the synchronous communication between P and B on PB, with the probabilities of 0.42, 0.28, 0.18, and 0.12 from the 0.6 vs. 0.4 of P by the 0.7 vs. 0.3 of B, ruled by the definitions of *ParCom* and *ProbabilityChoice* in Table 1. Notice that the middle 2 cases are of deadlock. From the left-most and the right-most compositions show the normal compositions without deadlock, from which another following synchronous communication between B and C on BC, with the probabilities of 0.40, 0.40, 0.10, and 0.10 from the 0.6 vs. 0.4 of P by the 0.7 vs. 0.3 of B, ruled by the same definitions in Table 1, resulting the compositions of two probabilities to be 0.168, 0.168, 0042, and 0.042 for the right-most, and 0.048, 0.048, 0.012, and 0.012 for the left-most. Notice that the middle 2 cases are of deadlock for both compositions. Finally we can see that the total probability of the safe execution paths without deadlock is 0.27, as shown at the bottom node of the graph.

Sometimes the results are not acceptable, and it is necessary to increase the total system probability by changing the probabilities of the nondeterministic choice operations for P and B, as well as B and C. For example, as the left side of Fig. 4 shows:

(3) *Producer* informs *Buffer* of the order of $R1$ and $R2$, or $R2$ and R1.
  ① The probability of choosing the order of $R1$ and $R2$ for *Producer* is 0.9; That of R2 and R1 is 0.1.

② The probability of choosing the order of *R1* and *R2* for *Consumer* is
0.79; That of *R2* and *R1* is 0.1.

(5) *Consumer* informs *Buffer* of the order of *R1* and *R2*, or *R2* and *R1*.

① The probability of choosing the order of *R1* and *R2* for *Consumer* is
0.9; That of *R2* and *R1* is 0.1.

② The probability of choosing the order of *R1* and *R2* for *Buffer* is 0.9;
That of *R2* and *R1* is 0.1.

As a result, the final probability is increased to .6724 from 0.27. Further it is
possible to define some function with the probability variables in order to control
dynamically the acceptable probability for the systems.

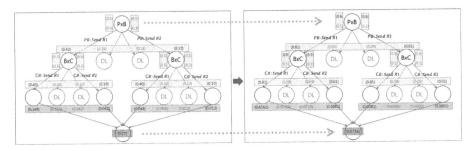

Fig. 4. Reachability execution trees for PBC example with probability

3.2   Risk Management

In the business applications, there are a number of transactions or decisions to be made
in the systems, while managing some risks. Similarly, in the industrial applications,
there are a number of interactions to be made by synchronization or nondeterministic
selections in the IoT systems, while managing some faults. In either case, it is necessary to evaluate the critical value to tolerate the risks or faults, while performing the
specified operations.

The left graph in Fig. 5 shows the case from the PBC example, where a specific
execution path is to be selected while performing the operations in order to satisfy the
risk or fault tolerance rate less than 0.2, which is the right-most path among all 4
possible paths. More specifically, from the top node, the right-most execution path, that
is, the synchronous communication between *P* and *B* on PB for transferring resource
R2 and *R1* in order, is selected since the risk or fault-tolerance rate is 0.01, which is less
than 0.2 in the requirement. Similarly, from that right-most node, the right-most execution path, that is, the synchronous communication between *B* and *C* on *BC* for
transferring resource *R2* and *R1* in order, is selected since the risk or fault-tolerance rate
is 0.01, which is less than 0.2 in the requirement. In case that there is no path that
satisfies the rate, it will be necessary to change the probabilities dynamically in order to
decrease the rate under the acceptable level.

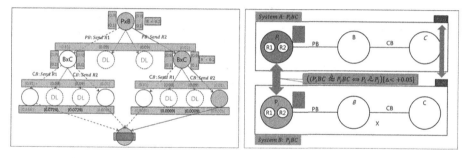

Fig. 5. Path selection for risk management and process substitution for capability management

3.3   Capability Management

Sometimes, it is necessary to substitute one IoT with another IoT while managing same capability in the IoT Systems. In order to satisfy the capability requirements for the substitution, there should be some way of evaluating the capability with respect to probability in order to control uncertain for substitution. In the dTP-Calculus, the probability determines the degree of nondeterminism during the choice operations and effects the final system probabilities. For example in the PBC example, the top system view from the right graph in Fig. 5 shows 0.27 of safe system executions without deadlock, where Process P_i has a successful choice operation with the 0.6 probability. Somehow there is a problem that P_i does not work properly and needs to be replaced. Then it is necessary to evaluate which process is suitable for replacement. As the bottom system of the figure shows that, if P_j has a successful choice operation with the 0.7 probability and satisfies the probability based system similarity with the tolerance of less than 0.05, that is, 0.29, it can be replaced for P_i. The process can represent any person, agent, thing, or device in a system.

4   A Smart City Example: SEES on SAVE

This section demonstrates the applicability of dTP-Calculus to a Smart City Example based on the IoT systems, known as *Smart Emergency Evacuation System* (SEES), on the SAVE tool, which is developed on the ADOxx Meta-Modeling Platform.

4.1   Specification

Figures 6 and 7 show both the dTP-Calculus specification and the system view for the SEES example. The processes in the example as defined as follows:

(1) *Control System*: The main process to control other processes in case of fire.
(2) *Sensor*: The process to detect fires on Stair *A* and Stair *B*.
(3) *Building*: The process to represent the building where the fire occurs. It contains all the related processes in the building, except *911*.
(4) *Floor*: The process to represent the floors in the building. There are two floors: *1st* and *2nd Floor*s. And two persons, *P*1 and *P*2, on *2nd Floor*.

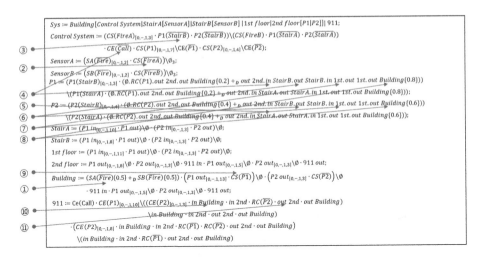

Fig. 6. dTP-Calculus code for SEES example

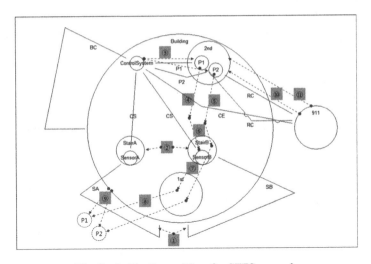

Fig. 7. In-The-Large View for SEES example

(5) *Stair*: The process to represent stairs. There are two stairs: Stair A and Stair B. A fire occurs at one of the stairs.

(6) *Person*: The processes to represent the persons in the building, P1 and P2.

(7) 911: The process to perform fire extinction and people rescue.

SEES performs its operations in order as follows. Note that each action is denoted with the number, representing action or interactions from Figs. 6 and 7:

(1) A fire occurs on *1st Floor* or *2nd Floor*: ①.

(2) Sensor detects the fire and sends a signal to *Control System*: ②.

(3) *Control System* informs *Person* of the fire and shows the escape route. And it sends the signal to *911*: ④.

(4) Each *Person* may get out of *Building* safely, or be confined on *2nd Floor*: ⑤, ⑥, ⑦, ⑧.

(5) *Building* detects the escape of *Person*, and sends the information of the escaped to *Control System*: ⑨.

(6) *Control System* sends the information of the confined to *911*: ⑩.

(7) *911* enters *Building*, extinguishes the fire on *2nd Floor*, and rescues *Person* if any: ⑪.

A fire occurs at Stair *A* or Stair *B* in Building, and each *Person* may or may not escape from *Building*. In SEES, three kinds of probabilistic choices are specified as follows:

(1) *Building:* $SA(\overline{Fire})\{0.5\} +_D SB(\overline{Fire})\{0.5\}$

(2) $P1 : \emptyset...\{0.2\} +_D$ *out 2nd*...$\{0.8\}$

(3) $P2 : \emptyset...\{0.4\} +_D$ *out 2nd*...$\{0.6\}$.

For simplicity, all the probabilities are defined to be of discrete distribution. For the first probability, it is assumed that the probabilities of detecting a fire from Sensor *A* and *B* are same: 0.50 vs 0.50. For the second probability, it is assumed that the probabilities for *Person* 1 to escape from *Building* by himself to be 0.80, and that of not escaping 0.20, in which case he is to be rescued by 911. Similarly, for the last probability, that of escaping for *Person* 2 to be 0.60, and that of not escaping to be 0.40.

4.2 Probability Analysis

The left side graph in Fig. 8 is the execution model for SEES, generated by SAVE. Note that there are total 8 paths in the figure, where each path represents the status how Person *P1* and *P2* are escaped or rescued safely. The right side of the figure shows the probability of each path, where *P1* or *P2* indicates the status of being escaped from Building and *P1'* or *P2'* indicates the status of being rescued by 911.

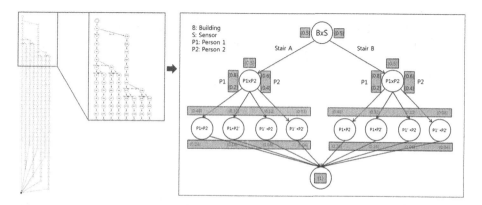

Fig. 8. Execution model for SEES and its probabilistic execution tree

The top node of the tree shows the probability of detecting a fire from Sensor *A* and *B* are same: 0.50 vs 0.50. The second nodes from the first nods show two probabilities: (1) the probability for *Person* 1 to escape from *Building* by himself to be 0.80, and that of not escaping 0.20, as shown in the left box from the nodes, and (2) the probability of *Person* 2 to be 0.60, and that of not escaping to be 0.40, as shown in the right box from the nodes. The third nodes from the second nodes show two types of all the combinations of the probabilities: (1) the combinations of probabilities for *P*1 and *P*2 are 0.48, 0.32, 0.12, and 0.08 from the 0.8 vs. 0.2 of *P*1 by the 0.6 vs. 0.4 of *P*2, as shown in the top box from the nodes, and (2) the combinations of its probabilities with the sensor probability are 0.24, 0.16, 0.06, and 0.04 by 0.5 of Sensor *A* or *B,* as shown in the bottom box from the nodes. From the tree, it can be analyzed that the probability for both *P*1 and *P*2 to escape from the building is 0.48 in total, the probability for either *P*1 or *P*2 to do is 0.44 in total, and the probability for both *P*1 and *P*2 not to do is 0.08 in total. If the final probabilities are not acceptable, it is possible to change dynamically the probabilities for detecting fires and guiding people to safe evacuation routes by increasing the number of sensors for better visibility and temperature in air.

5   SAVE

SAVE is a suite of tools to specify and analyze the IoT systems with dTP-Calculus. It is developed on the ADOxx Meta-Modeling Platform. SAVE consists of the following basic three components:

(1)   Specifier, as shown in Fig. 9, is a tool to specify the IoT systems with dTP-Calculus, visually in the diagrammatic representations [2]. The left side of Fig. 9 is the In-the-Large (ITL) model, or system view, representing both inclusion relations among components of the system and communication channels among them. The right side of the Fig. 9 is In-the-Small (ITS) models, or process view, representing a sequence of the detailed actions, interactions and movements performed by a process.

(2)   Analyzer is a tool to generate the execution model from the specification in order to explore all the possible execution paths, as the left side of Fig. 10 shows, and to perform the simulation of each execution from the execution model in order to analyze probabilistic behaviors of the specified system.

(3)   Verifier is a tool to verify a set of system requirements on the geo-temporal space output generated from each, as the right side of Fig. 10 shows. It checks the behaviors of the system for safety and security requirements and shows their results on the output.

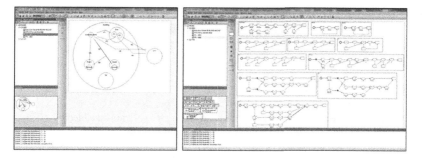

Fig. 9. Specification tool of SAVE

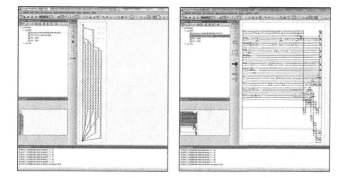

Fig. 10. Analysis and verification tool of SAVE

6   Conclusions and Future Research

This paper presented dTP-Calculus in order to model enterprise Smart IoT Systems, like Smart City, with uncertainty to safety and security of the systems. It showed that the algebra can be used to control the uncertainty with dynamic probability features on the unconditional nondeterministic choice operations, and that the algebra can provide good facilities to manage risks and capabilities with the systems. Further the paper presented the SAVE tool to demonstrate the feasibility of the approach with the calculus. It can be considered to be one of the innovative methods to handle the uncertainty for enterprise Smart IoT Systems.

The future research will include application of dTP-Calculus and SAVE to real enterprise industry examples to demonstrate their efficiency and effectiveness as method and tool.

Acknowledgment. This work was supported by Basic Science Research Programs through the National Research Foundation of Korea (NRF) funded by the Ministry of Education (2010-0023787), Space Core Technology Development Program through the National Research Foundation of Korea (NRF) funded by the Ministry of Science, ICT and Future Planning (NRF-2014M1A3A3A02034792), Basic Science Research Program through the National Research

Foundation of Korea (NRF) funded by the Ministry of Education (NRF-2015R1D1A3A01 019282), and Hyundai NGV, Korea, and Research Fund from Chonbuk National University (2018–2019).

References

1. Skouby, K.E., Lynggaard, P.: Smart home and smart city solutions enabled by 5G, IoT, AAI and CoT services. In: 2014 International Conference on Contemporary Computing and Informatics (IC3I), pp. 874–878. IEEE (2014)
2. Chin, J., Callaghan, V., Lam, I.: Understanding and personalising smart city services using machine learning, the Internet-of-Things and big data. In: 2017 IEEE 26th International Symposium on Industrial Electronics (ISIE), pp. 2050–2055. IEEE (2017)
3. Allam, Z., Dhunny, Z.A.: On big data, artificial intelligence and smart cities. Cities **89**, 80–91 (2019)
4. Choe, Y., Lee, M.: Algebraic method to model secure IoT. Domain-Specific Conceptual Modeling, pp. 335–355. Springer, Cham (2016). https://doi.org/10.1007/978-3-319-39417-6_15
5. Meldal, S., Walicki, M.: Nondeterministic Operators in Algebraic Frameworks. Stanford University, Stanford (1995)
6. Feng, C., Hillston, J.: PALOMA: a process algebra for located Markovian agents. In: Norman, G., Sanders, W. (eds.) QEST 2014. LNCS, vol. 8657, pp. 265–280. Springer, Cham (2014). https://doi.org/10.1007/978-3-319-10696-0_22
7. Lee, I., Philippou, A., Sokolsky, O.: Resources in process algebra. J. Logic Algebraic Program. **72**(1), 98–122 (2007)
8. Choe, Y., Lee, M.: Process model to predict nondeterministic behavior of IoT systems. In: Proceedings of the 2nd International Workshop on Practicing Open Enterprise Modelling within OMiLAB (PrOse) (2018)
9. Song, J., Choe, Y., Lee, M.: Application of probabilistic process model for smart factory systems. In: Douligeris, C., Karagiannis, D., Apostolou, D. (eds.) KSEM 2019. LNCS (LNAI), vol. 11776, pp. 25–36. Springer, Cham (2019). https://doi.org/10.1007/978-3-030-29563-9_3
10. Choe, Y., Lee, S., Lee, M.: dT-Calculus: a process algebra to model timed movements of processes. Int. J. Comput. **2**, 53–62 (2017)
11. Choe, Y., Lee, S., Lee, M.: SAVE: an environment for visual specification and verification of IoT. In: 2016 IEEE 20th International Enterprise Distributed Object Computing Workshop (EDOCW), pp. 1–8. IEEE (2016)
12. Fill, H.G., Karagiannis, D.: On the conceptualisation of modeling methods using the ADOxx meta modeling platform. In: Proceedings of Enterprise Modeling and Information Systems Architectures (EMISAJ), vol. 8, no. 1, pp. 4–25 (2013)

Enterprise Architecture for Security, Privacy and Compliance

Using an Enterprise Architecture Model for GDPR Compliance Principles

Gaëlle Blanco-Lainé[1], Jean-Sébastien Sottet[2(✉)], and Sophie Dupuy-Chessa[3]

[1] Univ. Grenoble Alpes, IUT2, 38000 Grenoble, France
Gaelle.Blanco-Laine@univ-grenoble-alpes.fr
[2] LIST, 5, Avenue des Hauts-Fourneaux, 4362 Esch-Sur-Alzette, Luxembourg
Jean-Sebastien.Sottet@list.lu
[3] Univ. Grenoble Alpes, CNRS, Grenoble INP, LIG, 38000 Grenoble, France
Sophie.Dupuy-Chessa@univ-grenoble-alpes.fr

Abstract. Nowadays, all enterprises must take into account the legal frameworks at all levels of their organization. Over the past two years, the focus has been on the GDPR. This regulation on data and their processing activities impacts on the vision of the enterprise information system. In order to identify these impacts, it is necessary to define an approach to conciliate regulatory and business points of view. Our proposal is to use an enterprise architecture modeling approach to integrate regulatory concerns. This article describes a high-level Archimate model for implementing a GDPR compliance approach.

Keywords: GDPR · Architecture enterprise · Regulation and compliance · Privacy · Model

1 Introduction

The legal framework is a major constraint for all enterprises, notably when dealing with an increasing number of legal regulations or when their complexity raises, e.g., in the financial sector [1]. Our work partially addresses this issue by dealing with the understanding of the new regulations and their consequences on the enterprise architecture. It promotes the use of models, notably Enterprise Architecture Models (EAM) to support enterprises with their obligation to regulatory compliance. In regard to this purpose, we have chosen to work on the new European regulations on the processing of personal data: the General Data Protection Regulation (GDPR) [2].

The effective date of the GDPR in May 2018 has fundamentally changed the way companies must collect and process personal data. They are now subject to an ongoing, proactive and continuous obligation to comply with the rules set out in the GDPR. Being and remaining compliant with the GDPR is currently a major issue for organizations worldwide. The problem relies on understanding legal requirements which is generally time-consuming and cumbersome [3].

© IFIP International Federation for Information Processing 2019
Published by Springer Nature Switzerland AG 2019
J. Gordijn et al. (Eds.): PoEM 2019, LNBIP 369, pp. 199–214, 2019.
https://doi.org/10.1007/978-3-030-35151-9_13

Without the assistance of data protection law experts, the operationalization of the GDPR can be jeopardized, especially for small- and medium-sized organizations. To address this issue, we suggest that a legal expert helps at defining a common model conciliating the legal and business approaches. As the GDPR constrains activities in terms of data and their processing, it can impact the information system at all levels: from the strategic level (to avoid sanctions) to the application and technological levels (to guarantee data security and privacy).

We aim at developing an reference architecture that depicts the principles of the GDPR so that it can be reused by enterprises with little legal knowledge. Our model highlights the links between the principles and the obligations supported by the regulation. It is implemented in an ArchiMate model, constituting a fragment that can be reused, by any organization for GDPR compliance.

The paper is organized as follow: first we describe related work about modelling the GDPR. Second, we introduce our approach: proposing an EAM for describing and explaining the GDPR. Third, we detail the GDPR model.

2   Related Work

With the goal of achieving compliance to the GDPR, [3] suggests that researchers and practitioners have investigated three main approaches: compliance checklists and assessment toolkits, operationalizing the GDPR with some specific data protection techniques and modeling of the regulation and its requirements.

The first approach has been developed by public agencies and private companies to support organizations in checking their compliance to the GDPR. Public agencies propose some guides for understanding the GDPR and its impact for organizations and citizen. Some of them [4] also make some self-assessment checklists. Private companies, like Microsoft [5], have provided their own toolkits to assess measures for protecting personal data. These assessment checklists and toolkits are good diagnostic tools as they can be useful to identify large gaps in compliance. However, they are not steering tools that provide concrete suggestions, particularly by taking the organizational aspects into account.

The second approach proposes some concrete data protection techniques, focusing then on a limited number of the GDPR concerns. For instance, Ayala-Rivera and Pasquale [3] define privacy controls inside system requirements, to ensure compliance to GDPR. Nevertheless they do not provide crucial legal requirements like the need for establishing a consent or a record of processing activities. Agostinelli et al. [6] propose a set of patterns for ensuring compliance of BPMN processes and fragmenting the GDPR principles for a better comprehension. However, the article focuses only on the obligations of the data controller and thus not necessarily provides rational and assistance to the overall GDPR management. Colesky et al. [7] also proposes a set of strategies and tactics to operate privacy protection. Although these works illustrate the usefulness of providing concrete suggestions for GDPR compliance, they do not provide a view of the GDPR impact on the enterprise architecture.

The last approach suggests to model the regulation concepts to achieve GDPR compliance. Some of these works rely on ontologies, using a well-known method for law modeling like [8]. This work consists of a domain ontology describing the basic elements that are required by the GDPR. A second step is to provide a set of rules [9] to ensure compliance and to identify the gap to be compliant, e.g., [10]. Following the ontological approach, [11] proposes a framework for a generic compliance tool (i.e. compliance to any legal model) that they apply to the GDPR. However the framework relies on questions that can be ambiguous, leading to an inappropriate assessment. Moreover, if an ontology-based approach is interesting to reason on a regulation, it does not provide an organizational view of the GDPR.

Another approach, similar to ontologies, is based on a semi-formal domain model. [12] proposes a preliminary model describing the concepts of the GDPR. It scopes the domain of discourse, by depicting the kind of data (i.e. the different personal data kinds) and processes to be considered. However it needs to be completed with other models to provide some concrete help. With such goal, the work described in [13] proposes a generic conceptual model for GDPR and a global approach based on it to check compliance. By focusing on softwares, it does not provide a global view of the impact of the GDPR on the organization.

Related work presents interesting approaches to provide guidance in checking compliance and in understanding the impact of the GDPR. Nevertheless, none of them proposes a global vision of the GDPR effects at all the levels of an organization. With such goal, we propose to model the GDPR regulation at the different levels of an enterprise architecture.

3   Towards a GDPR Architecture

3.1   Introduction to GDPR

In an attempt to clarify the area of work, it is important to review some elements of the GDPR. Following the European directive 95/46/EC on the protection of individuals with regard to the processing of personal data and on the free movement of such data, the GDPR reaffirms the obligation of enterprises to respect a set of obligations aimed at protecting personal data: prior consent collection, data minimisation, security, etc. These obligations, described in 7 key principles (see Fig. 1) have marginally changed between the two regulations.

The GDPR removes the obligation of prior notification to the authorities (Article 18 Directive 95/46/EC) and replaces it with the obligation for companies to prove at any time at the request of the supervisory authority that their processes comply with the regulations. This is the principle of accountability. This paradigm shift implies a reinforced obligation for enterprises to document and monitor all their processing operations relating to personal data. To ensure compliance with all the principles and ensure regulatory compliance within accountability, the processes corresponding to each of the 7 key principles must be defined. If the obligations within the GDPR are not scheduled, the nature of the data and processes to be put in place for compliance and maintenance leads to the definition of a logical order of implementation (see Fig. 6).

Moreover we introduce some definitions to facilitate the understanding of the rest of the paper: **data controller**, according to article 4(7) is: "the natural or legal person,[...], alone or jointly with others, determines the purposes and means of the processing of personal data". A **data subject** is natural person whom the data collection will identify directly or indirectly. The **Consent** means any informed agreement to the processing of personal data (article 11 GDPR).

3.2 Global Approach

Our approach aims at providing a global viewpoint of the GDPR in terms of the rights and requirements it conveys. It has been realized by a legal expert for interpreting and explaining the GDPR and a collaborative modeling work between the legal expert and computer scientists.

To provide a global viewpoint, EAM constitutes an interesting solution. It offers different perspectives, including in particular a regulative perspective [14] which is naturally of interest to our work. By nature, EAM embeds principles that can be related to regulation aspects, e.g, recommendations, requirements, impositions, etc. As a result, we depict the GDPR regulation as a part of an enterprise architecture. This idea is also conveyed in a reference model for regulation [15] and in reference organization/enterprise models [16]. The GDPR regulation and its objectives for compliance cover only a part of enterprise architecture concerns: so we will define some architecture fragments [17]. But the layers beyond the business one are specific to an implementation of the regulatory compliance solution; we did not study them.

We selected the ArchiMate language as it fits with our modelling goals: having a support for modelling regulation as architecture; being compatible and potential partially incorporated within an actual enterprise architecture model.

3.3 Domain and Goal Models

First of all, understanding a regulation implies understating its underlying vocabulary and semantics [8,12], i.e. establishing a domain model or an ontology. The legal text defines more or less explicitly, the relevant concepts and their relationship. To complete this initial model, we also looked at cases, jurisprudence which may refine the concepts of the law. The domain model notably defines, what are the type of personal data (e.g., marital status, genetic data, etc.) and the kind of processing activities (e.g., profiling, data transfer, etc.).

In a second time, we analyze the underlying principles of the regulation. They can be modeled as goals [18]. Those goals, also provide a rationale (i.e. belonging to the motivation layer) and the fundamental organization for the regulation architecture we provide. This approach requires a complete study of the regulation: each regulation contains explicit rights, principles which can then be translated into (regulatory) goals. Each goal is then refined into outcomes and requirements. Each requirement helps in defining the necessary measures to be put in place for compliance. It can be either a rule or a process or an organizational structure. To generalize this, we use the concept of business service.

3.4   Services and Processes

Business services define the entry points of actions, sub-systems, processes to be performed by an enterprise to be compliant with the regulation. They represent answers to the previously defined regulatory requirements. They can be grouped by important core regulatory functions, such as processing activities and personal data maintenance. Contrary to [18] which expresses GDPR links between goals, we define the dependency relationship between services: the legal principles, and so goals, are to be considered as self-contained elements. But, the business implementation may require information from another service. As a result, we have to define an orchestration between the services that express the regulation.

Then we study each regulatory service and we define their behavior using a high business processes description. Each service and their process implementation manipulate the related domain elements.

3.5   Implementation in Organizations

By having the regulation formalized as an architectural fragment, we aim at simplifying its integration into an existing architecture or one in the process of being defined (following the principle of compliance by design). We want to ensure that a process (application and infrastructures) is in place in order to support the corresponding business service. An Enterprise Architect has to bridge this fragment to its specific implementation in the enterprise. We try to be as much generic as possible regarding enterprises. As a consequence, we cannot go deeper into the applications and technical layers. For instance, the data retention period defined in the GDPR implies many different implementations of deletion when the retention period expires as it depends on the data support (paper, usb-key, internal information system, etc.).

4   Modeling GDPR in ArchiMate

4.1   GDPR Principles: Motivation View

As proposed in Sect. 3, we first need to understand the GDPR domain model and goals. As domain models have already been proposed [12,13], we focus here on regulatory goals.

We define an ArchiMate motivation view for the regulation (Fig. 1) which helps to clarify the regulatory obligations with regard to the key principles of the GDPR, set out in article 5 of the regulation.

First, the GDPR analysis highlights two important identifiable areas in terms of regulatory obligations, compliance and accountability associated with their control elements, Privacy Impact Assessment (PIA) and the record of processing activities (see Sect. 4.4). These two obligations are represented as drivers in the ArchiMate model. Then drivers give rise to goals that correspond to the 7 key principles for the protection of personal data as they constrain the activities of enterprises in terms of data and processing:

1. **Provide transparency on information about personal data usage** corresponding to the principle of transparency.
2. **Obtain consent** corresponding to the principle of free and informed data collect and usage.
3. **Ensure personal data accuracy** corresponding to the principle of data accuracy, requiring enterprises to provide procedures for updating data.
4. **Restrict personal data collect** corresponding to the principle of minimization of data collection, according to which all personal data collected must strictly comply with a purpose legitimately pursued by the enterprise.
5. **Restrict personal data processing activities scope** according to which the processing on data must be directly linked to the enterprise activity.
6. **Ensure right to oblivion** corresponding to the principle of respect for the right to be forgotten.
7. **Ensure personal data security** for the data security principle.

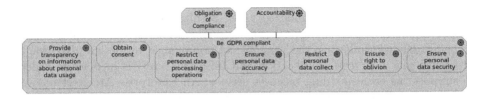

Fig. 1. GDPR motivation view

Article 5 of the GDPR sets out the obligation to obtain the data subject's consent (goal 2, Fig. 1). It must be free and informed, which implies that collecting consent must be accompanied by sufficient information arising from the obligation of transparency.

This obligation (goal 1 in Fig. 1), described in article 13 of the GDPR, is based on the ability for the enterprise to provide data subjects with sufficiently complete information at the time of personal data collection about the enterprise, the data collected, their storage period, the processing operations to ensure the right to oblivion (goal 6). In addition, it should describe all the processing operations using personal data, the purpose of these operations, as well as the data security measures (goal 7). These data security measures are set up within the enterprise to prevent any use not in line with the stated objectives, and to ensure their confidentiality and integrity. Depending on the enterprise activity, these elements will have to be supplemented by general information on how to exercise the rights to ensure data accuracy (goal 4) or forgetting, and the possible means of recourse available for the persons concerned. The GDPR also limits the collect and processing operations (goals 5 and 3) of personal data to data and operations strictly necessary for the enterprise activities.

4.2   Requirements and Business Service View

The GDPR obligations (i.e. regulatory goals) must now be refined into outcomes and requirements as explained in Sect. 3. The global compliance to the GDPR (i.e. goal "be GDPR compliant" in Fig. 1) involves implicitly a prerequisite of knowledge of enterprise's processes and data as well as an identification of the GDPR concerns related to these processes and data. So as outcome, a knowledge cartography (i.e, an annotated model of the enterprise information system) about the personal data and processing operation needs to be established. This cartography will then be used to reach most of the goals.

From requirements, four functional groups are defined. They represent the core GDPR functions: processing operations and personal data maintenance, consent management, data retention management, data security management.

Processing Operations and Personal Data Maintenance

One implicit claim of the GDPR is to be able to identify which data and processing operations are affected by the GDPR. Data can be of different kinds of personal (e.g. civil status, location data) and particular data (e.g. racial backgrounds, political opinions). As shown in Fig. 2, the requirement *Analyse personal data and processing operations regarding GDPR* comes directly from the overall goal *Be GDPR compliant*. To perform this analysis, a review of the enterprise processing operations (collection, profiling, archiving...) on personal data (depicted by the two requirements *Realize processing operations review* and *Realize personal data review* is necessary. From this review, we obtain a cartography of enterprise data and processing activities related to GDPR. This cartography must be kept up-to-date, giving rise to the *update processing operations* and *update data collection operations* requirements. As a result two business services

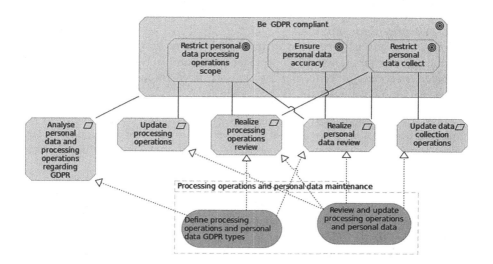

Fig. 2. Requirements for processing operations and data maintenance

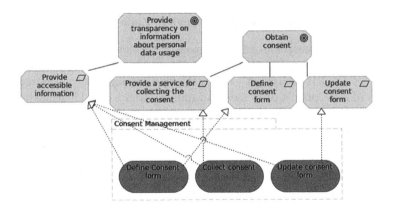

Fig. 3. Requirements and services for consent management

are needed to realize these operations: one for defining the enterprise cartography (of data and processes) and finding out what part of the enterprise system is impacted by the GDPR; and a second one for keeping the cartography related to GDPR up-to-date.

Consent Management
Is a central element of the GDPR regulation[1]. It determines the lawfulness of the processing operations envisaged by the data controller. As shown in Fig. 3, it contains the following requirements:

- *define a consent form* that will inform the data subject about his/her collected personal data, the processing operations that the enterprise will realize, the security means put in place. It contains all the legal information.
- *provide accessible information*: the form should be clear, understandable by the enterprise data subjects.
- *update the consent form*: the form should evolve as the enterprise evolve (information system, activities, providers, etc.) and as the regulation evolves.
- *provide a service for collecting the consent*: it corresponds to the collect of consents from data subjects.

These 4 requirements are implemented in 3 business services that will be detailed in Sect. 4.3. Two are related to the establishment and the update of the consent form. One is the service responsible of getting the consent information from the data subject.

Data Retention Management
Right to oblivion is a crucial right, that is historically present in national laws. Article 5.1.e of the GDPR states that *"Personal data shall be kept in a form which permits the identification of data subjects for no longer than necessary for the purposes for which the personal data are processed"*. This article gives rise to 2 requirements (Fig. 4):

---

[1] The consent itself is also seen as a deliverable, see Sect. 4.4.

- *Define personal data retention*: data retention may be limited in time regarding by legislation or by enterprise activities. A process should be put in place to ensure that the retention time is set according to the enterprise activity or to some existing legal limitation periods.
- *Delete data impacted by the right to oblivion*: personal data must be deleted after a user request or after the expiration of the retention period. Then it should be removed from the active system but it can be stored as archive.

The related services implementation (services in Fig. 4) should ensure that the retention period is set and updated according to the evolution of the regulation or of the information system. It should also defined all the processes of deletion, pseudonymization, anonymization of personal data according to articles 5.1.e and 89.1 of GDPR.

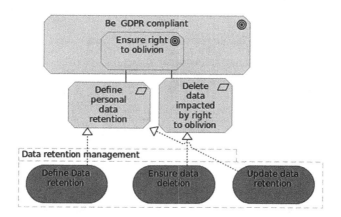

Fig. 4. Requirements and services for data retention management

Personal Data Security Management

The principle of data security laid down in the 2015 European Directive has been considerably strengthened with the GDPR. Article 32.2 of the GDPR refers in particular to *"risk of accidental or unlawful destruction, loss, alteration, unauthorized disclosure of, or access to personal data transmitted, stored or otherwise processed"*. So the GDPR introduces two new obligations for the controller: the impact analysis and the obligation to notify if security breaches occur. These obligations correspond to 4 requirements to ensure personal data security (Fig. 5): *Formalize a security policy, Identify personal data security risk, Define personal data security risk mitigation* and, in a lesser extend, *Secure data transmission*. Indeed they are also needed to produce a Privacy Impact Assessment (see Sect. 4.4) and most of them touch on the risk analysis (threats identification, impacts and mitigation).

4.3   Details of Business Services and Their Orchestration

Currently, we have identified 10 business services related to the GDPR. As recommended in Sect. 3, these services are studied in more detail by specifying their links through an orchestration and their implementation through processes.

Business Services Orchestration
The business services orchestration is shown in the Fig. 6. Two symmetrical paths can be followed: one when the system is put in place and another one for the system evolution. In the first case, everything starts with the identification of processing operations and data types related to the GDPR. It makes it possible the definition of both the data security and the data retention processes. It also impacts the definition of the consent form. Indeed the latter should reflect the enterprise policy (including security, retention, communication to third parties, etc) related to the previously mapped personal data and processing operations.

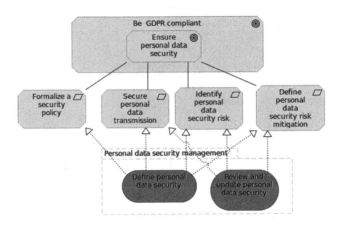

Fig. 5. Requirements and Services for Data Security Management

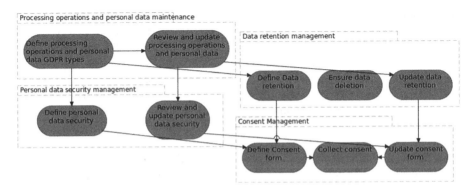

Fig. 6. Business service orchestration

For the remainder of this section, we will focus on some representative business services (one per group of Fig. 6.): *Define processing operations and personal data mapping to GDPR types, Define data retention, Define personal data security, Define consent form.*

As explained previously, we assume that a cartography of all the enterprise data and processing operations has been performed beforehand. For sake of clarity, the cartography is separated into two distinct business objects *Cartography of System Data* and *of System operations*, which are interleaved in practice.

Define Processing Operations and Personal Data Mapping to GDPR Types

This service is fundamental for all other services related to GDPR. Figure 7 presents the process of tagging the system data with GDPR types like gender or genetic data. These GDPR types are provided typically by the GDPR domain analysis (e.g. like in [12] or [8]).

The first sub-process consists in checking the system regarding privacy. It answers the question: is there any personal data managed in my enterprise? Then it tags the data with the correct GDPR type (e.g. biometrics, religion, etc.). A similar activity must be realized for operations that manipulates these tagged data. Only data (to be collected) and the processes which are actually related to the enterprise activity (defined potentially in a business plan model) are retained. Finally, we restrict the collect of the personal data which are related to the previously kept processing operations. This helps in building the actual cartography as well as providing the records of processing operations.

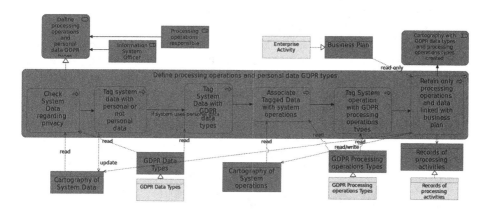

Fig. 7. Business service: mapping GDPR types on personal data and related processing operations

Define Data Retention

This service is essential when a legal retention period exists (e.g., video monitoring should not exceed one month) or when the exploitation period finishes, or following some recommendations (e.g., the personal data about a prospect who does not answer is ideally not kept above 3 months). Such a service is thus relying on the cartography of personal data and processing operations. It starts by *Getting personal data* (Fig. 8). Then, a retention period is assigned, either according to a legal regime or according to the enterprise activity, and the cartography is updated.

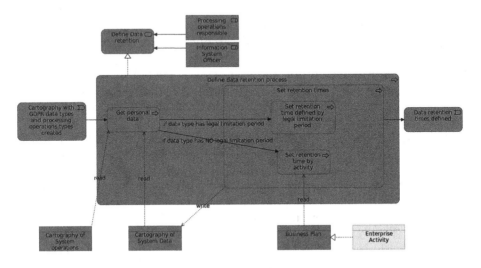

Fig. 8. Business service: data retention

Define Personal Data Security

It is aligned with the traditional risk analysis and mitigation processes: it contains part of the privacy risk assessment (i.e. the IT security aspect). As shown in Fig. 9, the process consists in identifying the impacted data and processing operations, then in defining the risk - threats, impact (having three main security concerns: unauthorized deletion, modification and transmission of data). Finally, it consists in defining the security control and policy: the expected security result

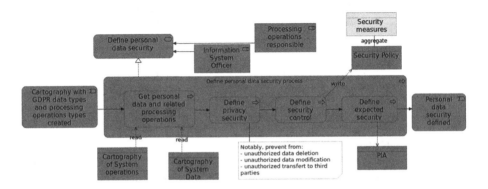

Fig. 9. Business service: define data security

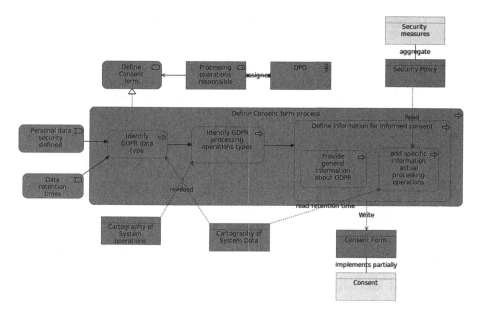

Fig. 10. Business service: define consent form

will be involved in the PIA, the records of processing operations deliverable and described in the consent form.

Define Consent Form

Establishing a clear consent that informs correctly the data subject is a difficult task. The consent can only be established after all other main services were executed as it depicts the personal data, their related processing operations and their finality (in relation with the enterprise business), the retention times, the GDPR legal information and the policy necessary to ensure the data security (Fig. 10).

4.4   Deliverable Viewpoint

We finally propose a viewpoint concerning deliverables. The GDPR is based on a documentation obligation that includes two essential elements that must be produced at the request of the supervisory authorities: the record of processing operations provided for in Article 30 and the PIA provided for in Article 35 GDPR. These mandatory deliverables are linked with the previously identified requirements (Fig. 11).

Article 30 of GDPR lists the mandatory elements to be mentioned in the records of processing operations: information identification of the controller and recipients of the data, information relating to the categories of data (types), their retention, processing activities and purpose, and a description of the technical and organizational measures put in place to guarantee the security of personal

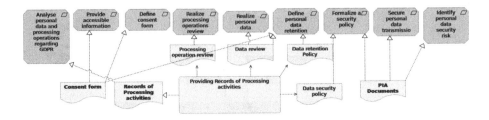

Fig. 11. Deliverable view

data. The records of processing operations carried out as part of accountability must be regularly updated. With such goal, four intermediate deliverables are defined to ensure continuous compliance (Fig. 11): processing operation review, data review, data retention policy and data security policy.

The PIA, 2nd mandatory element, must contain the elements of description and justification of the relevance of the envisaged processing operations. Article 35.7 of GPDR also requires the documentation of a risk analysis and management. For such requirement, standards such as ISO 27001 [19] can be useful. Finally, the consent form is a central document for GDPR compliance (Fig. 11). Even if it is not explicitly cited as an obligation, it is essential for compliance to the GDPR.

5   Conclusion

This paper addresses the modelling of a given regulation (GDPR) as an EAM fragment that needs to be integrated into a more global EAM. We defined an approach for specifying a reference EAM for a given regulation: providing a motivation, services and process that an enterprise has to deal with. Moreover, an EAM fragment, depicting a regulation, helps enterprise stakeholders to understand the regulation itself, its rationale and its impacts. Notably it provides some guidance to implement the GDPR by identifying services and processes to be realized and integrated by an enterprise to be compliant. This contribution is concretized in an ArchiMate model of the GDPR.

In a future work, we will test our model on privacy by design real case studies. Then, we will try to set up a tool to help with conformance checking against existing enterprise architecture and conformance maintenance. We will address in more details some services and processes like the data transfer to third parties (notably outside the GDPR zone), the data migration right and notification of security breaches. Finally we also want to generalize the approach to many regulations and define its generic foundations.

References

1. Gozman, D., Currie, W.: Managing governance, risk, and compliance for post-crisis regulatory change: a model of is capabilities for financial organizations. In: 2015 48th Hawaii International Conference on System Sciences, pp. 4661–4670. IEEE (2015)
2. European Commission: General Data Protection Regulation (2018). https://ec.europa.eu/commission/priorities/justice-and-fundamental-rights/data-protection/2018-reform-eu-data-protection-rules
3. Ayala-Rivera, V., Pasquale, L.: The grace period has ended: an approach to operationalize GDPR requirements. In: 2018 IEEE 26th International Requirements Engineering Conference (RE), pp. 136–146. IEEE (2018)
4. Data Protection Commission - Ireland: Self-assessment checklist (2019). https://www.dataprotection.ie/en/organisations/self-assessment-checklist
5. Microsoft: GDPR assessment (2017). https://assessment.microsoft.com/gdpr-compliance/compliance-risk-results-133MC-2218RO.html
6. Agostinelli, S., Maggi, F.M., Marrella, A., Sapio, F.: Achieving GDPR compliance of BPMN process models. In: Cappiello, C., Ruiz, M. (eds.) CAiSE 2019, vol. 350, pp. 10–22. Springer, Cham (2019). https://doi.org/10.1007/978-3-030-21297-1_2
7. Colesky, M., Hoepman, J.H., Hillen, C.: A critical analysis of privacy design strategies. In: 2016 IEEE Security and Privacy Workshops (SPW), pp. 33–40. IEEE (2016)
8. Palmirani, M., Martoni, M., Rossi, A., Bartolini, C., Robaldo, L.: Legal ontology for modelling GDPR concepts and norms. In: JURIX, pp. 91–100 (2018)
9. Gordon, T.F., Governatori, G., Rotolo, A.: Rules and norms: requirements for rule interchange languages in the legal domain. In: Governatori, G., Hall, J., Paschke, A. (eds.) RuleML 2009. LNCS, vol. 5858, pp. 282–296. Springer, Heidelberg (2009). https://doi.org/10.1007/978-3-642-04985-9_26
10. Sunkle, S., Kholkar, D., Kulkarni, V.: Explanation of proofs of regulatory (non-) compliance using semantic vocabularies. In: Bassiliades, N., Gottlob, G., Sadri, F., Paschke, A., Roman, D. (eds.) RuleML 2015. LNCS, vol. 9202, pp. 388–403. Springer, Cham (2015). https://doi.org/10.1007/978-3-319-21542-6_25
11. Agarwal, S., Steyskal, S., Antunovic, F., Kirrane, S.: Legislative compliance assessment: framework, model and GDPR instantiation. In: Medina, M., Mitrakas, A., Rannenberg, K., Schweighofer, E., Tsouroulas, N. (eds.) APF 2018. LNCS, vol. 11079, pp. 131–149. Springer, Cham (2018). https://doi.org/10.1007/978-3-030-02547-2_8
12. Tom, J., Sing, E., Matulevičius, R.: Conceptual representation of the GDPR: model and application directions. In: Zdravkovic, J., Grabis, J., Nurcan, S., Stirna, J. (eds.) BIR 2018. LNBIP, vol. 330, pp. 18–28. Springer, Cham (2018). https://doi.org/10.1007/978-3-319-99951-7_2
13. Torre, D., Soltana, G., Sabetzadeh, M., Briand, L., Auffinger, Y., Goes, P.: Using models to enable compliance checking against the GDPR: an experience report. In: To appear in the Proceedings of the IEEE/ACM 22nd International Conference on Model Driven Engineering Languages and Systems (MODELS 19). ACM/IEEE (2019)
14. Bommel, P.V., Buitenhuis, P., Hoppenbrouwers, S., Proper, E.: Architecture principles-a regulative perspective on enterprise architecture. Enterprise Modelling and Information Systems Architectures-Concepts and Applications (2007)

15. Cleven, A., Winter, R.: Regulatory compliance in information systems research – literature analysis and research agenda. In: Halpin, T., et al. (eds.) BPMDS/EMMSAD -2009. LNBIP, vol. 29, pp. 174–186. Springer, Heidelberg (2009). https://doi.org/10.1007/978-3-642-01862-6_15
16. Timm, F., Sandkuhl, K.: A reference enterprise architecture for holistic compliance management in the financial sector (2018)
17. Lagerström, R., Saat, J., Franke, U., Aier, S., Ekstedt, M.: Enterprise meta modeling methods – combining a stakeholder-oriented and a causality-based approach. In: Halpin, T., et al. (eds.) BPMDS/EMMSAD -2009. LNBIP, vol. 29, pp. 381–393. Springer, Heidelberg (2009). https://doi.org/10.1007/978-3-642-01862-6_31
18. Ghanavati, S., Amyot, D., Rifaut, A.: Legal goal-oriented requirement language (legal GRL) for modeling regulations. In: Proceedings of the 6th International Workshop on Modeling in Software Engineering, pp. 1–6. ACM (2014)
19. ISO: ISO/IEC 27001 - information technology - security techniques - information security management systems - requirements. Standard, International Organization for Standardization, Geneva, CH, March 2013

Challenges for Risk and Security Modelling in Enterprise Architecture

Gudmund Grov$^{(\boxtimes)}$, Federico Mancini, and Elsie Margrethe Staff Mestl

The Norwegian Defence Research Establishment (FFI), Kjeller, Norway
{Gudmund.Grov,Federico.Mancini}@ffi.no

Abstract. From our experience cooperating with the Norwegian Armed Forces, we outline two interconnected challenges for modelling risk and security in an enterprise architecture: (1) modelling what is protected and why it is protected with sufficient detail whilst being simple enough to facilitate analysis; and (2) establishing automated support for analysing and reasoning about the security models, something we deem crucial to exploit the full potential of an enterprise security architecture. In addition, we sketch out our approach to tackle these challenges and outline our future direction of work.

Keywords: Enterprise security architecture · Diagrammatic risk and security modelling · Automated reasoning

1 Introduction

One the aims of an *enterprise architecture* (EA) is to create a consistent model, or blueprint, of an enterprise's structure and organisation, from its goals and processes to its information systems. The model links different aspects, or domains, that can be considered as architectures in their own right, and which can be visualised through different *views* tailored for the specific domain and actors concerned. Security is one such domain, which we will henceforth refer to as *enterprise security architecture* (ESA), but which is often considered as one of the least developed EA domains [21]. A very important element of ESA is risk[1], and the challenges presented here are a result of ongoing work with the Norwegian Armed Forces to integrate risk and security aspects with their EA (see [8]).

There are several relevant concepts related to risk and security, which are often defined differently according to context. For this paper we use the following[2]:

---

[1] For the Norwegian defence sector security is increasingly risk-driven, and a requirement in the law of national security for classified systems.

[2] The definitions of threat and risk are adapted from NIST SP800-30 Rev. 1, while security has its origin in NIST SP800-160.

© IFIP International Federation for Information Processing 2019
Published by Springer Nature Switzerland AG 2019
J. Gordijn et al. (Eds.): PoEM 2019, LNBIP 369, pp. 215–225, 2019.
https://doi.org/10.1007/978-3-030-35151-9_14

Definition 1 (Threat). *Any circumstance or event with the potential to adversely impact organisational operations, organisational assets, individuals, other organisations, or the nation.*

Definition 2 (Risk). *A measure of the extent to which a threat can cause adverse impact if realised (impact) and the likelihood of its occurrence.*

Definition 3 (Security). *The state of being free from unacceptable risks.*

An ESA should therefore model how unacceptable risks are dealt with at all levels of the organisation. There has been considerable work in developing theoretical frameworks for realising an ESA, such as SABSA [16], or integrating security aspects into EA frameworks [2,3,13,21]. We are, however, not familiar with work focusing on more practical challenges in using and developing an ESA. During the course of our work with the Norwegian Armed Forces, two such challenges have become apparent:

1. Modelling, at a suitable level of detail, both what is protected and why it is protected, and at the same time keeping the complexity of the models at an appropriate level for analysis.
2. The lack of support for automated tools to perform analysis and reasoning about the models as their scale and complexity increases.

The main motivation for developing an ESA should be to help ensure that the modelled security measures are indeed the correct ones to handle the identified risks, and do so effectively and efficiently. This requires adequate solutions to both of our identified challenges; if not solved, the ESA may become nothing more than yet another system to statically document security. Over the next two sections we address these two challenges independently. For each, we introduce the problem with related work, and outline how we chose to approach them. Section 4 concludes the paper by addressing these challenges as a uniform problem and briefly discusses the road ahead.

2   Challenge 1: Risk and Security Modelling in EA

Security is unique in the sense it does not provide any enterprise functionality in itself – it enables secure use of other functionalities. Without an asset to secure, or a threat to the asset, there is no point in adding security. The other peculiarity is that determining whether something is indeed secure is very hard, and depends on the context one considers. It is therefore crucial that the ESA includes both the security measures chosen for the enterprise, and the motivational aspect of security, in the form of the underlying risk, in order to provide the right context for the security. This will ease the assessment of security measures, and make their adjustment more effective in case of changes in the enterprise's risk profile. How to model this in practice is the real challenge, especially with regard to risk.

Risk and security are usually decomposed into several constituent. These are then related to one another in order to ease the systematic analysis of relevant threats and possible mitigations. Although one can find minor variations in the definitions of these factors, the underlying concept is typically that we have a threat (event), where an actor exploits one or more vulnerabilities to gain access to a valuable asset and cause a negative impact to an enterprise. Mitigations are then put in place according to how severe the risk associated with the threat is. Many of these factors can already be modelled in an EA. Security, in particular, is relatively straightforward to model, as mitigations usually take the form of requirements, capabilities, services and processes that are already routinely modelled in an EA. Many risk factors can be modelled in EA languages such as ArchiMate [3,21] and *Unified Architecture Framework* (UAF), however the support in *NATO Architecture Framework* (NAF) [8], which is used by the Norwegian Armed Forces, is more limited. Proposals even exists for integrating Information System Security Risk Management (ISSRM) with ArchiMate [2,13].

The challenge is to find the right level of granularity of ESA models. On the one hand, the list of possible threats, and the level of detail in which they can be described, can quickly become unmanageable. On the other hand, a generic threat can cover multiple cases, but be almost useless in designing appropriate mitigations. Furthermore, it is not clear how risks in different domains of the EA can be placed in relation to one another to achieve traceability and consistency. A high-level business threat may correspond to several technical threats, while attacks on actual systems may have consequences on business processes that rely on them. These downwards, upwards and sideways dependencies in the EA show the need for a holistic approach to enterprise security: we must be able to trace the identified risks and threats across the EA. This contrasting need for a level of detail which conveys enough information to properly assess the enterprise-level security, but at the same time keeps complexity low enough to make analysis feasible, is a major challenge for our work.

Some assistance can come from modelling approaches to risk and security not specifically designed for ESA. *CORAS* [11] is a language developed specifically to model and analyse risk. It includes assets, vulnerabilities, threat actors, threats, unwanted incidents, risks and security controls, and supports a very granular level of detail. *Misuse cases* [17] exhibit security extensions of UML use cases to model and relate threats in the form of scenarios that could, but should not happen, together with mitigating scenarios. *Attack trees* [15] give a hierarchical depiction of attacks using AND-OR trees, where each level of the tree increases the granularity of the attack description. *Attack-defence trees* [9] augment attack trees with security controls to protect or mitigate the attacks or sub-attacks. *Bowtie diagrams* [14] enable diagrammatic separation of preventative and reactive security mechanisms in relation to the underlying threat, and have also been combined with attack trees [1]. *Assurance cases* can provide structural argumentation for the security [19], and have been studied in an EA context [22].

Figure 1 summarises the support for risk and security modelling in the approaches discussed in this section. Here, we have separated support into: *dedicated* (●), *some* (◐) and *no support* (○). Some support implies that it is either

	Event	Threat	Risk	Asset	Actor	Vuln.	Impact	Mitigation
ArchiMate (AM)	●	○	●	●	●	○	○	●
AM + ISSRM [2,13]	●	●	●	●	●	●	○	●
AM extended [3]	●	●	●	◐	●	●	○	●
UAF	◐	○	●	●	◐	○	○	●
NAF	●	○	○	◐	◐	○	○	●
CORAS [11]	◐	●	●	●	●	●	○	●
Misuse cases [17]	●	●	○	◐	●	○	○	●
Attack trees [15]	◐	●	○	○	○	○	○	○
Attack defence trees [9]	◐	●	○	○	○	○	○	●
Assurance cases [19]	○	◐	○	○	○	○	○	◐
Bowtie diagrams [14,1]	●	●	○	●	○	○	●	●

Fig. 1. Risk and security support. Over line: EA frameworks; under: non-EA.

partially supported or that it can be indirectly modelled through other means without dedicated support. There will naturally be some borderline cases where our classification is open for debate.

2.1 Outline of Our Approach

In Fig. 1 we saw that threat is the risk factor that nearly all non-EA risk modelling approaches support. Therefore, we decided to investigate how to best model and achieve traceability of this risk component in an ESA, and leave the modelling of the other ISSRM concepts for future iterations, if at all necessary. We use NAF (version 3) as a reference EA framework, as it is what is currently used by Norwegian Armed Forces, albeit we consider both the challenges and the approach easily transferable to other frameworks, given their generic nature.

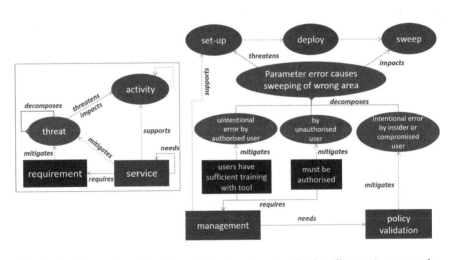

Fig. 2. Left/boxed: explanation of threat extension. Right: illustrative example.

As a first step, we propose extending NAF with a *threat* component. Figure 2 (right) shows an illustrative example using this component, while the left-hand side of the figure explains relevant components and relations. The example is based on a fragment of a mine-sweeping operation employing unmanned and autonomous vehicles [12]. Three of the activities are shown: first the unmanned boat is configured and set-up for the mission; then it is deployed at sea where it will autonomously reach the area to sweep for mines; and finally, it will autonomously sweep for mines, based on some configuration parameters.

The threat component implicitly defines the assets to be protected and the impact of the threat, by using the *threaten* and *impact* relations, respectively. Note that both are needed as the impact may be on different parts of the model from where the assets are, and that we only show where the impact is, not its severity. In our case, the set-up activity is what needs to be protected to prevent incorrect sweeping parameters being input, and impacting the mission by causing the wrong area to be swept. We stress that the extension shown in Fig. 2 (left) is simplified for the example and any EA assets that need protection can be the subject of a threat. In this case it is an activity, but it can for example also be information objects, services or software.

A management service supports the configuration of the system in the set-up activity, so the threat to the activity has to be mapped to this service. In order to map threats across layers of the EA, they may need to be decomposed and refined to reflect different concerns and levels of abstraction. This may also be required as there may be sub-threats that are mitigated in different ways. To achieve this we have introduced a *decomposes* relation for threats, illustrated in the example by decomposing the overall threat into three sub-threats.

As a bridge between a threat and its mitigation we can use *requirement* components, which specify the mitigations needed to reduce the risk associated to the threat. In our example, this translates into the properties the management service should have in order to protect the set-up process from some of the identified sub-threats. This "requirement bridge" has been inspired by "safety constraints" found in the system-oriented STPA approach for safety [10] (and security [23]). Requirements are not always necessary to express the motivational aspect and achieve traceability, as in the case of the "policy validation" service, where the threat is related directly to a concrete mitigation. What one may lose in this case though, is the part of the motivational aspect used to show why a mitigation is indeed correct and sufficient for the threat. This could be useful to manage changes more efficiently at a later time. The example further shows that by decomposing the threat, we can relate specific mitigations to different aspects of the threat. This can also enable reasoning about completeness of the threat mitigation.[3]

Summary and Next Steps. To summarise, we have started the first iteration of our work by extending NAF with threat components which can be decomposed

---

[3] For our illustrative example the decomposition is incomplete with other sub-threats omitted for simplicity.

and traced across the EA, and used requirements as a bridge between threats and their mitigation. This bridge provides a logical abstraction of the mitigations needed to handle the threat. One interesting extension would be to use assurance cases as a formal basis for arguing that a given threat has been handled sufficiently. There are also several other ways to further extend the work. While we use a single threat element, [2] separates it into 'loss event', 'threat event' and 'vulnerability' (among others), and associates each part with different layers of the ESA. These can then be related and traced. For instance, a loss event can, via a threat event, be related to a technical vulnerability. Although such classification of different types of threats may be desirable, and will not necessary lead to larger models, we still believe a decomposition as illustrated by our example is the right way ahead as there will not always be a one-to-one mapping between threats at different parts of the ESA. Integrating other risk components beyond threats and possibly vulnerabilities, would mean integrating a complete risk analysis framework in the ESA. The question then remains as to whether this is really desirable or it should be handled by a dedicated risk framework. Our example has shown that just by incorporating threats, the size and complexity of the model is substantially increased. Further extensions may make it harder to achieve holistic reasoning about the ESA, thus reducing the effect the ESA has on improving the enterprise security. The use of a dedicated risk analysis framework, closely aligned with the ESA may be a good compromise between the conflicting need for both detail and abstraction.[4]

3   Challenge 2: Automated Reasoning for ESA[5]

From the previous section we may conclude that complexity is unavoidable, and accept that (purely) manual reasoning and analysis is unfeasible and automation is required. Such automation is the topic of our second challenge. As an anecdote, configurations for Amazon Web Services have become too complex to analyse manually, and automated reasoning techniques are now being used to ensure security properties of these configurations [4].

The types of question one would like to reason about in an ESA, partially mentioned in the previous section, include: Are the security controls sufficient to handle the identified risks? What are the consequences for security when changing existing processes or systems? What are the consequences for the security of the enterprise when cancelling or delaying a project? Which business processes will be impacted by given attacks or vulnerabilities?

Automated reasoning techniques require unambiguous semantics of the modelling languages, which currently do not exist for NAF, ArchiMate or UAF. Sunkle et al. [18] developed a translator for ArchiMate models that produces a representation which enables analysis of how changes made to one part of the

---

[4] As a result the ESA will also act as a document management system, such as the ASCE tool by Adalard for assurance cases [https://www.adelard.com/asce].

[5] More detail about this section is available in a (Norwegian) report [7].

enterprise effect other parts. It also generates a more holistic view of the technical details, which can be used for communication of the EA to a less technical audience. This illustrates two potential applications of automated reasoning. There are though reservations about such formal underpinnings to the modelling, in particular with respect to mapping the EA to other representations with conflicting semantics.[6] Such mappings are not relevant for our particular application domain, but even if they were, our belief is that multiple ways of interpreting the same model are undesirable beyond analysis. Interoperability is obviously important, but if each model has to come with an explanation of how to interpret it, then one can question why we need the model in the first place. For security, this is particularly problematic as it cuts across many aspects of an enterprise, which typically are developed by different architects (with their own semantics), and this amalgamate of different interpretations needs to be combined into a uniform and holistic judgment of the security of the enterprise. We therefore believe that a common understanding and semantics of the ESA are crucial, possibly with the parts of the models that are not required for our security analysis to be left undefined.

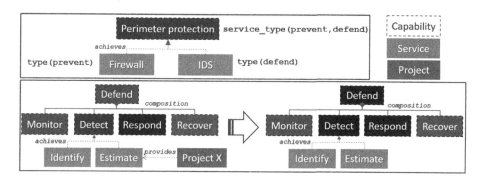

Fig. 3. Examples of security attributes and automated reasoning support.

3.1   Outline of Our Approach

To show feasibility for automated reasoning in an ESA context, we have developed a proof-of-concept prototype for a subset of NAF and implemented it for Sparx Enterprise Architect (EA). Several examples have been developed to illustrate a range of different usages:

Vertical coherence across architecture layers. There needs to be coherence between the architecture layers, e.g. to ensure that the enterprise operations are secured in a technical layer, and that technical security mechanisms serve a business purpose. Figure 3 (top) illustrates an example where reasoning

---

[6] See the Open Group's ArchiMate 3 documentation [http://tiny.cc/amch5].

is used to ensure that a security capability is realised at the service layer. This is augmented by additional security properties specified by the security architect, which we return to below.

Visualisation of capability strength across diagrams. *NATO CIS Security Capability Breakdown* (SCB) [6] provides a hierarchical structure for security capabilities, where each capability can be given a *strength level*, which indicates the maturity of the capability. This strength level can be defined recursively in terms of the strength of its sub-components, and be visualised by colouring the capability box by using a scale typically ranging from dark red (non existing) to dark green (perfect). We can use our reasoning engine to automate the colouring of capabilities, either by providing the numerical level directly or computing it from other components. Changes to one component will then automatically cause dependent capabilities to be re-coloured. Figure 3 (bottom) illustrates such colouring for a subset of SCB. Here, we can see that 'Defend' depends on other sub-capabilities and a change of colour in one of them ('Detect'), causes the recolouring of 'Defend' (rightmost diagram).

Change management. In the bottom example of Fig. 3 the 'Estimate' service is being delivered by a project (l.h.s. of arrow) and when this project is removed (r.h.s. of arrow) then the consequence in terms of reduced capabilities is automatically derived and visualised. In Fig. 3 (bottom), this is visualised by recolouring 'Detect' as a result of cancelling the project delivering the 'Estimate' service, and recolouring 'Defend' as a result of recolouring 'Detect'. This is an example of automated reasoning for change management. Changes to plans or solutions may have impacts elsewhere, e.g. cancelling, or changing the deliverables of a project may have considerable impacts on other services or capabilities of the enterprise. Our techniques can reason about direct, and indirect consequences to give an instant response to the architect, e.g. in the form of alarms or colouring as we have illustrated.

Law, regulation and policy compliance. By encoding laws, regulations and policies directly (in a formal way), compliance can automatically be verified. One simple example is the requirement for certain Evaluation Assurance Level (EAL) certification for software systems applied at given classification levels. An alarm can then be raised if the requirement is not met.

To achieve support for automated reasoning, the models are translated into a formal representation, which is analysed with the help of an external state-of-the-art automated reasoning engine [5]. Both the nodes and edges of NAF diagrams (in Sparx EA) are typed via a mechanism called UML stereotypes.[7] In addition, the nodes can be augmented with additional security properties via a mechanism we call *security attributes*[8] (SA). A SA is a piece of *formal text*, which the reasoning engine can interpret and use in the analysis. SAs are intertwined with informal natural language description of the component, and

---

[7] For simplicity, stereotypes have been omitted in Fig. 3, however we have given the types of the nodes in the top corner, and some commentary for the edges.

[8] This should not be confused with the business attributes found in SABSA [16].

the formal and informal texts are separated by a dedicated markup.[9] We have illustrated SAs in Fig. 3 (top), but note that it is also the mechanism used to achieve the colouring and change management (Fig. 3 (bottom)). The example shows an additional security attribute, which states that the capability has to be realised by services labelled by both 'prevent' and 'defend'. Here this is the case, but an alarm would have been raised if not.

Summary and Next Steps. This proof-of-concept has shown the feasibility of automated reasoning in an ESA setting, however we have only applied it to toy examples and for a limited set of problems. We have not yet attempted to reason about mitigations with regards to given threats or risks, which is an important element of our future work.

4 Towards a Combined Challenge

We have identified modelling and automated reasoning challenges for ESA based on our experience in the Norwegian Defence sector, and sketched out our approaches for tackling them. Whilst described as separate challenges, they are indeed interconnected: what and how is modelled will impact what we can reason about; but what we want to reason about, may change what we need to model. Both challenges are also complicated by the nature of risk and security: they are a permeating aspect of the EA and are context-dependent, so that they cannot be addressed in isolation. Finding a suitable level of abstraction and modelling it consistently to enable meaningful holistic automated reasoning is therefore crucial, since it will be impossible to analyse the ESA manually.

Security is inherently risk dependent – if there is no risk then there is no need for security. We must therefore address the reasoning challenge in a risk setting, e.g. to analyse if modelled threats and risks are sufficiently mitigated in the enterprise. This may require additional modelling elements, such as use of structured argumentation of why the threat is mitigated via assurance cases [19, 22], and possible use of bowtie diagrams to separate preventive and reactive security. The automated reasoning engine could then utilise "local arguments" about a given threat to reason holistically about the security of the entire enterprise. By solving this combined challenge, we believe the potential of ESA can be fully exploited and play a major role in securing future enterprises.

References

1. Abdo, H., Kaouk, M., Flaus, J.M., Masse, F.: A safety/security risk analysis approach of industrial control systems: a cyber bowtie-combining new version of attack tree with bowtie analysis. Comput. Secur. **72**, 175–195 (2018)
2. Band, I., et al.: How to Model Enterprise Risk Management and Security with the ArchiMate Language. The Open Group white paper no. W172 (2017)

---

[9] This has been inspired by *anti-quotations* from the Isabelle proof assistant [20].

3. Van den Bosch, S.: Designing secure enterprise architectures - a comprehensive approach: framework, method, and modelling language. Master's thesis, University of Twente (2014)
4. Cook, B.: Formal Reasoning About the Security of Amazon Web Services. In: Chockler, H., Weissenbacher, G. (eds.) CAV 2018. LNCS, vol. 10981, pp. 38–47. Springer, Cham (2018). https://doi.org/10.1007/978-3-319-96145-3_3
5. de Moura, L., Bjørner, N.: Z3: an efficient SMT solver. In: Ramakrishnan, C.R., Rehof, J. (eds.) TACAS 2008. LNCS, vol. 4963, pp. 337–340. Springer, Heidelberg (2008). https://doi.org/10.1007/978-3-540-78800-3_24
6. Gay, S.: CIS security capability breakdown version 2.00, NATO NCIA Technical report 2017/NCB010400/13, NATO Unclassified (2017)
7. Grov, G., Mestl, E.M.S., Mancini, F., Nordbotten, N.A.: Kan resonnering rundt sikkerhetsarkitektur automatiseres? en studie i sikkerhetsattributter og automatisk resonnering, FFI-report 18–01982 (2019)
8. Jørgensen, H.D., Liland, T., Skogvold, S.: Aligning TOGAF and NAF - experiences from the Norwegian Armed Forces. In: Johannesson, P., Krogstie, J., Opdahl, A.L. (eds.) PoEM 2011. LNBIP, vol. 92, pp. 131–146. Springer, Heidelberg (2011). https://doi.org/10.1007/978-3-642-24849-8_11
9. Kordy, B., Mauw, S., Radomirović, S., Schweitzer, P.: Foundations of attack–defense trees. In: Degano, P., Etalle, S., Guttman, J. (eds.) FAST 2010. LNCS, vol. 6561, pp. 80–95. Springer, Heidelberg (2011). https://doi.org/10.1007/978-3-642-19751-2_6
10. Leveson, N.: Engineering a Safer World: Systems Thinking Applied to Safety. MIT Press, Cambridge (2011)
11. Lund, M.S., Solhaug, B., Stølen, K.: Model-Driven Risk Analysis: The CORAS Approach. Springer, Heidelberg (2010). https://doi.org/10.1007/978-3-642-12323-8
12. Mancini, F., et al.: Information security for unmanned and autonomous vehicles - main challenges and relevant operational concepts, FFI-report 19/00888 (exempt from public disclosure) (2019)
13. Mayer, N., Aubert, J., Grandry, E., Feltus, C., Goettelmann, E., Wieringa, R.: An integrated conceptual model for information system security risk management supported by enterprise architecture management. Softw. Syst. Model. 18(3), 2285–2312 (2019)
14. de Ruijter, A., Guldenmund, F.: The bowtie method: a review. Saf. Sci. 88, 211–218 (2016)
15. Schneider, B.: Attack trees: modelling security threats. Dr. Dobb's J. Softw. Tools 24(12), 21–29 (1999)
16. Sherwood, N.A.: Enterprise Security Architecture: A Business-Driven Approach. CRC Press, Boca Raton (2005)
17. Sindre, G., Opdahl, A.L.: Eliciting security requirements with misuse cases. Requirements Eng. 10(1), 34–44 (2005)
18. Sunkle, S., Kulkarni, V., Roychoudhury, S.: Analyzing enterprise models using enterprise architecture-based ontology. In: Moreira, A., Schätz, B., Gray, J., Vallecillo, A., Clarke, P. (eds.) MODELS 2013. LNCS, vol. 8107, pp. 622–638. Springer, Heidelberg (2013). https://doi.org/10.1007/978-3-642-41533-3_38
19. Weinstock, C.B., Lipson, H.F., Goodenough, J.B.: Arguing Security - Creating Security Assurance Cases, white paper by the Software Engineering Institute (Carnegie Mellom University) (2007)
20. Wenzel, M., Chaieb, A.: SML with antiquotations embedded into Isabelle/Isar. In: Workshop on Programming Languages for Mechanized Mathematics (2007)

21. Wierda, G.: Mastering ArchiMate Edition III: A Serious Introduction to the Archi-Mate Enterprise Architecture Modeling Language. R&A (2017)
22. Yamamoto, S., Kobayashi, N.: Mobile security assurance through archimate. IT CoNverg. PRAct. (INPRA) **4**(3), 1–8 (2016)
23. Young, W., Leveson, N.G.: An integrated approach to safety and security based on systems theory. Commun. ACM **57**(2), 31–35 (2014)

Cybersecurity Evaluation of Enterprise Architectures: The e-SENS Case

Tanja Pavleska[1(✉)], Helder Aranha[2], Massimiliano Masi[3],
Eric Grandry[4], and Giovanni Paolo Sellitto[5]

[1] Jozef Stefan Institute, Jamova 39, Ljubljana, Slovenia
atanja@e5.ijs.si
[2] Public Administration Shared Services Entity, I.P., Alfragide,
Amadora, Portugal
helder.aranha@espap.pt
[3] Tiani Spirit GmbH, Vienna, Austria
massimiliano.masi@tiani-spirit.com
[4] Ministry of Mobility and Public Works, Luxembourg, Luxembourg
eric.grandry@tr.etat.lu
[5] Autorità Nazionale Anticorruzione, Rome, Italy
g.sellitto@anticorruzione.it

Abstract. Technology management through enterprise architectures has already become a widespread practice across large enterprises. Modeling and evaluating the cybersecurity aspect of it, however, has just begun to get the needed attention. This paper presents a cybersecurity evaluation methodology developed for the reference architecture of the e-SENS project and derives a generic framework for cybersecurity evaluation of an enterprise architecture. The evaluation addresses both the high-level design artefacts (the reference architecture) and operational solutions. Therefore, both a conceptual and an empirical framework are developed as part of the methodology. The former extends a goal-based security model with a threat-view incorporating standardized guidelines on security measures, whereas the latter captures and systematizes implemented project-specific security practices. The resulting methodology effectively supports the evaluation and is easy to grasp by non-technical people. Moreover, it is lendable to formalization, supporting a semi-automatic process of solution architecture design.

Keywords: Cybersecurity · Enterprise architecture · e-SENS · Evaluation methodology · Framework

1 Introduction

Supporting the management of technology by enterprise architectures, while essential and useful, poses additional requirements for effectiveness and efficiency, such as: accounting for the life cycle of the different aspects and attributes of the architecture (interoperability, (cyber)security, change management, variability, etc.). Various models to address these requirements have been proposed [1–3]. However, they mainly address small-scale solutions, lack an account of a standardized process of technology

© IFIP International Federation for Information Processing 2019
Published by Springer Nature Switzerland AG 2019
J. Gordijn et al. (Eds.): PoEM 2019, LNBIP 369, pp. 226–241, 2019.
https://doi.org/10.1007/978-3-030-35151-9_15

management or require fully manual work on the issue under consideration. In this paper, we present a cybersecurity evaluation methodology developed for the reference architecture of the e-SENS project.[1] The aim is to derive a generic framework for cybersecurity evaluation of enterprise architectures that would be interoperable, applicable to both small and large-scale scenarios, understandable by non-technical people, but also technically sound to the extent that it is fully automatable and reusable.

The Electronic Simple European Networked Services (e-SENS) project aimed at delivering reusable architecture Building Blocks (BBs throughout this paper) for the implementation of cross-border and cross-sector digital services. In addition to developing BBs as elementary parts of the e-SENS Reference Architecture (e-SENS RA), corresponding implementations in several domains were piloted (eHealth/ ePrescription, eProcurement, eJustice, Business LifeCycle and eAgriculture), providing a proof of the architecture feasibility and effectiveness. The e-SENS approach adopts the TOGAF9 concept of a building block [1]. The BBs are combined and consolidated into Solution Architecture Templates (SATs), as used by the European Interoperability Reference Architecture[2], and address specific real-world use-case. The BBs are described along common dimensions, captured by the e-SENS Metamodel [4]. The availability of solution templates not only facilitates the use of the BBs, but guides developers in the realization of custom solution architectures. In doing so, significant challenges appear due to the requirements for architecture solutions and the standards and security solutions. Thus, an evaluation methodology is needed that is applicable at architectural level, but which also presents the various features in a uniform way for all of the BBs.

The evaluation presented in this paper includes model-based assessments at SAT-level from the aspect of (cyber)security. Although designed for e-SENS, the methodology has been generalized and proven applicable for other contexts as well [5]. It combines two complementary evaluation frameworks: conceptual and empirical. The former builds on a standard goal-based security model known as the Reference Model for Information Assurance & Security (RMIAS) [6]. This model was augmented by a threat-view incorporating the ENISA guidelines on security measures [7] to provide a holistic account of the security properties of the reference architecture. The empirical framework, on the other hand, is an evaluation tool for the pilots, designed according to the conceptual framework. It captures and systematizes the security practices deployed in the solutions based on the reference architecture and provides recommendations on how the BBs' specifications can be fine-tuned to meet the security goals.[3]

This paper is structured as follows: the next section introduces the two parts of the evaluation methodology – the conceptual and empirical evaluation frameworks. Each is supported by a relevant discussion or recommendations related to the obtained results.

---

[1] https://www.esens.eu/.

[2] https://ec.europa.eu/isa2/solutions/eira_en.

[3] Note that the terms "security" and "cybersecurity" are used interchangeably throughout the paper: while the RMIAS addresses information security (& assurance) in general, the evaluation described here focuses on cybersecurity, as information in e-SENS is mainly in electronic form.

Then, our work is placed among the state of the art approaches. Finally, we conclude and point to some future work plans.

2   Methodology: The Conceptual Framework

The conceptual framework aims at assessing how the technical specifications contribute to meet the security goals. Two approaches are usually followed in the practice of information assurance and security: a goal-based and a threat-based approach [8]. The former defines the security goals, and then selects the countermeasures to reach these goals [9]. The latter analyzes the threats and vulnerabilities of the system to be secured, and then selects countermeasures mitigating the threats and vulnerabilities [10]. In a cybersecurity evaluation at architecture level, a goal-based approach is usually taken, as a threat-based requires detailed analysis of all system vulnerabilities, and a detailed knowledge of the system behavior history. Such data is not available at system design.

The objective of the proposed methodology is twofold: (1) the core security goals must be general enough to address all of the domain needs; and (2) they should be applicable to any architecture derived from the BBs. Therefore, both a goal-based and a threat-based approach are combined in this work in a coherent manner.

Figure 1 depicts the application of the conceptual framework to the e-SENS System, which is represented in the core diagram with all its assets: Network, Hardware, People, Information, etc.

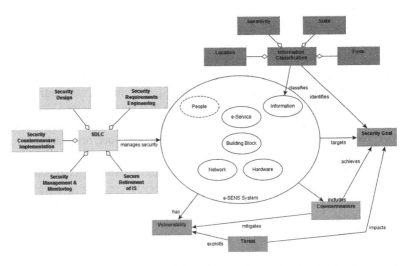

Fig. 1. The conceptual framework of the cybersecurity evaluation (Color figure online)

The security aspects (i.e. dimensions) composing the RMIAS goal-based view are: *Security Development Life Cycle SDLC* (represented in green), *Information Classification* (which corresponds to the RMIAS *taxonomy*), *Security Goals* (in orange) and *Countermeasures* (in blue).

- SDLC illustrates how security is built up along the system development life cycle;
- Information Taxonomy characterizes the nature of information being protected;
- Security Goals contain a broadly applicable list of eight security goals: Confidentiality; Integrity; Availability; Accountability; Authentication (and Trustworthiness); Non-repudiation; Privacy and Auditability.
- Countermeasures categorize the countermeasures available for information protection.

To address the threats and vulnerabilities of the system, the goal-based model is complemented by a threat-view, which is represented by the purple blocks in Fig. 1.

2.1 RMIAS and the Goal-Based View

The evaluation is preceded by goal-based modeling, performed along each of the RMIAS dimensions. Information classification helps to understand the relevant security goals associated with the system under evaluation. Information is classified by:

- Form: in e-SENS information is exclusively manipulated in electronic form;
- State: in e-SENS it can be in one of the following states: Creation, Transmission, Storage, Processing, Destruction;
- Sensitivity: in e-SENS it can be either confidential, or non-confidential;
- Location: in e-SENS it is always at controlled locations.

The e-SENS System can be described through different views; in this evaluation, we concentrate on the architecture description relevant to the various eServices. The evaluation includes the cross-border SATs that were most employed by the pilots while carrying the bulk of the security mechanisms: eID, eDelivery, Non-repudiation, Trust Establishment, eDocuments, and Semantics [11–13].

The goal-based assessment is performed as follows:

1. The architecture of the system to be protected is described, and the various stages of information manipulation are identified;
2. For each stage, the information is categorized according to the information view of the security model. The associated security goals are deduced by the security expert performing the evaluation (See Table 1 for example);

Table 1. Information classification template for the SATs; an example.

Information	Sensitivity	Location	State	Security goal
Authentication request	Non-confidential	Controlled	Transit	Integrity
Secure message transfer	Confidential	Controlled	Transmission, storage	Authentication, Non-repudiation
…	…	…	…	…

3. The security goals devised are then analyzed and classified in relation to the relevant architecture (as shown in Table 2). The most generic description for each column is Node_X - Node_Y; this refers to information exchange in three general cases: (a) National infrastructure (b) Cross border infrastructure and (c) Direct end-to-end.

Table 2. Template for goal-based end-to-end analysis of each SAT

		Name of the SAT being evaluated			
		Point of assessment			
S E C U R I T Y G O A L		**End-point 1**	**Node A**	**...** **Node X**	**End-point Y**
	Access Control	Yes	Yes	...	Yes
	Authentication	Yes	Yes	...	Yes
	Confidentiality	No	Yes	...	No
	Integrity	Yes	Yes	...	Yes
	Non-repudiation	No	No	...	...
	Accountability	...	...	...	...
	Auditability	...	...	...	...
	Privacy	...	...	...	...

2.2 ENISA Guidelines on Security Measures and Threat-Based View

The ENISA guidelines on security measures sublime an extensive list of national and international EU electronic communications standards into a set of security objectives divided by domain [7]. They outline 25 security objectives, each analyzed through various security measures and supported by evidence testifying that an objective was met. The security measures are grouped in 3 sophistication levels, whereas the security objectives are divided in 7 domains of application. This provided a suitable framework of complementary views to the goal-based security evaluation.

As information is the main security asset in e-SENS, many of the ENISA security measures and objectives were not addressed by the evaluation. To determine those that are relevant for e-SENS, a mapping of the contextual and security traits between the e-SENS security needs and the ENISA provisions is performed, as presented in Fig. 2 showing the whole set of ENISA security objectives divided by domains. To represent the relevance for the e-SENS context the boxes are colored and assigned the following semantics: red denotes the relevance of that particular security objective (SO) for the evaluation in the concrete domain (Dx); green represents the SOs for which e-SENS can provide recommendations to future adopters of e-SENS building blocks; and transparent (white) boxes denote that the SO is not relevant for the evaluation purposes. Mapping the contextual and the security traits of RMIAS to the ENISA framework

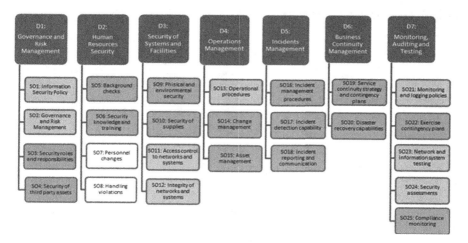

Fig. 2. Relevance of the ENISA guidelines in the context of e-SENS

provides sufficient practical and scientific rigor in accomplishing the task of a holistic cybersecurity evaluation. Moreover, it enables the extraction of specific guidelines and recommendations for the security measures that must be adopted to meet the objectives.

2.3 Integrating RMIAS Dimensions and ENISA Objectives

Mapping RMIAS to the ENISA technical guidelines establishes correspondence between each of the RMIAS dimensions and the ENISA Security objectives by domain. It is represented as a matrix: each entry that lays at the intersection of an RMIAS row-entry and an ENISA column-entry contains the information about the reciprocal relevance of the two. The same matrix can also contain the results of the assessing of relevance in the specific context. Such results are denoted by red-green-white coloring the particular entry, with the same meaning as presented in the previous section.

As Information is the main asset to be protected by the security mechanisms specified by the e-SENS RA and implemented by the pilots, the mapping of Information Taxonomy is granulated into: Creation, Processing, Storage, Transmission, and Destruction. The result is a 25×25 matrix (see Table 3) with one additional dimension for *Relevance* represented by a particular color, as explained previously. This additional dimension can be further fine-grained, for example by giving it numerical weights. It enables a threat-view by domain for each goal-based dimension and its sub-dimensions. Providing a threat-view starts as a subjective assessment, as the decision to denote a particular table entry as relevant or not depends on the analyst's expertise and experience. This is also one of the inherent drawbacks of a threat-based method. To ensure the least bias possible, the evaluation has been reviewed by more experts who were involved in both the design of specifications and in pilot implementations. The most important result from this cybersecurity evaluation, however, is the methodology

Table 3. Mapping RMIAS to ENISA guidelines by relevance for e-SENS security mechanisms

ENISA guidelines RMIAS			D1				D2				D3				D4			D5			D6		D7				
			SO1	SO2	SO3	SO4	SO5	SO6	SO7	SO8	SO9	SO10	SO11	SO12	SO13	SO14	SO15	SO16	SO17	SO18	SO19	SO20	SO21	SO22	SO23	SO24	SO25
Security goals		Confidentiality																									
		Integrity																									
		Availability																									
		Privacy																									
		Authentication																									
		Non-repudiation																									
		Accountability																									
		Auditability																									
Information taxonomy	State	Creation																									
		Processing																									
		Storage																									
		Transmission																									
		Destruction																									
		Form (Electronic)																									
		Sensitivity																									
		Location																									
System Counter-measures		Technical																									
		Legal																									
		Organizational																									
		Human-oriented																									
Security lifecycle		Design																									
		Implementation																									
		Management and monitoring																									
		Redundancy and fault-tolerance																									
		System retirement																									

itself, which not only is it not subjective, but is based on rigorous standards and scientific approaches.

To give an example, we can refer to the goal-based analysis of the pilots (presented in Sect. 3.2). There, we show that the security goal *Availability* requires proper account. In Table 3, there are 19 security objectives that provide a threat-view of Availability relevant for e-SENS across all 7 domains. Eight are mandatory (in red) for specification and implementation, whereas for 11 (in green) e-SENS provides recommendations to future adopters. Depending on the domain, a catalogue of security objectives can be designed to guide the specification and implementation of relevant security measures. Governance and risk management can be similarly addressed.

Finally, it is worth noting that this table can further be checked for compliance with international standards by comparing it against the mapping of ENISA's domains and security objectives to international standards in Sect. 6 of the ENISA report [7].

2.4 Discussion

The evaluation of the e-SENS SATs demonstrated that the specifications are grounded on well-established security standards and solutions. Furthermore, all security goals can be addressed by adopting one or a composition of BBs. Information in all its states and locations can be adequately accounted for, depending on its sensitivity, in order to devise a certain security goal. One of the most important traits of the e-SENS RA is that its BBs are fully interoperable. This implies that by interconnecting the relevant BBs, a certain security property can be leveraged to meet a desired security goal.

By presenting a high-level overview of the architecture to which a security mechanism applies, and by providing a catalogue of the security goals addressed by each of the SATs, a non-technical person is able to grasp the potential of a certain solution to satisfy given security requirements. Moreover, by providing a detailed elaboration of the technical processes behind a solution and reference to the standards on which it is based, a technical person gets the support to build a conceptual evaluation model to satisfy the desired security goals. Hence, the analysis performed here provides a common ground for understanding between various levels of experts in a given organization. It also helps to organize the security policies spread over multiple domains. Furthermore, it not only permits tracing contradictory security policy statements, but also facilitates the identification of weak or omitted security policies. Complemented with the more domain-specific security measures offered by the threat-based analysis, it may contribute to more cost-effective and efficient solutions for both public administrations and private organizations. Finally, the modularity of the analysis by security domain, objective, goal and countermeasures allows to detect opportunities for further improvement of both the system/architecture and the implemented security mechanisms.

3 Methodology: The Empirical Framework

To provide a holistic view of the cybersecurity evaluation of the architecture and validate the conceptual framework as a generic methodological tool, an empirical framework was devised. This framework aims to close the gap between concept and realization. A questionnaire[4] was deemed as the most effective method to gather information, given the time-frame available. It was designed to extract expert knowledge and experience from the implementation of security mechanisms in the pilots. In addition to the security aspects, some general system properties were also investigated. The results obtained with the empirical evaluation framework directly answer to the objectives of this work, while providing insights into the interdependencies between the BBs' specifications and their implementations.

3.1 Questionnaire Design

The questionnaire design follows the RMIAS premises. It contains five sections: four focus on the RMIAS dimensions (Security goals, Countermeasures, Information Taxonomy and System Security Lifecycle), and one obtains information about Trust models implemented by the pilots. The results from the questionnaire in turn fed the threat-view analysis of the architecture, providing the needed knowledge about the system behavior and establishing a feedback loop between the design specifications and the architecture implementation. Moreover, they provided valuable insights into how the SATs address the same security objectives as the architecture building blocks they are composed of.

---

[4] http://tiny.cc/yjwfaz.

3.2   Results and Analysis

The questionnaire was filled in by the relevant experts of all piloting domains. Following are the comparative and qualitative analysis of their feedback, divided by sections.

Security Goals. The first section investigated the employment of security mechanisms to address the desired security goals. As shown in Fig. 3, all security goals set to be addressed by the specifications have been a requirement that was also addressed by one or more of the pilots. One of the pilots, (eTendering) employed mechanisms for addressing almost all security goals, which was to some extent expected, considering that it was structurally the most complex and had to cope with all information states during its lifecycle.

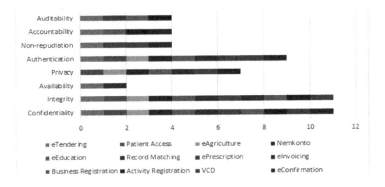

Fig. 3. Security goals addressed by the pilots

Confidentiality and Integrity were addressed by almost all of pilots, whereas the results for Availability reveal that further considerations are needed in this direction. On the one hand, assuring Availability of all resources and hardware, fault-tolerance and redundancy is country-dependent. However, considering the fact that Hardware, Software and Networks are among the security assets stated by the pilots, Availability is expected to be among the top security goals to be addressed. The fact that no pilot has reported consideration of Redundancy and Fault-tolerance, is thus of no surprise. At the same time, it reveals a need for better consideration and proper accounting for Availability as one of the major security goals.

Information Taxonomy. Information in e-SENS is tackled in all states in its lifecycle: Creation, Transmission, Storage, Processing and Destruction. Some pilots did not employ mechanisms to handle information securely in every state (see Fig. 4a), but all pilots ensure secure transmission of information. However, dealing with information in a particular state is highly context-dependent. Thus, no claim can be made on whether some security mechanisms are lacking or if information is not handled securely. Secure processing and creation of information were addressed to a greater or lesser extent.

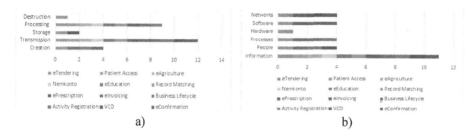

Fig. 4. (a) The state in which Information is being dealt with; (b) Entities concerned by the security mechanisms implemented in the pilots

Variety of entities for which Information is the main asset are concerned in the implementation of security mechanisms (as shown in Fig. 4b). Software, Networks, Processes and People are also major security assets, whereas Hardware is only rarely addressed. However, the number of security assets and the frequency of implementation of certain security mechanism are of less importance; the impact of the particular asset for the overall system and the impact of the failure of a certain security mechanism are crucial. The choice of entities to be addressed by the security goals is both context- and mechanism-dependent. However, as humans are at the core of all systems, it can be observed that the human-factor is poorly addressed by the security mechanisms. This is especially important if one considers that countermeasures can be legal, organizational and purely human-oriented. Next, broader analysis of this issue are presented.

Countermeasures. Regardless of whether a certain pilot implemented security mechanisms with a concrete threat-model in mind, countermeasures could still be in place due to mere operational system requirements. The countermeasures' types investigated here are: (i) Technical; (ii) Legal; (iii) Organizational; and (iv) Human-oriented. Technical countermeasures that are widely employed by the pilots are encryption and authentication. They are complemented with legal countermeasures in the form of agreements/contracts, whose type depends on the pilot's needs. Policies are the organizational countermeasures implemented, whereas audit was reported by only one of the pilots (eConfirmation). Human-oriented countermeasures are largely lacking, with 'Motivation' and 'Operational guidelines' being the only ones considered.

The implementation of countermeasures is highly context-dependent. Not every pilot has the same assets to secure or deals with the same risks. For e.g., whereas most pilots employ only encryption and authentication as technical countermeasures, the eHealth pilot also implements policy-based access control for authorization, and patient-informed consent to address Privacy. However, starting from the lowest level possible, training of both public administration, citizens and workers must be enforced, since user knowledge and behavior are the first line of defense against cyber-threats.[5]

---

[5] ENISA guidelines (SO6) in D2: Human resources security.

Trust. Trust mechanisms facilitate the accomplishment of Integrity and Account-ability. Confidentiality, although mainly addressed through encryption, is also strengthened by trust in the underlying infrastructure. All pilots employ one or more types of trust mechanisms, depending on the needs of the intra-domain or the cross-domain trust establishment. Although the Trust Network PKI[6] is the most widely employed BB, all of the Trust Establishment BBs are used by some of the pilots. One trust issue reported by the pilots is that self-signed certificates are still widely used. Although they may decrease the overall security risk of a transaction in some situations, self-signed certificates cannot be revoked, allowing an attacker with authorized access to monitor and inject data into a connection, or spoof an identity if a private key was compromised. This points to the need for adequate risk analysis, which was not done by any of the pilots.

Trust analysis does not only help in the consolidation of security policies across a system architecture, but it points to the fact that trust in the overall architecture is as important as securing the information that flows through that architecture. The presented methodology enables this kind of trust reasoning and can be used to assure the adopters of any of the architectural solutions of their desired trust properties.

Security System Lifecycle. This section explored the general lines of development of the security mechanisms. In a way, it extracts the bigger picture of the security design and management of the system.

Most e-SENS pilots base the choice for employing trust and security mechanisms on an inherited infrastructure (from previous Large Scale Pilots[7]). The results are to a certain extent a testimony of the ability to adapt novel security mechanisms to earlier security infrastructures. This adaptability of security solutions is also an argument for the architecture sustainability with respect to the BBs' security capabilities. Therefore, the fact that all pilots claim low expectations for frequent mechanism updates comes as no surprise. In terms of stability of the security mechanisms, all security experts responded that small changes in the security mechanisms would not have a big impact on the remainder of the system. However, most of the pilots reported no redundancy considerations in the security mechanism design. This again points to the need for risk-modelling and analysis, and introduction to proper countermeasures during system design.

Overall Evaluation of the e-SENS Security Measures. After performing the cybersecurity evaluation of all SATs, the overall e-SENS security measures have been evaluated and assigned a sophistication level according to ENISA guidelines. The security measures are grouped in three sophistication levels as shown in Table 4.

Each level corresponds to some criteria judging of its attainment. The results are backed by evidence gathered in support of the judgement. The levels are cumulative, so the evidence for attaining level 2 applies to level 1 as well.

---

[6] PKI stands for Public Key Infrastructure.

[7] EPSOS (eHealth), PEPPOL (eProcurement), E-CODEX (eJustice), to name a few.

Table 4. Evaluation of sophistication level of e-SENS security measures according to ENISA descriptions

ENISA description of sophistication levels	Assessment of the e-SENS security measures	
	Level attained	Evidence
Level 1 (basic) - Basic security measures that could be implemented to reach the security objective - Evidence for that	**Yes**	Basic security measures are in place - the arguments were detailed in the BB's security evaluation and the pilots security evaluation
Level 2 (industry standard) - Industry standard security measures to reach the objective and an ad-hoc review of the implementation, following changes or incidents - Evidence for that	**Yes**	Industry security measures are in place - demonstrated in the pilots security evaluation and in the assessment of technical maturity of the e-SENS RA's building blocks
Level 3 (state of the art) - State of the art (advanced) security measures, and continuous monitoring of implementation, structural review of implementation, taking into account changes, incidents, tests and exercises, to proactively improve their implementation - Evidence for that	**Not Yet**	Not all e-SENS BBs have reached full technical maturity and scalability readiness; no comprehensive documentation is provided to claim accounting for changes, incidents and tests to improve the implementation of the security measures However, solid basis for reaching level 3 can be provided: the current analysis is a form of a structural review and a proactive step towards recommendations to improve the security measures implementation

The possibility of e-SENS RA to be adapted to the domain needs and to evolve with the system speaks of its flexibility to retain the reached sophistication level. This wraps up the complementary view on the goal-based approach and provides the cybersecurity evaluation with operational recommendations for securing the e-SENS RA solutions.

3.3 Discussion

While not all pilots address all security goals or employ countermeasures, the fact that all security goals were addressed, information has been accounted for in all of its states, all entities were tackled by some of the security mechanisms and technical, legal, human and organizational countermeasures are in place, testifies that the e-SENS RA satisfies the cybersecurity requirements by the pilots. However, not all recommendations for a secure system operation and maintenance can and should be addressed by a single project; imposing technical, legal, and organizational requirements is dealt with on national or domain level. While desirable good practices may be part of its recommendations, mandatory security measures are not.

Complementing a reference architecture with a methodology to encompass the security goals from design time with tools to support the cybersecurity assessment is of paramount importance for meeting the regulatory requirements as well. Clearly, the mechanisms employed depend on the particular context and use case and cannot be joined by a universal security mechanism. The results from the questionnaire demonstrate that the generic security properties provided by the e-SENS RA are also reflected in the pilot implementations.

To validate the adoption of e-SENS building blocks, special events named connect-a-thons were organized within the eHealth pilot, where conformance and interoperability tests were performed assisted by tools[8] and skilled personnel [12]. The secure and successful cross-border exchange of patient summaries and ePrescriptions was simulated among at least 4 countries. It is the first attempt to reuse this testing methodology for architectural assets created outside the eHealth domain.

This cybersecurity analysis joins the benefits of a goal-based approach with the systemic nature of a threat-view on security management. It also helps to organize the security policies spread over multiple domains. Furthermore, it not only permits tracing possible contradictory security policy statements, but facilitates the identification of weak or omitted security policies as well.

4 Related Work

The EU is making significant steps toward cross-border eServices interoperability and implementation. The 2018 edition of eGovernment summarizes related policies and activities in 34 countries and enlists cybersecurity as an emerging topic [14]. The NIS Directive aims at ensuring a high level of network and information security across Europe [15]. As a response to the directive requirements, ENISA, national governments and National Regulatory Authorities engaged in joint work in order to achieve harmonized implementation. Three non-binding technical documents were provided as guidance to the NRAs across EU member states [7, 16, 17]. The presented analysis is a contribution in similar direction and an effort to bridge technical solutions with regulatory policies and standardization.

There are approaches that cover one or more aspects addressed by our work [18, 19]. In addition, [20] describes a thorough process to include and evaluate security aspects in all stages of the Information System lifecycle: requirement elicitation, acquisition, design and implementation, operation and maintenance, and disposal. Although security evaluation is included in the process, it follows a threat-based approach and offers no evaluation framework or any reference or enterprise architecture the systems might conform to. Evaluating certain cybersecurity attributes of enterprise architectures was approached in [2, 3], which mainly rely on human effort. The same stands for addressing interoperability in enterprise architectures [21]. Zuccato et al. [22] provide a holistic account of "security requirements profiles" in an organization by

---

[8] The Gazelle test suite, http://gazelle.ihe.net.

assembling a set of "modular security safeguards". However, they are concerned only with the technical aspects and mainly serve the solution developers.

There is criticism about security design frameworks deemed to be too focused on the technical aspects and falling short in detecting and addressing potential design conflicts [23]. An example of this is a system that should implement both anonymity and auditability. By joining the goal-based approach with a threat-view, the issue of contradictory requirements in technology management through enterprise architectures is addressed from design time. Finally, the generic framework presented here is easy to understand by a non-technical person, while offering sufficient technical guidance for the (cyber)security experts.

5 Conclusion and Future Work

Secure information exchange platforms are crucial to the correct functioning of the services they support. The methodology presented here can be successfully applied for a model-based evaluation in a practical setting. It bridges technical and business solutions with the latest regulatory policies and frameworks. The employment of RMIAS in practice has led to a goal-based security analysis of each architecture construct, identifying how the technical specifications associated with them contribute to meeting the security goals. The empirical security evaluation showed that although the implementations were able to address the security goals, additional availability measures, proper risk analysis, and provision of human-oriented countermeasures require refinement of the architecture to provide further tools to reach the security objectives.

Designing a methodology to analyze security measures provided by the implemented security mechanisms and integrating the outcomes of such analysis into the specifications allows for a technical person to cope more easily with the dynamics of security changes that a system may require. Furthermore, by enabling a non-technical person to understand the needs for implementing a certain security measures and the implications of not addressing it adds value in terms of usability of the system itself and for aligning the managerial requirements with the technical possibilities that an architecture offers.

Although each e-SENS pilot performed the evaluation of the architecture via domain-specific methodologies (e.g., connect-a-thons in eHealth), we pursue two independent approaches for the security assessment of the building blocks. Firstly, we plan to evaluate the eHealth pilot architecture with a tool such as securiCAD[9]. Secondly, we will formalize the conceptual framework of the methodology in order to enable a semi-automatic solution architecture design and help the architect deal with the variability and optionality of the design choices. An immediate step towards the automation of solution architecture design is thus the automation of the quality-attributes check. One way to do that is by employing denotational semantics as the formal apparatus, but other possibilities will also be tested. Therefore, an open-access

---

[9] https://www.foreseeti.com/community/.

implementation tool will be created to allow reusability and testing of the methodology, and moreover, implementation into real-world setting.

References

1. Korman, M., Lagerström, R., Välja, M., Ekstedt, M., Blom, R.: Technology management through architecture reference models: a smart metering case. In: 2016 Portland International Conference on Management of Engineering and Technology, pp. 2338–2350 (2016)
2. Sommestad, T., Ekstedt, M., Holm, H.: The cyber security modeling language: a tool for assessing the vulnerability of enterprise system architectures. IEEE Syst. J. **7**(3), 363–373 (2013)
3. Holm, H., Shahzad, K., Buschle, M., Ekstedt, M.: P^{2}CySeMoL: predictive, probabilistic cyber security modeling language. IEEE Trans. Dependable Secure Comput. **12**(6), 626–639 (2015)
4. Grandry, E., e-SENS Architecture team: D6.7 e-SENS European Interoperability Reference Architecture. European Commission, 31 Mar 2017
5. Masi, M., Pavleska, T., Aranha, H.: Automating smart grid solution architecture design. In: 2018 IEEE International Conference on Communications, Control, and Computing Technologies for Smart Grids (SmartGridComm), pp. 1–6 (2018)
6. Cherdantseva, Y., Hilton, J.: A reference model of information assurance & security. In: Proceedings of the 2013 International Conference on Availability, Reliability and Security, Washington, DC, USA, pp. 546–555 (2013)
7. ENISA: Technical Guideline on Minimum Security Measures — ENISA (2014)
8. Röhrig, S.: Using Process Models to Analyse IT Security Requirements. University of Zurich (2003)
9. Anton, A.I., Earp, J.B., Reese, A.: Analyzing website privacy requirements using a privacy goal taxonomy. In: Proceedings IEEE Joint International Conference on Requirements Engineering, pp. 23–31 (2002)
10. Pfleeger, C.P., Pfleeger, S.L.: Security in Computing, 4th edn. Prentice Hall PTR, Upper Saddle River (2006)
11. DG CONNECT: Introduction to the Connecting Europe Facility eDelivery building block. European Commission (2015)
12. eHDSI Business Analyst: Non-repudiation mechanism - eHealth DSI Operations - CEF Digital (2019). Accessed 02 Aug 2019
13. What is eID: CEF Digital. https://ec.europa.eu/cefdigital/wiki/cefdigital/wiki/display/CEFDIGITAL/What+is+eID. Accessed 02 Aug 2019
14. Digital Government Factsheets – 2018. Joinup. https://joinup.ec.europa.eu/collection/nifo-national-interoperability-framework-observatory/digital-government-factsheets-2018. Accessed 01 Aug 2019
15. European Commission: The Directive on security of network and information systems (NIS Directive). Digital Single Market, 09 May 2017. Accessed 31 Aug 2017
16. ENISA, "Technical Guideline on Threats and Assets — ENISA." 14-Sep-2014
17. ENISA: Technical Guideline on Incident Reporting — ENISA, 24 Oct 2014
18. ISO/IEC/IEEE 24748–1:2018: ISO. http://www.iso.org/cms/render/live/en/sites/isoorg/contents/data/standard/07/28/72896.html. Accessed 01 Aug 2019
19. Bowen, P., Hash, J., Wilson, M.: SP 800-100. Information Security Handbook: A Guide for Managers. National Institute of Standards & Technology, Gaithersburg, MD, United States (2006)

20. Cyber Security Agency of Singapore: CSA Singapore Security-by-Design Framework v1.0. Cyber Security Agency, Singapore, 09 November 2017
21. Ullberg, J., Johnson, P., Buschle, M.: A language for interoperability modeling and prediction. Comput. Ind. **63**(8), 766–774 (2012)
22. Zuccato, A., Daniels, N., Jampathom, C., Nilson, M.: Report: modular safeguards to create holistic security requirement specifications for system of systems. In: Massacci, F., Wallach, D., Zannone, N. (eds.) ESSoS 2010. LNCS, vol. 5965, pp. 218–230. Springer, Heidelberg (2010). https://doi.org/10.1007/978-3-642-11747-3_17
23. Mercuri, R.: Uncommon criteria. Commun. ACM **45**(1), 172 (2002)

Author Index

Printed in the United States
By Bookmasters